PLAYS
for
YOUNG PUPPETEERS

Plays *for* Young Puppeteers

25 *puppet plays for easy performance*

by
Lewis Mahlmann
AND
David Cadwalader Jones

Publishers   PLAYS. INC.   *Boston*

Library of Congress Cataloguing-in-Publication Data

```
Mahlmann, Lewis.
  Plays for young puppeteers : 25 puppet plays for easy
  perfomance/by Lewis Mahlmann and David Cadwalader Jones.
  p. cm.
  Summary: A collection of twenty-five easy-to-stage puppet
  plays based on such familiar tales as "Beauty and the
  Beast," "Puss-in-Boots," and "Cinderella." Includes
  production notes on such aspects as costumes, special
  effects, and the presentation of puppet shows.
  ISBN 0-8238-0298-1
  1. Puppet plays, American. 2. Children's plays, American.
  [1.Puppet plays. 2.Puppet theater. 3.Plays. 4.Folklore.]
  I. Jones, David Cadwalader. II. Title. III. Title: Puppet
  plays for young puppeteers.
  PN1980.M345 1993                                  92-38529
  812'.54--dc20                                         CIP
                                                         AC
```

Manufactured in the United States of America

CONTENTS

PLAYS
for
YOUNG PUPPETEERS

PETER PAN

Adapted from a play by J. M. Barrie

Characters
NANA THE NURSE
JOHN DARLING, *10*
MICHAEL DARLING, *5 1/2*
WENDY DARLING, *12*
TINKERBELL, *a fairy*
PETER PAN
NARRATOR *(Wendy at 25)*
CAPTAIN HOOK, *a pirate*
SNEE, *his partner*
CROCODILE
ANNA, *Wendy's little girl, 6*

Scene One

BEFORE RISE: *There is a musical introduction. NARRATOR speaks from offstage (or speeches may be pre-recorded and played during performance).*

NARRATOR: This is the story of a boy who never wanted to grow up. His name was Peter Pan. But our story begins with the Darling family. They live in a pretty house in a very nice neighborhood in London. There are Mr. and Mrs. Darling and their three children: Wendy, who is twelve and very grown-up for her age; John, ten; and Michael, five-and-a-half. They have a nurse called Nana, and we find her asleep on the nursery floor. . .for she is a newfoundland dog.

* * *

3

SETTING: *Nursery. There are three beds. Large open window on backdrop.*

AT RISE: NANA *is asleep on the floor.* JOHN *and* MICHAEL, *dressed in pajamas, come running in.*

JOHN: Look, Michael. Nana is asleep.

MICHAEL: Let's pull her tail. (*They do so.* NANA *wakes up, and there is much barking and laughter.*)

WENDY (*Entering; scolding*): John! Michael! Stop teasing Nana! It's time to go to bed.

MICHAEL: I won't go to bed, Wendy. I won't. (NANA *barks.*)

WENDY: Now, mind Nana. She is your nurse and you will do what she tells you.

JOHN: I won't mind going to bed. I'm tired. (*Yawns, gets into bed*)

MICHAEL: I'm not tired. (NANA *gives big, deliberate bark.* MICHAEL *relents.*) O.K., Nana. Maybe I am a little tired. (*Gets into bed.* NANA *barks again, then exits.*)

WENDY: I'm tired, too. (*She goes to bed, falls asleep.*)

NARRATOR: All was peaceful and everyone was asleep. . .but we expect that something is about to happen. (*There is a musical cue. Window flies open and* TINKERBELL *flies in and hides.* TINKERBELL'*s music is heard.*)

PETER (*Flying in and standing on windowsill; speaking softly*): Tinkerbell, where are you? Stop hiding!

WENDY (*Sitting up; curiously*): Hello there, boy.

PETER: Hello. Who are you?

WENDY: I am Wendy Morra Angela Darling. Who are you?

PETER: My name is Peter Pan.

WENDY: Is that all? Didn't your mother give you a full name?

PETER: Oh, I don't have a mother. I ran away the day I was born.

WENDY: Oh, how sad! I have a mother and a father and two

4

brothers, John and Michael. (*Pause*) Why did you run away?

PETER: I heard my mother and father talk about what I was to be when I grew up. I just wanted to stay a boy all my life. So I ran away and lived among the fairies.

WENDY (*Interested*): The fairies? I'd love to meet a fairy.

PETER: There's one here, hiding in this room. Tinkerbell! Come out wherever you are! (TINKERBELL *flies out and her music is heard.*)

WENDY: Oh, how pretty she is! Hello, Tinkerbell! (*Music*) I'd love to live among the fairies.

PETER: You would? Tink can take us to Never-Never-land.

WENDY: Truly? Oh, yes. Let's go. Can John and Michael come, too?

PETER: If you like.

WENDY (*Rushing over to* JOHN *and* MICHAEL; *waking them*): John! Michael! Wake up. (*They wake up.*) Peter Pan and Tinkerbell are going to take us to Never-Never-land to live among the fairies.

JOHN *and* MICHAEL (*Ad lib; excitedly*): The fairies! Never-Never-land! Let's go! (TINKERBELL *flies out while her music is heard.*)

PETER: There goes Tinkerbell.

WENDY: But how do we get to Never-land?

PETER: It's easy. We'll fly. I'll teach you to jump on the wind's back and away we'll go. (*Boys get out of bed.*) Just watch me. (PETER *flies.*)

JOHN: He can fly!

WENDY: How sweet!

PETER (*Still flying*): I'm sweet, I'm sweet, I'm sweeeet!

MICHAEL (*Excitedly*): Teach me! Teach me to fly!

PETER: First I have to drop some fairy dust on you. (*Sprinkles children with glitter.*) There! Now, just think good thoughts and wiggle your shoulders. (JOHN, MICHAEL, *and*

5

WENDY *wiggle their shoulders, and one by one, they levitate.*)

JOHN: Look at me! I'm flying!

MICHAEL: I'm flying! This is wonderful!

WENDY: Oh, how lovely!

JOHN: The window is open.

MICHAEL: Why don't we fly out?

PETER (*In warning tone*): There are pirates in Never-Never-land.

JOHN: There are? (*Exuberantly*) Then let's go!

MICHAEL: Yes. Let's go.

WENDY: To Never-Never-land! (*They all fly out window. Curtain*)

* * *

Scene Two

NARRATOR: Never-Never-land is not a big island, but small and nicely crammed. You could never discover Peter's home, for he didn't live above ground, but beneath a hollowed-out tree. . .like a furry little mole. Here come Peter and the children now.

* * *

SETTING: *Forest in Never-Never-land. Peter's house is a hollowed-out tree trunk.*

AT RISE: PETER, WENDY, JOHN, *and* MICHAEL *fly in.*

WENDY (*Looking around*): How lovely it is here, Peter.

MICHAEL: Where are the pirates?

PETER: First I'll show you where you are to live. (*Pause; hopefully*) Wendy, won't you be our mother?

WENDY: Oh, how lovely. All right. Now, all of you get to bed. (*Pirates are heard singing in the distance.*)

PETER: Quick! Into the tree and down below.

JOHN: Pirates! (*They exit quickly.* CAPTAIN HOOK *and* SNEE *enter.*)

HOOK: Snee! I want you to comb every inch of this island and find Peter Pan.

SNEE: What for, Captain?

HOOK: 'Twas he that cut off my arm in a sword fight. And I almost got him, too. He threw my arm to the crocodile. I've waited a long time to shake his hand with this hook.

SNEE: But you've often said the hook has come in handy for combing your hair and other homely uses.

HOOK: That crocodile follows me wherever I go. From land to land and sea to sea. . .licking his lips for the rest of me. By chance, he swallowed a clock, and when I hear that clock ticking I know he is nearby. (*Sits on tree stump*) Hm-m-m, what's this? This tree stump is hot.

SNEE: It looks like a chimney.

HOOK: Aha! This is where Peter Pan and his friends live. We've got them, Snee! We'll put a sweet poisoned drink in their house. They will drink it and they will die. (*Laughs evilly. Ticking of clock is heard.*)

SNEE: Listen, Captain. A ticking clock. (CROCODILE *slithers on.*)

HOOK (*Frightened*): Hobbs, Bobs, Hammer and Tongs. The crocodile! Let's run! (*They run off, followed by* CROCODILE. *Curtain*)

*   *   *

Scene Three

SETTING: *Peter's home underground, with chairs, table, ladder.*

AT RISE: PETER, MICHAEL, JOHN, *and* WENDY *are onstage.* TINKERBELL *flies in and hides.*

7

PETER: How do you like your new home?

WENDY: It's lovely, Peter. So cozy.

PETER: I'd better see if the pirates are around. I won't be long. Don't leave until I get back.

WENDY: Goodbye, Peter. You be careful! (PETER *exits up ladder.*)

JOHN: You sound just like Mother, Wendy. (*They don't see* MICHAEL *ascending ladder and exiting.*)

WENDY: Well, we must be careful, because. . .(*Notices* MICHAEL *is gone*) Where is Michael? Oh, no! He has gone after Peter!

JOHN: Don't worry. I'll bring him back. (JOHN *ascends ladder, exits.*)

WENDY (*Calling after him*): Be careful, John! Oh, I do so worry about them. What's a mother to do? (*She doesn't see* HOOK *and* SNEE *climbing down ladder. They grab her.*) Let me go! Let me go! Who are you?

HOOK: The *un*honorable Captain Hook — at your service. Snee, take her to the ship and hold her. She'll be our mother.

WENDY: Let me go!

HOOK: Take her away, Snee. (*There is a ruckus while* SNEE *takes* WENDY *up ladder and off.*) Now I am by myself. (TINKERBELL *darts behind him. He doesn't notice her.*) Just to put this poisoned sweet drink upon the table and then. . .Ha, ha, ha! It's doom for Peter Pan. (*He places glass on table, exits. There is a pause, then* PETER *descends ladder.*)

PETER (*Looking around*): Wendy! John! Michael! (*Puzzled*) Where could they have gone? . . .Oh, well, they'll be back soon. (*Noticing glass*) What's this? A lovely drink. I'll bet Wendy made it for me, knowing I'd be thirsty when I got back. (*He is about to drink when* TINKERBELL *flies around him and annoys him.*) What's the matter, Tink? (*Music*) Wendy and the boys are gone? (*He climbs ladder to look*

8

outside. TINKERBELL *drinks potion and falls to the ground. Music gets fainter.* PETER *returns to table.*) Wendy and the boys captured by the pirates? (*Suddenly*) What's wrong, Tink? Wake up! Oh, no, Tink! Dear Tink! Are you dying? (*Music gets slower and softer.* PETER *addresses audience; desperately*) Her music is growing fainter. If the music stops, that means she's dead. (*To* TINKERBELL) What is it, Tink? (*He leans over her, then addresses audience again.*) She says that she will get well again if children believe in fairies. Do you believe in fairies? Please say that you do. If you believe, clap your hands. Clap your hands! (*Clapping sound is heard; audience joins in.* TINKERBELL *moves, her music gets louder and faster, and then she gets up, flies around.* PETER *addresses audience.*) Oh, thank you! Thank you! And now I must get to the pirate ship, to save Wendy and the boys! (*He and* TINKERBELL *fly off. Curtain*)

* * *

Scene Four

SETTING: *Pirate ship. There is a plank running across stage.*
AT RISE: HOOK *brandishes sword.*
HOOK: While most children are in bed dreaming of good things, these children here are about to walk the plank. 'Tis the hour of triumph!
SNEE (*Pushing children on*): What shall I do with these three, Captain?
JOHN (*Belligerently*): You let us go! Just wait until Peter gets here! (MICHAEL *kicks* SNEE.)
SNEE: Ouch! This little one kicked me. My shin, my shin, my shinny shin shin! (*Again* MICHAEL *kicks* SNEE, *who howls in pain.*)

9

HOOK: Take the boys below. I'll deal with the girl first.

SNEE (*Laughing*): Get down there with the rats and the bilge. Ouch! Stop biting! (*They exit.*)

HOOK (*To* WENDY): Now, as for you. . .now you will be *my* mother!

WENDY: I'll never be your mother. I'd rather die first.

HOOK: Then die you will. Onto the plank and overboard. (*He forces her on the plank.*) It isn't too much farther. Just a bit more out to the edge.

PETER (*Offstage*): Cock-a-doodle-doo!

SNEE (*Returning; frightened*): What was that?

PETER (*Appearing with sword in hand*): It is I, Peter Pan the Avenger!

HOOK: Snee, take the girl below. (SNEE *exits with* WENDY.) Proud and insolent youth, prepare to meet thy doom.

PETER: Rare and sinister man, have at thee! (*They have sword fight, with sound effects.* PETER *backs* HOOK *onto plank.*) You are a rare swordsman, Captain Hook, but not a match for Peter Pan! (PETER *knocks sword from* HOOK'*s hand.*)

HOOK (*Surprised; at edge of plank*): You knocked the sword out of my hand. What sort of a fiend are you?

PETER (*Exultantly*): I'm youth! I'm joy! I'm freedom!

HOOK: Better to die at sea than in the hands of a fiend. (*Sound of ticking clock is heard.*) Ah, Crocodile, my yawning Crocodile. I greet thee as a friend. (HOOK *jumps; splash of water is heard.*)

PETER (*Calling off*): Wendy! John! Michael! You can come out now! (*Children enter.*)

JOHN: We overpowered Snee and tied him up.

MICHAEL: He'll learn his lesson.

WENDY: Peter, please take us home!

PETER: Away we go! (*All fly off.*)

*   *   *

Scene Five

NARRATOR: So off they flew, back to the nursery and home.

* * *

SETTING: *Same as Scene 1.*

AT RISE: PETER *and children are onstage.*

WENDY (*Happily*): We're home! John, Michael — go tell Mother and Father not to worry. We're home.

JOHN: Right away. Come, Michael. (JOHN *and* MICHAEL *exit.*)

WENDY: Peter. . .I think Mother and Father would be willing to adopt you.

PETER: Would they send me to school?

WENDY: Yes.

PETER: And then to an office?

WENDY: I suppose so.

PETER: Soon I'd be a man.

WENDY: Very soon.

PETER: I don't want to learn solemn things. No one is going to catch me and make me a man. I just want to be a little boy and have fun.

WENDY: But you will be lonesome without us, Peter.

PETER: I still have Tink and the fairies. (*He gets on windowsill.*) Goodbye, Wendy. (*Starts out*)

WENDY (*Rushing to window*): Goodbye, Peter! And don't forget me! (WENDY *waves, then slowly walks offstage. Musical interlude to indicate passage of time.*)

* * *

NARRATOR (*Entering*): I am Wendy. I grew up, and now I'm a mother.

ANNA (*Running in*): Mommy, I'm ready for bed.

NARRATOR: That's good, my sweet. Now, jump into bed.

11

(ANNA *gets into bed.* NARRATOR *kisses her, then exits. There is a musical cue and the sound of rushing wind.*)

PETER (*Flying in*): Wendy! (ANNA *sits up.*) Oh! You're not Wendy. Who are you?

ANNA: My name is Anna.

PETER: Would you like to visit the fairies? You'll be back by morning.

ANNA (*Eagerly*): Oh, yes! Yes!

PETER: I just have to sprinkle you with fairy dust and away we go. (*He sprinkles her with glitter. She laughs as she rises and they both laugh and fly out window. Curtain*)

THE END

Production Notes

PETER PAN

Number of Puppets: 11 hand or rod puppets, including crocodile and dog.

Playing Time: 20 minutes.

Costumes: Children wear nightclothes, then change to costumes appropriate for the period. Peter wears green tights, leotard. Captain Hook and Snee, pirate's outfits; Hook also wears eyepatch and has hook. Narrator puppet, dress.

Properties: Glitter; swords.

Setting: Scenes 1 and 5, nursery: three beds and open window; Scene 2, forest in Never-Never-land, with hollowed-out tree trunk; Scene 3, Peter's underground home, with ladder at one side, chairs and table; Scene 4, pirate ship. There is a plank running across stage.

Sound: Tinkling sound for Tinkerbell; musical interludes; ticking clock; rushing wind.

BEAUTY AND THE BEAST

Characters

NARRATOR, *boy or girl*
PRINCE LEON
THE BEAST
OWL
ENCHANTRESS
FATHER
BEAUTY
BRENDA ⎱ *her sisters*
AGATHA ⎰
FOREST ANIMALS

SCENE 1

BEFORE RISE: NARRATOR *addresses audience.*
NARRATOR: Here is the story of Beauty and the Beast —
where a lesson is learned in a most unusual way. There
was once a proud and selfish young prince, who liked to
hunt in his woods. (*Curtain opens.*)

*   *   *

SETTING: *A dark forest backdrop, with one large tree at
one side and bush with one rose on the other side.*
AT RISE: FOREST ANIMALS (*rabbits, squirrels, etc.*) *run
about.* OWL *flies in.*

OWL: Whooo! Whooo! You had better hop out of this part
of the forest. Prince Leon hunts in these woods, and your

life isn't worth much jumping about here. Whooo! Whooo! Here he comes now...scoot! (ANIMALS *run off, as a shot is heard.*)

PRINCE (*Entering*): Missed him.

OWL (*Flying about*): Whooo! Whooo!

PRINCE: Oh, be quiet, Owl. Don't bother me with your hooting. This forest belongs to me, and I'll hunt any animal I wish.

ENCHANTRESS (*Appearing*): And any forest spirit as well?

PRINCE (*Crossly*): Who are you?

ENCHANTRESS: Forest Enchantress supreme....

PRINCE: You're in my forest. *I'm* supreme here, and I'll ask you to leave right away.

ENCHANTRESS: It seems you should be taught a lesson — to be humble, young man. The life of a lonely animal would teach you a good lesson.

PRINCE: Forest enchantress, indeed!

ENCHANTRESS (*Chanting*):
> Prince Leon, selfish and vain,
> Who knows nothing of humility and pain —
> Turn into a beast, ugly but pure,
> And remain as such, till love does cure....

(PRINCE *turns into* BEAST. *See Production Notes.*) Now, my proud beast, hunt no more my beautiful forest creatures. And let no one touch my trees or flowers or else he will die. Goodbye, Prince Leon. (*She exits. Sound of a rainstorm is heard suddenly, and* BEAST *hides behind tree.* FATHER *enters, with large bag.*)

FATHER: What a dark, sinister glen this is! I've lost my way to the main road. (*Looks around*) I hope I find my way home soon. This storm is getting worse. (*Goes to tree*) There seems to be some protection under this tree. (*Sound of rain decreases.*) Let's see now. (*Looks into bag*) I have all my gifts for my daughters. A scarf for

15

Agatha. A bracelet for Brenda. But poor Beauty. She wanted a single rose, but there was none to be had, with winter so near... (*Rain stops*) Oh! A bush with *one* rose left. (*Goes to bush*) Beauty will be pleased. She is such a good child, and I especially want to make her happy. (*He plucks rose.*) For Beauty! (BEAST *appears suddenly.*)

BEAST: Who dares to pick the Enchantress's rose?

FATHER (*Frightened*): A terrible beast! Help!

BEAST (*Approaching him*): There's no one to help you here. This is my forest.

FATHER: I didn't know. What can I do to make amends?

BEAST: Send me one of your daughters, or else you die!

FATHER (*Pleading*): But I love all my daughters...

BEAST: Just until I learn what love is... or else you die.

FATHER: You have much to learn. I do not wish to die, so I'll send a daughter. Goodbye, Beast. (*They exit on opposite sides.* OWL *flies in.*)

OWL: Whooo! A lesson to be learned. (*Curtain*)

* * * * *

SCENE 2

TIME: *A short time later.*

SETTING: *Beauty's cottage. There are a large chest, table and chairs.*

AT RISE: FATHER *enters with bag.*

FATHER (*Calling*): Girls! Agatha, Brenda, Beauty. I'm home. (AGATHA, BRENDA *and* BEAUTY *run in.*)

AGATHA: What do you have for us?

BRENDA: Did you bring my bracelet?

BEAUTY: Welcome home, Papa! Did you have a nice trip?

FATHER: Yes. I sold all my goods and bought what you asked for. (*Takes blue scarf out of bag*) Your scarf, Agatha.

AGATHA (*Taking scarf*): It's not the right shade of blue. And it's too short.

FATHER: That's all I could afford. Brenda, your bracelet. (*Takes bracelet from bag and hands it to* BRENDA)

BRENDA: Hm-m-m. It looks like glass to me.

FATHER: Here, Beauty, is your rose. (*Takes rose from bag*)

BEAUTY (*Taking it*): It's beautiful, Father. Thank you.

AGATHA: A rose? It will just wither and die.

BRENDA: Much good it will do you.

BEAUTY: But where did you find a rose at this time of year?

FATHER (*Sadly*): Please don't ask me.

BEAUTY: Something is wrong. Tell us.

FATHER: I plucked the rose from a bush in an enchanted forest. Its keeper is an ugly Beast, who has threatened to kill me unless I send one of you to teach him about love. But I cannot send any of you away.

AGATHA: Well, I'm certainly not going to live in a spooky old forest.

BRENDA: I'm not going to care for an ugly Beast.

BEAUTY: I will go, Father. It was for me that you picked the rose.

FATHER: But, Beauty, I cannot let you go...

BEAUTY: Goodbye, Brenda. Goodbye, Agatha. Take care of Papa. Goodbye, Father. (*She exits. Curtain.*)

*   *   *   *   *

SCENE 3

TIME: *A short time later.*
SETTING: *The Beast's castle.*
AT RISE: BEAUTY *enters.*

BEAUTY: This is such a mysterious, spooky castle, but I — I won't be afraid.

OWL (*Flying in*): Whooo! Whooo!

BEAUTY (*Startled*): Oh-h-h!

OWL: Welcome — to the Beast's castle. Who are you?

BEAUTY: Hello, little Owl. I am Beauty, and I have been sent to care for the Beast.

OWL: He'll be here soooon. . . soooon.

BEAUTY: I'll be brave, even though my father says he is an ugly Beast.

OWL: Brave. . . brave. . . Whooo! Whooo! (*Flies off*)

BEAUTY: Perhaps I'll be happy here. At least I'll try.

BEAST (*Appearing*): Be happy?

BEAUTY (*Seeing him, turning away, frightened*): Oh-h-h.

BEAST: I shall do all in my power to make you happy. Please don't be afraid of me. You said you wouldn't be afraid. (*Pleading*) I need you.

BEAUTY (*Bravely*): How can I help you, Beast?

BEAST: You can brighten my days. You alone can save me from my fate.

BEAUTY: What can I do?

BEAST: You can teach me love. You can marry me.

BEAUTY: I will not be afraid of you, and I will be good to you, but I cannot marry you.

BEAST: We will have good times in my woods, and I'll show you my castle — and every fortnight, I will again ask you to marry me. Come. . . (*He leads her out.*)

NARRATOR (*Speaking from offstage or entering to address audience*): So Beauty and the Beast grew to know each other. A year passed, and the Beast began to learn humility, while Beauty grew to love the Beast. (BEAUTY *and* BEAST *enter. She is now dressed in magnificent gown and jewels.*)

BEAST: Beauty, once again I ask you to marry me.

BEAUTY: I've grown fond of you, but I still cannot marry you.

OWL (*Flying in*): Beauty! Beauty! Your father is very sick. Hurry home. Hurry home. (*Flies off*)

BEAUTY: Poor Papa. I must go to him. Please let me go, Beast. I've never asked for anything, but I'm needed at home.

BEAST: If you leave me, I shall die of loneliness.

BEAUTY: I'll hurry back to you. I'll remember you.

BEAST: All right, but just three days. No more, or I shall perish.

BEAUTY: I'll be back soon. Goodbye, dear Beast.

BEAST: Soon! (*They exit on opposite sides. Curtain*)

* * * * *

SCENE 4

BEFORE RISE: NARRATOR *speaks*.

NARRATOR: So Beauty rushed back to her sick father, and with her loving care he became well again. The days passed quickly, and all were happy — except Beauty's two greedy sisters... (*Curtain opens*)

* * *

SETTING: *The cottage. Chest filled with glittering dresses and jewels is open at one side.*

AT RISE: AGATHA *and* BRENDA *look through chest.*

BRENDA: Just look at the dresses Beauty brought with her...

AGATHA: And her jewels. Yet she wears her shabby rags here. Why she wears them after living in such finery, I'll never know.

BRENDA: She wants to keep them all to herself, that's why. She doesn't want us to see them. How can we get these lovely things away from her?

19

AGATHA: We'll just keep her here until we find a way. (BEAUTY, *in her old clothes, and* FATHER *enter.* AGATHA *quickly closes chest.*)

FATHER: I believe I'm much better now.

BEAUTY: Dear Father, I would not want anything to happen to you, but now that you are well, I must return to my Beast.

AGATHA (*Sweetly, pleading*): Please stay. Just a few days more.

BRENDA: The Beast will never miss you, and we've been so lonely without you.

FATHER: Yes, please stay a while longer.

BEAUTY: Well...maybe....

OWL (*Flying in*): Whooo! Whooo! Beauty! Three *weeks* have passed. The Beast is dying.

AGATHA: How did that owl get in here?

BRENDA: I'll get the broom.... (OWL *flies out.*)

BEAUTY: My Beast — dying? Has it been three weeks? Oh, I must go at once to my poor Beast.

FATHER: But we don't want to lose you.

AGATHA (*Aside*): Or the jewels.

BRENDA (*Aside*): Or the fine clothes.

BEAUTY: I must go to my Beast. Goodbye, Father. Goodbye, sisters.

FATHER: Goodbye, Beauty. (BEAUTY *rushes out.* FATHER *follows.*)

AGATHA: Ah-ha! She left her beautiful clothes behind.

BRENDA: And her jewels.

AGATHA: Let's get them.

BRENDA: Finders keepers. (*They open chest and pull out tattered rags and strings of onions and garlic.*)

AGATHA: The gowns are torn and falling apart.

BRENDA: The jewels have turned to garlic and onions!

BOTH: Oh, no! (*Curtain*)

*   *   *   *   *

20

SCENE 5

SETTING: *The Beast's garden.*

AT RISE: BEAST *is lying on ground, dying.* ENCHANTRESS *enters.*

ENCHANTRESS: Poor Prince Leon. I never meant for this to happen — from a handsome, vain prince to a lonely, dying Beast.

BEAST (*Weakly*): It's too late. I found out what love is, when Beauty came, but too late...

ENCHANTRESS: My magical powers are not strong enough to save you from such human misery. Farewell ... and I am sorry for you. (*Exits*)

BEAST: Beauty! Beauty! It's too late. (BEAUTY *rushes in.*)

BEAUTY: Beast, Beast — my Beast!

BEAST (*Faintly*): Too late...too late.

BEAUTY: It's not too late. Ask me again!

BEAST: Will you...will you be my wife?

BEAUTY: Yes, Beast. With all my strength and heart. (*She kisses his forehead.*)

BEAST: Beauty.... (BEAST *is transformed into* PRINCE, *and* BEAUTY *appears in her fine clothes. See Production Notes.*)

BEAUTY: It's impossible...you're a Prince!

PRINCE: I thought it was impossible to feel love — to know sharing and humility. But now your love has transformed me and changed me back into a Prince. Stay with me always, Beauty, and never leave my side again.

BEAUTY: I will be with you forever... my Beast! (*Curtain*)

THE END

Production Notes

Number of Puppets: 9 hand or rod puppets or marionettes
(there should be 2 Beauty puppets: 1 in shabby clothes
and 1 in a rich dress and jewels); additional puppets for
Forest Animals.

Characters: 1 male or female for Narrator.

Playing Time: 15 minutes.

Description of Puppets: Beauty, sisters and Father wear
shabby clothes, with an elaborate dress for one Beauty
puppet, as described above. Enchantress wears beautiful
fanciful costume. Prince wears appropriate royal outfit;
Beast wears similar clothes, but with an ugly beast's head
(often a lion's head; see illustrations in a book of fairy
tales for ideas).

Properties: Bag containing blue scarf, bracelet, rose; chest
containing rich dress and jewels, ragged dress and
strings of onions and garlic.

Setting: Scene 1: Dark forest backdrop with large tree on
one side of stage, bush with one rose on the other; Scenes
2 and 4: Beauty's cottage, with chairs, table, and large
chest; Scene 3: Beast's castle; Scene 5: Beast's garden.

Special Effects: For the Beast's transformations, if using
marionettes, include a hillock in the setting behind
which the second marionette is hidden, and exchange
them. Hand or rod puppets simply disappear and are
replaced by second puppet. To change Beauty's dress at
end, have her back off stage (in surprise) and exchange
puppets. In the last scene, the garden might be dark,

with dying flowers, etc., with a second backdrop of a beautiful garden to drop into place after Beast turns into Prince. For a "gunshot" quickly strike a flat stick on table top or wooden floor. Storm can be a sound effects record of rain, or the puppeteers can make loud noises from offstage. Owl can be rod puppet attached to a light-colored stick and controlled from below, or on string and "flown" from above.

Lighting: No special effects.

Music: You might use Ravel's "Mother Goose Suite."

THE WIZARD OF OZ

Adapted from the book by L. Frank Baum

Characters

NARRATOR
DOROTHY
TOTO, *her dog*
AUNT EM ⎱
UNCLE HENRY ⎰ *offstage voices*
GOOD WITCH OF THE NORTH
MAYOR OF THE MUNCHKINS
MUNCHKIN LADY
MUNCHKIN BOY
MUNCHKINS
SCARECROW
TIN WOODSMAN
LION
GATE KEEPER
WICKED WITCH OF THE WEST
OZ, *as a dragon*
OZ, *as a large, ugly head*
OZ, *as himself*
CAT

Scene One

SETTING: *Side yard of a little house on the great Kansas prairies. There is a cut-out of side view of house onstage, against a plain background.*
AT RISE: *Stage is empty.*

NARRATOR: Dorothy lived in the midst of the great Kansas prairies, with her Uncle Henry and her Aunt Em. They lived in a one-room house, and not a tree or farm broke the broad sweep of flat country that reached the edge of the sky in all directions.

DOROTHY (*Entering*): Come out, Toto! (TOTO, *her dog, comes out from behind house.*) Let's play ball, Toto. (DOROTHY *holds up ball.*) Come on, Toto—fetch! (*Wailing sound is heard in distance. She throws ball and* TOTO *brings it back.*) Aunt Em! See how Toto plays ball with me! Uncle Henry!

AUNT EM (*From offstage*): Uncle Henry's too tired from working so hard. And I'm doing the dishes, Dorothy.

DOROTHY: Listen, Toto. Hear that strange noise? (*Wailing sound becomes louder*)

TOTO (*Whimpering*): Hmm-hmm-hmm!

UNCLE HENRY (*From offstage*): There's a cyclone coming, Em!

AUNT EM (*From offstage*): Quick, Dorothy! Run for the cellar. (TOTO *runs offstage.*)

DOROTHY: I have to get Toto first. (*She exits after* TOTO.)

UNCLE HENRY (*From offstage*): Come down here, Em!

AUNT EM (*From offstage*): Dorothy! Dorothy! I'm coming, Henry! (*Wind howls furiously. House shakes.* DOROTHY *re-enters with* TOTO.)

DOROTHY: Hurry, Toto. We have to get in the cellar, too.

TOTO (*Barking*): Arf! Arf! Arf! (*They exit behind house just as it is lifted into the sky.*)

DOROTHY (*From offstage, as if in house*): Help! Aunt Em! Uncle Henry! Help me! (*House flies offstage and is quickly exchanged for a smaller model of house which twirls around in mid-air.*)

NARRATOR: Dorothy and Toto didn't get into the cellar in

time. The north and south winds met in the middle of the cyclone, and the great pressure of the winds on every side of the house raised it up higher and higher until it was at the very top of the funnel of air. The cyclone carried Dorothy miles and miles away from Kansas. (*Curtain*) After many hours she landed with a kerplunk in the middle of a strange and beautiful countryside.

* * *

Scene Two

SETTING: *The land of the Munchkins, a field with brightly colored flowers all around. Dorothy's house is onstage, center. Two bony legs with silver slippers on the feet are sticking out from under house.*

AT RISE: DOROTHY *enters from house.*

DOROTHY: Toto! It's all right. Come on out. I wonder where we are? What a pretty place this is. (TOTO *comes out.*) And look at the little people coming to say hello! (MAYOR, LADY *and* BOY MUNCHKINS *enter, followed by* GOOD WITCH OF THE NORTH.)

WITCH OF NORTH (*To* DOROTHY): You are welcome, most noble sorceress, to the land of the Munchkins.

MAYOR: We are grateful to you for having killed the Wicked Witch of the East and for setting my people free.

DOROTHY: You are very kind, but there must be some mistake. I am only Dorothy, a little girl. I have never killed anything.

WITCH OF NORTH: Your house did anyway, and that is the same thing. (*Points to house*) See! There are her two toes —still sticking out.

DOROTHY: Oh, dear! The house must have fallen on her. Whatever shall we do?

MAYOR: There is nothing to be done. She has held all the Munchkins in bondage for many years, making them slave for her night and day.

LADY: Now we are all set free. Thank you, Dorothy. Come out, little one. (BOY MUNCHKIN *steps forward, holding flowers.*) He's shy.

BOY (*Singing to tune of "Row, Row, Row Your Boat"*):
> Here are flowers for you,
> We're grateful, thanks a lot,
> Keep the flowers fresh and nice,
> Leave them in the pot.

(*Gives flowers to* DOROTHY)

WITCH OF NORTH: Come out, Munchkins. (MUNCHKINS *enter.*)

MUNCHKINS (*Singing to tune of "Row, Row, Row Your Boat"*):
> Thank you very much,
> Won't you be our friend?
> Please, oh please live here with us
> Right in Munchkin land.

DOROTHY: Thank you all very much. (*To* WITCH OF NORTH) Are you a Munchkin too?

WITCH OF NORTH: No, but I am their friend. I am the Witch of the North.

DOROTHY: Oh, gracious! Are you a real witch?

WITCH OF NORTH: Yes, indeed! But I am a *good* witch.

DOROTHY: Can you help me get back home?

WITCH OF NORTH: There is only one who can help you. He is the great Wizard of Oz. He is more powerful than all the rest of us together. He lives in the City of Emeralds.

LADY: Look! (*Points to house*) The Witch of the East is

gone! (*Legs are pulled under house, leaving only silver shoes.*)

MAYOR: There is nothing left of her but her silver shoes!

WITCH OF NORTH: She was so old that she dried up. That is the end of her. Now there is only one truly bad witch still alive, and she lives in the West. (*Taking silver shoes*) The silver shoes are yours, Dorothy. (*Gives shoes to DOROTHY.*)

DOROTHY: Thank you. But I must see the Great Wizard of Oz. How do I find him?

WITCH OF NORTH: You must follow the yellow brick road and continue on it until you come to the gates of the Emerald City of Oz. Here is a kiss. (*She kisses DOROTHY on forehead.*) It will protect you from harm. Goodbye, my dear.

MUNCHKINS (*Together*): Goodbye, Dorothy!

DOROTHY: Goodbye, all my dear little friends. And thank you, Good Witch of the North! (DOROTHY *exits with* TOTO *as all wave goodbye.*)

MUNCHKINS: Goodbye! Goodbye! (*Curtain*)

*   *   *

Scene Three

SETTING: *A cornfield. Stick with Scarecrow on it is at one side.*

AT RISE: DOROTHY *and* TOTO *enter. She carries a basket.*

DOROTHY: Let's rest a while, Toto. We've walked so far and I'm tired. (*She sits down.*)

SCARECROW: Good day!

DOROTHY (*Looking at* SCARECROW): Did you speak?

SCARECROW: I think so. How do you do?

DOROTHY: I'm pretty well, thank you. How do you do?

SCARECROW: I'm not feeling well. It's very tedious being perched up here night and day to scare away the crows . . . and they won't scare. They just laugh at me.

DOROTHY: Can't you get down?

SCARECROW: No—this pole is stuck up my back. If you can, please, get me down. (DOROTHY *takes* SCARECROW *down.*) Thank you very much. I feel like a new man. Where are you going?

DOROTHY: To the Emerald City of Oz, to ask the great Oz to send me back to Kansas.

SCARECROW: Where is the Emerald City—and who is Oz?

DOROTHY: Why, don't you know?

SCARECROW: No, indeed. I don't know anything. You see, I am stuffed, so I have no brains at all.

DOROTHY: Oh, I'm awfully sorry for you.

SCARECROW: Do you think if I go with you that Oz would give me some brains?

DOROTHY: I can't tell, but you may come with me if you like. If Oz will not give you any brains, you will be no worse off than you are now.

SCARECROW: That's true! So off we go.

TOTO (*Growling*): Grr-r-r-r! (SCARECROW *jumps.*)

DOROTHY: Don't mind Toto. He never bites.

SCARECROW: I'm not afraid. He can't hurt the straw. I'll tell you a secret. There is only one thing in the world I'm afraid of and it's a lighted match. Come on—let's go. (*They exit. Curtain.*)

* * *

Scene Four

AT RISE: TIN WOODSMAN *is standing at one side, holding ax in air, not moving.* DOROTHY, TOTO *and* SCARECROW *enter.*

DOROTHY: It's getting dark . . . and the trees are getting thicker.

SCARECROW: If this road goes into the forest, it must come out. And as the Emerald City is at the other end of the road, we must go wherever it leads us.

DOROTHY: Why, anyone would know that!

SCARECROW: Certainly—that is why I know it. If it required brains to figure it out, I never should have said it.

TIN WOODSMAN (*Groaning*): Mmmmm!

DOROTHY: What was that?

SCARECROW: I can't imagine.

TIN WOODSMAN (*Groaning again*): Mmmmm!

DOROTHY (*Seeing* TIN WOODSMAN): Why, it's a man all made of tin. (*To* TIN WOODSMAN) Did you groan?

TIN WOODSMAN: Yes, I did. I've been groaning for more than a year and no one has ever heard me before—or come to help me.

DOROTHY: What can I do for you?

TIN WOODSMAN: Get my oil can and oil my joints. There is one at my feet. (DOROTHY *picks up oil can.*) Oil my neck first. (*She does.*) Now oil the joints of my arms and legs. (*She does. He tries to move legs and arms. Squeaking sounds are heard. He lowers arms.*) Ah-h-h! That feels good. This is a great comfort. I have been holding that ax in the air ever since I rusted. I'm glad to be able to put it down at last! I am very grateful to you.

DOROTHY: Oh, that's all right.

TIN WOODSMAN: I might have stood there always if you hadn't come along. So you have certainly saved my life. How did you happen to be here?

DOROTHY: We are on our way to the Emerald City to see the great Oz.

TIN WOODSMAN: Why do you wish to see Oz?

DOROTHY: I want him to send me back to Kansas, and the Scarecrow wants him to put a few brains into his head.

TIN WOODSMAN: Do you suppose Oz could give me a heart?

DOROTHY: Why, I guess so. It would be as easy as giving the Scarecrow brains.

SCARECROW: Come along!

DOROTHY: We would be pleased to have your company.

TIN WOODSMAN: All right. Off we go! And bring my oil can, too. (DOROTHY *puts oil can into basket and all four start to move off together. Suddenly* TOTO *begins to bark.*)

TOTO (*Loudly*): Arf! Arf! Arf!

DOROTHY: What is it, Toto?

LION (*From offstage, roaring loudly*): Gr-r-r! (LION *comes bounding in.*) Gr-r-r! (LION *sends* SCARECROW *and* TIN WOODSMAN *sprawling.* DOROTHY *screams.* LION *starts for* TOTO, *who is still barking.* DOROTHY, *furious, hits* LION *on nose. He suddenly begins to whimper and cry.*)

DOROTHY: Don't you dare to bite Toto! You ought to be ashamed of yourself. A big beast like you—biting a poor little dog.

LION (*Still crying*): I didn't bite him.

DOROTHY: No—but you tried to. You are nothing but a big coward.

LION: I know it. I've always known it. But how can I help it?

DOROTHY: I don't know, I'm sure. To think of you striking a stuffed man like the poor scarecrow!

LION: Is he stuffed?

DOROTHY: Of course he's stuffed. (DOROTHY *picks up* SCARE-
CROW.)

LION: Is the other one stuffed also?

DOROTHY: No. He's made of tin.

LION: That's why he nearly blunted my claws. What is that
little animal made of? Straw or tin?

DOROTHY: Neither. He's a—a—a meat dog.

LION: Now that I look at him, no one would think of biting
such a little thing except a coward like me.

DOROTHY: What makes you a coward?

LION: It's a mystery to me, but I've learned that if I roar
very loudly, every living thing is frightened and gets out
of my way.

SCARECROW: But that isn't right. The King of the Beasts
shouldn't be a coward.

LION: I know it. (*Sobs*) It is my great sorrow and makes my
life very unhappy. But whenever there is danger, my heart
begins to beat fast.

TIN WOODSMAN: Perhaps you have heart trouble.

LION: It may be.

SCARECROW: I am going to the great Oz to ask him to give
me some brains.

TIN WOODSMAN: And I am going to ask him to give me a
heart.

DOROTHY: And I am going to ask him to send Toto and me
back to Kansas.

LION: Do you think Oz could give me courage?

DOROTHY: Perhaps he can.

LION: Then, if you don't mind, I'll go with you.

DOROTHY: You are very welcome. (*They start off together.
Curtain.*)

*　　*　　*

32

Scene Five

SETTING: *The gates of the Emerald City of Oz.*
AT RISE: DOROTHY, TOTO, LION, SCARECROW *and* TIN
WOODSMAN *enter.*

DOROTHY: Look! That must be the Emerald City of Oz.
SCARECROW: I'll push this button and see if someone will let
us in. (*He touches gate.*)
GATE KEEPER (*Entering*): What do you want in the Emer-
ald City of Oz?
DOROTHY: We wish to see the great Oz.
GATE KEEPER: It has been many years since anyone asked to
see Oz. He is powerful and terrible, and if you come on an
idle or foolish errand to bother his wise reflections, he
might be angry and destroy you all in an instant.
SCARECROW: But it is not a foolish errand, nor an idle one.
It is important. We have been told that Oz is a good
Wizard.
GATE KEEPER: Yes, he is . . . and he rules the Emerald City
wisely and well. But to those who are not honest, or who
approach him from curiosity, he is most terrible. However,
since you have asked to see the great Oz, I must take you
to his palace. Come in! (*They all cross and exit. Curtain.*)

*　　*　　*

Scene Six

SETTING: *Oz's throne room. There is a throne at center. At
one side is a curtained booth.*
AT RISE: Oz, *in the form of a dragon, is sitting on throne.*

DOROTHY, TOTO, LION, TIN WOODSMAN, *and* SCARECROW *enter.*

Oz: I am Oz, the great and terrible. Who are you and why do you seek me?

DOROTHY: I am Dorothy, the small and meek. This is the Scarecrow, the Tin Woodsman, the Cowardly Lion, and my dog, Toto. We have come for your help.

Oz: Where did you get those silver shoes?

DOROTHY: I got them from the Wicked Witch of the East when my house fell on her and killed her.

Oz: And where did you get that mark upon your forehead?

DOROTHY: That is where the Good Witch of the North kissed me when she sent me to you.

Oz: What do you wish me to do?

SCARECROW: Please, I would like to have some brains.

TIN WOODSMAN: And I would passionately like to have a heart.

LION: And I would like to have courage.

Oz: And you, girl?

DOROTHY: Please send me back to Kansas and my Aunt Em and Uncle Henry.

Oz: Why should I do this for you?

DOROTHY: Because you are strong and we are weak; and because you are a great Wizard and we are helpless.

Oz: You have no right to expect me to do these things unless you will do something for me in return. In this country everyone must pay for everything he gets.

SCARECROW: What must we do?

Oz: Kill the Wicked Witch of the West. She is the only wicked witch left in all this land.

TIN WOODSMAN: But we cannot!

Oz: The girl killed the Witch of the East, and now she wears the silver shoes which bear a powerful charm. When you can tell me the Wicked Witch of the West is dead, I will do all you ask of me . . . but not before. Now—go! (DOROTHY, TOTO, SCARECROW, TIN WOODSMAN *and* COWARDLY LION *exit, leaving* OZ *on throne. Curtain.*)

* * *

Scene Seven

SETTING: *The red castle of the Wicked Witch of the West.*
AT RISE: DOROTHY, TOTO, SCARECROW, LION *and* TIN WOODSMAN *enter.*

LION: I don't know why we came. This is such a spooky place. Maybe we had better go back and tell Oz we won't do it.

TIN WOODSMAN: Don't be such a scaredy-cat. Everything will be all—(WICKED WITCH OF THE WEST *enters, carrying a torch.*)

WITCH OF WEST: So. . . . You have come to visit me, have you? You have escaped my slaves, have you? The Tin Woodsman killed my wolves, the Scarecrow destroyed my crows and the Lion scared away my Winkies . . . but my winged monkeys brought you here to me. Now I will get rid of you myself.

SCARECROW: Don't you dare touch any of us, you ugly Witch of the West. Dorothy is protected by the kiss of the Good Witch of the North.

WITCH OF WEST: Ah, yes. The little girl. (*To* DOROTHY) How did you get those silver shoes? Give them to me.

DOROTHY: But the Witch of the North said they were mine now.

WITCH OF WEST: Give them to me, I say! (*She starts for* DOROTHY.)

LION (*Roaring*): Gr-r-r-r-r! Don't go near Dorothy or I'll bite you.

WITCH OF WEST: Ah! A spirited lion. Good! You will be my slave and draw my black carriage.

LION: Never!

WITCH OF WEST: Tin Woodsman, you can build me a new castle with your ax.

TIN WOODSMAN: I'll use this ax on you!

WITCH OF WEST: Scarecrow, you would make a nice little fire! (*She starts toward* SCARECROW *with her torch.*)

SCARECROW: No! No! Stay away. I'm afraid of fire. Stay away!

WITCH OF WEST: He-he-heee! Just a little taste, my straw friend. He-he-heee!

DOROTHY: You leave my friends alone, you ugly, bad Witch! (DOROTHY *picks up a bucket of water.*)

WITCH OF WEST (*Frightened*): What are you going to do with that water? Put it down! Put it down!

DOROTHY: You stay away from the Scarecrow! (DOROTHY *throws the water on* WITCH. *A loud hissing sound is heard.* WITCH *begins to melt.*)

WITCH OF WEST (*Shrieking*): Ah-h-h-h! See what you have done? In a minute I shall melt away!

DOROTHY: I'm very sorry!

WITCH OF WEST: Didn't you know water would be the end of me?

DOROTHY: Of course not. How could I have known?

WITCH OF WEST: Well, in a few minutes I shall be all melted

and you will have this castle to yourself. I never thought a little girl like you would end my wicked deeds. Look out —here I go. . . . (WITCH *disappears. Only her hat is left.*)

ALL: Hurray! The Wicked Witch of the West is dead!

SCARECROW: Quickly! Back to the Wizard of Oz. (*All rush out as curtains close.*)

*   *   *

Scene Eight

SETTING: *The same as Scene 6.*

AT RISE: Oz, *in the form of a large, ugly head, is sitting on throne.* DOROTHY, TOTO, SCARECROW, TIN WOODSMAN, *and* LION *enter.*

OZ: What? You have returned already? Go away and come back tomorrow. I need time to think over your requests.

TIN WOODSMAN: You've had plenty of time already.

SCARECROW: We won't wait a day longer.

DOROTHY: You must keep your promises to us. (LION *roars.*)

LION: Give me my courage—*now!*

TOTO (*Barking*): Arf! Arf! Arf! (TOTO *runs over to booth and pulls open curtain revealing* WIZARD OF OZ, *a short, kind-looking man, standing at a control panel.*)

TIN WOODSMAN: Who are you?

OZ (*Meekly*): I am Oz, the great and terrible, but please don't strike me. Please don't! I'll do anything you want me to.

DOROTHY: What? Aren't you a great wizard?

OZ: Hush, my dear. Don't speak so loudly or you'll be overheard—and I shall be ruined. I'm supposed to be a great wizard!

DOROTHY: And aren't you?

OZ: I'm afraid not, my dear. I'm just a common man.

SCARECROW: You're more than that. You're a humbug!

OZ (*Pleased*): Exactly so. I am a humbug.

LION: But what about the things you promised us?

OZ: I have them right here. (*Takes diploma from control booth and hands it to* SCARECROW.) Scarecrow, here is a diploma, to prove that you have brains.

SCARECROW (*Taking diploma*): Thank you. I feel brilliant already.

OZ (*Taking small heart from control booth*): Tin Woodsman, here is your heart—but I think you are wrong to want it. It makes most people unhappy. (*Places heart on* TIN WOODSMAN's *chest*)

TIN WOODSMAN: Thank you. I shall never forget your kindness. (OZ *takes bottle from control booth and gives it to* LION.)

OZ: Lion, drink this little bottle of courage. (LION *drinks, making gulping sounds.*)

LION: Oh, that's delicious! It tastes like cinnamon cider. Thank you very much.

DOROTHY: What about me?

OZ: I think I have found a way to get us both back to Kansas, Dorothy. Tomorrow you and I will sail away in a large balloon—back to Kansas.

DOROTHY: Oh, thank you! (*Curtain.*)

*   *   *

Scene Nine

SETTING: *The same as Scene 5.*

AT RISE: *There is a large balloon with a basket hanging below it at center. Oz is in the basket. DOROTHY and TOTO
are on the ground, talking to SCARECROW, TIN WOODS-
MAN, and LION.*

OZ: Hurry, Dorothy! Get into the basket. Hurry, or the
balloon will fly away without you.

DOROTHY: Goodbye, my friends. I will miss you all very
much.

OZ: Goodbye, everyone. Hurry, Dorothy! (CAT *suddenly
runs onstage.* TOTO *barks and begins to chase it.* DOROTHY
chases TOTO. *Balloon starts to float into the air.*)

DOROTHY (*To* OZ): Come back! I want to go too! (*Balloon
rises.*)

OZ: I can't come back, my dear. Goodbye! (*He sails out of
sight in balloon.* CAT *exits and* TOTO *returns to* DOROTHY's
side.)

DOROTHY: Oh, no! (*She begins to cry.*) What shall I do? I'll
never get back to Kansas now! (*Weeps.*)

SCARECROW: Don't cry, Dorothy.

TIN WOODSMAN: You are making me cry, too. (*Sniffs*) I
must have a heart, for it is making me very unhappy now.

LION: Poor Dorothy! (WITCH OF NORTH *enters.*)

WITCH OF NORTH: Dorothy, your silver shoes will carry you
home, whenever you want to go. They can carry you any
place in the world, in three steps. All you have to do is
knock the heels together three times, and command them
to take you home.

DOROTHY: Then I shall return home at once. Goodbye, all
my wonderful friends.

ALL: Goodbye, Dorothy.

DOROTHY: I love you all and shall never forget you.

ALL: Goodbye. (*She picks up* TOTO. *He barks.*)

DOROTHY: Silver shoes, take me home to Aunt Em. (*She clicks heels of shoes together three times, and flies offstage with* TOTO *as all wave. Curtain.*)

* * *

Scene Ten

SETTING: *Kansas. This scene is played in front of curtain.*

BEFORE CURTAIN: DOROTHY *and* TOTO *enter.*

DOROTHY: Aunt Em! Uncle Henry! I'm home. I'm back home again! (DOROTHY *and* TOTO *cross stage and exit.*)

THE END

Production Notes

The Wizard of Oz

Number of Puppets: 13 hand puppets, marionettes, or rod puppets, or any combination of these, plus cut-outs for as many Munchkins as desired, cut-out of Oz as dragon, and cut-out of Oz as large, ugly head.

Playing Time: 20 minutes.

Description of Puppets: Use imagination in designing these puppets. Dorothy is a little girl with a simple dress. If her feet are visible, she wears silver shoes from Scene 3 on. She has a basket over her arm from Scene 3 on. Good Witch of the North and Wicked Witch of West are dressed alike, in long gowns, but Good Witch has a white gown and Wicked Witch a black gown. Wicked Witch wears a peaked black hat. If the Wicked Witch is a marionette, make a head and hands attached to a full, loose costume, so that when she melts, the costume sinks to the floor and her head goes into her hat. Tin Woodsman may be made of a series of tin cans, or cardboard rolls painted silver. Scarecrow is in patched shirt and pants, with straw sticking out of clothing. He wears a floppy hat. Lion is in an appropriate animal costume. Toto and Cat are loosely stuffed animal toys. A removable rod should be attached to Toto so that he can be in Dorothy's basket during Scenes 5, 6, and 7. Munchkins are short, cute little people in bright, colorful clothes.

Properties: Ball for Dorothy and Toto in Scene 1 (put it on a wire so that it can be controlled from backstage); pair of legs with silver shoes on them; bouquet of flowers; oil can; torch (red foil on a stick) sewn to hand of Wicked Witch;

41

diploma; heart (put tape or a pin on back of heart so that it will stick to Tin Woodsman's body); bottle; bucket containing shredded cellophane for "water"; cut-out of balloon with basket hanging below it; small, three-dimensional model of Dorothy's house, on a heavy wire or dowel, for Scene 1.

Setting: There are seven basic settings: Scene 1, Dorothy's house in Kansas—there is a cut-out of the house, side view, onstage. The background is plain. Scene 2, the land of the Munchkins—background shows a field with flowers growing all about. Scene 3, cornfield—background is plain and a cut-out or drawing of a fence is on it. There is a stick for Scarecrow at one side. Scene 4, forest—background shows dark, gnarled trees, cut-outs or painted on backdrop. Scenes 5 and 9, gates of the Emerald City of Oz—impressive, large green gates are painted on backdrop. Scenes 6 and 8, throne room—green draperies at rear, throne center, and small booth with curtain across it at one side. Curtain should be hung on rings so that it can be easily slid back—tie a string to it and pull curtain aside from backstage when Toto tugs at curtain. Suggestion of dials, knobs, levers, etc., should be drawn on control panel inside booth. Scene 7, red castle of Wicked Witch—painting on backdrop of red, forbidding castle with stone arches, turrets, spikes and chains hanging from walls, etc.

Lighting: No special effects.

Sound: Whining sound of wind for cyclone; squeaking sound for Tin Woodsman; hissing sound for Wicked Witch when water hits her; all as indicated in text.

THE NUTCRACKER PRINCE

Characters

KING WINTER
QUEEN BLANCHE
CLARA
CLARA'S MOTHER, *offstage voice*
PRINCE MARZIPAN (NUTCRACKER)
MOUSE KING
SUGAR PLUM FAIRY PRINCESS
SNOWFLAKES
CANDIES
OTHER DANCERS

SCENE 1

SETTING: *A dark sky with snowflakes.*
MUSIC: *Miniature Overture, Tchaikovsky's "Nutcracker Suite."*
AT RISE: KING WINTER *enters flying.*

KING WINTER (*Laughing*): Ho, ho, ho. Good Queen Blanche, come here! See what I see.
QUEEN BLANCHE (*Flying in*): What is it, King Winter?
KING: It seems that the silly Mouse King is making trouble for the Candy people of Sugar Plum Land.
QUEEN (*Concerned*): Oh, dear! And just before Christmas. Shame on him for stirring up trouble. You shouldn't laugh at a time like this. Should we stop him?

KING: What? And spoil the fun? Only if we are needed, Queen Blanche. The Candy people are as wise as they are sweet. But we will watch over them just in case. (*They fly off. Curtain*)

*   *   *   *   *

SCENE 2

SETTING: *Clara's living room, with small Christmas tree. Large window is at back, and toys are strewn about.*
AT RISE: CLARA *is playing with toys.*

CLARA'S MOTHER (*Offstage*): Clara! It's getting late. Put your new toys away and go to bed.
CLARA: Yes, Mother. (*To herself*) I wish I could stay up all night. Christmas is my favorite day of the year.
MOTHER (*Offstage*): Clara!
CLARA: I'm coming, Mother. (*To herself*) I think that of all the toys I got for Christmas, I like my nutcracker the best. (*Holds up small nutcracker shaped like man.*)
MOTHER (*Offstage*): Clara, I'll send that nutcracker back to Uncle Drosselmeyer if you don't mind me.
CLARA: I'm off to bed, Mama! (*To nutcracker*) Now, go to sleep, and we'll play in the morning. (*Puts down nutcracker and exits.*)

NARRATOR: So Clara went to bed, still with visions of sugar plums and nutcrackers in her head. (MOUSE KING *and* PRINCE MARZIPAN *enter fighting with swords.*)
MUSIC: *Mouse King Battle.*
NARRATOR: But what is this? Someone new has come on the scene. It is the hero, Prince Marzipan from Sugar Plum Land, and he is fighting the evil Mouse King.

PRINCE: Take that . . . and that, you evil sorcerer! You'll not get your grimy paws on my beautiful Sugar Plum Fairy Princess.

MOUSE KING (*Still fighting*): You are quite a swordsman, Prince Marzipan. And your spoken word is as strong as your sword arm.

PRINCE: Come on and fight!

MOUSE KING: Stand back! (*They stop fighting.*) This swordplay has gone on long enough. I shall turn you into that Nutcracker over there! Now your jaws will get a workout. Just you see.

PRINCE: You won't get away with this!

MOUSE KING: Oh, won't I? Into the nutcracker with you. (PRINCE *disappears.*) Ah-ha! Now back to Sugar Plum Land and the Princess. Yum, yum. (*Exits.* KING WINTER *and* QUEEN BLANCHE *fly by the large window and enter.*)

QUEEN: Oh, such an evil little mouse. We shouldn't allow this to happen. What should we do?

KING: I've awakened Clara with a strong gust of wind and snow on her window panes. Our Prince has certain elfin charms himself. Just watch and see. (*They exit.* CLARA *enters softly and looks about. She picks up small nutcracker.*)

CLARA: My beautiful nutcracker. I couldn't sleep thinking of you. A strong gust of wind and . . . (NUTCRACKER *appears.*)

NUTCRACKER: Please. You must help me.

CLARA: Nutcracker, are you talking? Who are you?

NUTCRACKER: I'm Prince Marzipan, trapped inside your Christmas toy. The evil Mouse King has put me inside it, and he has gone off to capture my Fairy Princess in Sugar Plum Land. Come with me!

CLARA: But how can I help? I'm only a little girl.

NUTCRACKER: I'm not sure, but come with me anyway. You will be back by morning.

CLARA: An adventure on Christmas! And I get to stay up all night, too. How exciting! (*They exit. Curtain*)

*   *   *   *   *

SCENE 3

SETTING: *Dark sky with snowflakes.*
MUSIC: *Dance of the Flutes.*
AT RISE: KING WINTER *and* QUEEN BLANCHE *fly in.*

QUEEN: Clara and the Nutcracker Prince are coming. Now, stop your snowing until they get safely to Sugar Plum Land.
KING (*Laughing*): Ho, ho! Snow! Snow! My snow will surround them and guide them. So dance, Snowflakes! Dance!
QUEEN: We must keep them in sight and protect them. (*They exit as* SNOWFLAKES *dance.*)
MUSIC: *Snowflake Waltz.*
CLARA (*Entering with* NUTCRACKER): Look at the beautiful snowflakes dancing. Let's watch.
NUTCRACKER (*Pulling her along*): No — we must save the Princess and my Candy people from the Mouse King. (*They exit. Curtain*)

*   *   *   *   *

SCENE 4

SETTING: *Sugar Plum Land, with buildings made of candy.*
AT RISE: CANDIES *enter, then* SUGAR PLUM FAIRY PRINCESS, *who dances.*
MUSIC: *Dance of the Sugar Plum Fairy.*

46

Sugar Plum Fairy (*At end of dance*): Quickly, now, cinnamon stick, chocolate, and all the rest. Let's get ready for Prince Marzipan's return. It's Christmas night, and he will be back soon from his battle with the horrible Mouse King. (Mouse King *enters as they rush about.*)

Mouse King: Horrible, indeed! (*He grabs* Sugar Plum Fairy. Candies *scream and run off.*)

Sugar Plum Fairy: Let me go! Go away! What has happened to my Prince Marzipan?

Mouse King: I turned your precious prince into a nutcracker by my magic. (*Laughs*)

Sugar Plum Fairy: Oh, sweet heavens!

Mouse King: And now you will be my bride, and all the Candies will be food for my mice.

Sugar Plum Fairy: You cruel, ugly villain.

Mouse King: All I have to do is squeal on my silver horn, and all my companions will run here, scramble over everything, and gobble up Sugar Plum Land.

Sugar Plum Fairy: No! Please don't! I'll go with you. Don't hurt my friends.

Mouse King: I'll count to three. (*Puts horn to mouth*) One! (*Breath*) Two! (*Breath*) Thr— (Clara *and* Nutcracker *rush in and knock horn from* Mouse King's *hand.*)

Nutcracker: Put down that villainous horn, Mouse King, and take up your sword.

Sugar Plum Fairy: Who can this be?

Mouse King (*Taking out sword*): So we meet again. (Sugar Plum Fairy *and* Clara *stay at one side as* Mouse King *and* Nutcracker *fight.*)

Nutcracker: Our swords cross again.

Mouse King: Yes, but I have the upper hand. I will win this battle, and the Sugar Plum Fairy Princess will be mine. (Mouse King *drives* Nutcracker *to ground.*)

SUGAR PLUM FAIRY: Oh, what shall we do?

CLARA: I have an idea! I'll do what Mama does when mice get into the pantry. I'll just take off my shoe. (*She does so.*) Now, watch this. (CLARA *hits* MOUSE KING *with her shoe, and he falls to ground, dying.*)

MOUSE KING: Ah-h-h! (*Disappears*)

ALL: Hooray!

SUGAR PLUM FAIRY (*To* CLARA): Thank you very much, my dear. But who are you, and where did you both come from?

NUTCRACKER: This is Clara, and she is from Everland.

SUGAR PLUM FAIRY (*To* NUTCRACKER): I seem to recognize your voice, but I do not know your face.

CLARA: This is your Prince Marzipan. The Mouse King put a spell on him and placed him in my Christmas nutcracker.

NUTCRACKER: If you will open the nutcracker's mouth all the way, out I'll spring.

CLARA: All right. Here, Princess. You pull on one end of this stick, and I'll pull the other. (CLARA *and* SUGAR PLUM FAIRY *pull on the* NUTCRACKER's *back stick and hold the jaw, and out pops* PRINCE. *See Production Notes.*)

ALL: Hooray!

PRINCE: That was a tight squeeze!

SUGAR PLUM FAIRY (*Embracing him*): My dear, sweet Prince Marzipan.

PRINCE (*To* CLARA): We thank you, dear Clara, for saving us from the Mouse King and his pack of mice.

SUGAR PLUM FAIRY: Please stay and celebrate Christmas with us.

CLARA: All right, but I must be home before dawn.

SUGAR PLUM FAIRY: You shall be. Now be seated over there, and the celebration will begin. (PRINCE, SUGAR

PLUM FAIRY *and* CLARA *exit as* DANCERS *enter and dancing begins. One or all of the following dances may be performed. See Production Notes.*)

MUSIC: *Chinese Dance, Russian Dance, Arabian Dance.*

KING WINTER (*Entering with* QUEEN BLANCHE *as dances conclude and stage is empty*): And so this is how Clara and the Candies of Sugar Plum Land spent their Christmas.

QUEEN BLANCHE: And we hope you spend as happy a one.

KING *and* QUEEN: Merry Christmas! (*They exit. Dance may end play. See Production Notes.*)

MUSIC: *Waltz of the Flowers.*

THE END

THE NUTCRACKER PRINCE

Number of Puppets: 7 hand or rod puppets or marionettes, including Prince as himself and as Nutcracker. Any number of dancing Candies or Snowflakes, plus other dancers for Chinese dance, Russian dance, Arabian dance, and Waltz of the Flowers.

Playing Time: 20 minutes.

Description of Puppets: King Winter and Queen Blanche are in white with glitter all over them to look like snow. Clara can be in a long nightdress. Prince wears regal clothes and Mouse King has a red cape and a crown between his ears. Sugar Plum Fairy wears glittery pink tights and a small crown. Dancers: Snowflakes may be abstract snowflakes or little people dressed like snowflakes. Candies may be all different kinds of candy — candy canes, gumdrops, etc. For Chinese dance, use one, two or three little mushroom-like people with coolie hats. For Russian dance, two or four fur-hatted and full-bloomered dancers. For Arabian dance, a beautiful lady in veils and full skirt. For Waltz of the Flowers, use stylized dancers like flowers with petals as skirts. The Nutcracker should look like a man, with wide jaws. When Prince Marzipan pops out of Nutcracker's mouth, the effect is created by having Clara and Sugar Plum Fairy stand in front of Nutcracker as they open its mouth, hiding it from sight. The two puppets are exchanged.

Properties: Small nutcracker and toys, swords, silver horn, shoe.

Setting: Scenes 1 and 3: A dark night sky with snowflakes. Scene 2: Clara's living room with a small Christmas tree and a large window at back. Scene 4: Sugar Plum Land, with buildings made of candy.

Lighting: Scenes 1 and 3 are dark, scenes 2 and 4 are bright.

Sound: Use the music from Tchaikovsky's "Nutcracker Suite," as indicated in text. Use only short parts of each number to keep each dance to one or two minutes.

ALI BABA AND THE FORTY THIEVES

Adapted from The Arabian Nights

Characters

ALI BABA, *a woodcutter*
KASSIM, *his brother*
MORGANA, *Ali Baba's wife*
SHAHRIAR, *Kassim's wife*
MUSTAPHA, *robber chief*
ABDULLA, *Mustapha's helper*
NARRATOR

SCENE 1

SETTING: *Outdoor area in front of a cave. A large rock and tree are at one side.*
AT RISE: ALI BABA *enters.*

NARRATOR: This is the story of how Ali Baba and his wife Morgana outwitted forty dangerous thieves. It all began one day as Ali Baba was returning from selling his wood in the marketplace.

ALI BABA: Oh, I am exhausted! I've been up since dawn, and have sold all the firewood that I gathered. (*Looks at hand*) These pennies will not help Morgana and me very much. There isn't much you can buy with a few pennies nowadays. If only my family hadn't lost all its money and possessions to that terrible band of thieves. They have looted all the families of the countryside. Just what will we do? (*Sound of band of thieves singing is heard from offstage.*) That must be the forty thieves now! I had better hide somewhere—but where? (*Looks up*) I know! Up in that tree. No. (*Looks at rock*) Better still, behind that rock. (*He hides.*)

MUSTAPHA (*Entering with* ABDULLA, *carrying bags*): Have the men camp over there, Abdulla. (*Points offstage*) You and I will enter the cave by ourselves.

ABDULLA: As you wish, Chief Mustapha. (*Calls offstage*) Comrades! Camp right where you are for a few minutes. Your chief and I will be joining you soon.

MUSTAPHA: Good. (*Facing cave*) Now, I'll say the magic words. (*Calls*) OPEN SESAME! (*Set piece covering mouth of cave moves aside, and precious jewels and gold are seen within cave.*)

ABDULLA: It always thrills me to see all this gold and these jewels. (*He puts the bag he carries inside cave.*) This is a perfect place to hide my—er—our treasure.

MUSTAPHA: Don't allow yourself to be tempted, Abdulla! If you ever decided to come to the cave by yourself, we would see to it that you would not get out again. You'd be a prisoner in the cave forever.

ABDULLA: Great chief, I had no such thoughts.

MUSTAPHA: You had better not! (*They finish placing bags inside cave.*) Come on, now. We must be on our way. We have more poor folk to rob before the sun sets.

ADBULLA (*Archly*): And a few to rob after the sun sets, as well.

MUSTAPHA: Of course! (*They both laugh.*) Now, stand aside. (*Calls*) CLOSE SESAME. (*Cave closes. They go offstage, laughing. Sound of thieves' song is heard again, as they exit.*)

ALI BABA (*Coming out cautiously*): Hm-m-m. Have they gone? Yes! The coast is clear. I heard the words they said to open the cave. Do I dare to try them? I think I shall. (*Calls*) OPEN SESAME! (*Cave opens.*) Look! (*In awe*) Caskets of jewels, bags of gold, costly rugs and tapestries and bolts of silks. (*Shocked*) Wait! Look! Those clothes and jewels belonged to my family. They were stolen from us years ago. It would not be wrong to take what is rightfully ours. (*He takes objects out of cave.*) There! Now to close the cave. (*Calls*) CLOSE SESAME! (*The cave closes.*) I'd better go home before the robbers return. Oh, what luck I have had today! (*He exits. Curtain*)

* * *

SCENE 2

SETTING: *Interior of Ali Baba's humble house.*
AT RISE: MORGANA *is cleaning the house, talking to herself.*

MORGANA (*Worried*): Where can Ali Baba be? He is unusually late today. I hope nothing has happened to him.
ALI BABA (*Running in, carrying riches*): Oh, Morgana, good wife, see what I have brought home. All the riches that once were ours! We are no longer poor.
MORGANA (*Amazed*): Oh, my! Can it be? Do my eyes deceive me? Let's see if it is all there. I have borrowed Shahriar's measuring cup, and we can measure the gold coins with that. (*Gets cup*)
ALI BABA: Good! Now, let's see. (*Measuring the coins*) Here are some coins.
NARRATOR: Ali Baba and his wife carefully measured the gold and counted their jewels to see if everything was there. The next day, Morgana returned the measuring cup to her sister-in-law, Shahriar. (*Curtain*)

* * *

SCENE 3

SETTING: *Room in the well-appointed house of Kassim and Shahriar. Rugs and tapestries are draped about.*
AT RISE: *Sound of a knock is heard.* SHAHRIAR *enters and crosses the stage.*

SHAHRIAR (*Calling*): Yes, yes! I'm coming. (*Crossly*) Who could that be? It's very early for a caller. Come in. Come in!

MORGANA (*Entering, with measuring cup*): Good afternoon, Shahriar, dear sister-in-law.

SHAHRIAR: What do you mean afternoon? Is it that late already? What do you want anyway?

MORGANA: I've only come to return your measuring cup. (*Hands cup to* SHAHRIAR) Thank you very much.

SHAHRIAR (*Angrily*): Well, it's about time you brought it back! (*Stops*) Hm-m-m. (*Distracted; turns away from* MORGANA) You can go now.

MORGANA: Thank you again.

SHAHRIAR: Yes, yes. Be off now. (MORGANA *exits.*) Hm-m-m. (*Calls*) Kassim. Kassim, my husband, come out here!

KASSIM (*From offstage*): What is it?

SHAHRIAR: I have something important to show you. Come here. (*She holds up a large gold coin.*)

KASSIM (*Entering*): What is it? (*Sees coin*) Where did you get that? It's pure gold!

SHAHRIAR: From your brother's wife, Morgana. It was stuck in the bottom of the measuring cup she had borrowed from me. (*Sarcastically*) Your brother, the wood-cutter, is so poor that he borrows a cup to measure his gold coins, eh?

55

KASSIM: Hm-m-m. I'm going to have to find out where he got that. Give it to me. (*Tries to take coin*)

SHAHRIAR (*Moving away*): No! I found it, so it's mine.

KASSIM: Keep it, then. I'll find others. (*He runs out.*)

NARRATOR: And so Kassim rushed to Ali Baba's house and forced Ali Baba to tell him where he got the gold. Then he rushed to the cave. (*Curtain*)

*   *   *

SCENE 4

SETTING: *Same as Scene 1.*
AT RISE: KASSIM *rushes in.*

KASSIM (*Facing cave*): Now, what is that word? (*Alarmed*) Oh, no! Did I forget the right words? Let's see. OPEN BARLEY! No, that's not it. (*Pauses*) Hm-m-m. OPEN WHEAT! No, that's not it, either. I remember. (*Calls*) OPEN SESAME! (*Cave swings open, revealing* MUSTAPHA *and* ABDULLA *inside cave.* KASSIM *cries out in fright.*)

MUSTAPHA (*Slyly*): So—you want to be in the cave of riches, do you? Assist him, Abdulla. (ABDULLA *rushes to capture* KASSIM *and pulls him inside cave.* MUSTAPHA *and* ABDULLA *leave cave.*) Now, stay there forever, thief! (*Calls*) CLOSE SESAME!

KASSIM (*As cave closes*): Ohhhhhhhh!

MUSTAPHA: Now, let that be a lesson to anyone who tries to steal thieves' gold! (*He and* ABDULLA *rush out. Lights may dim briefly to indicate passage of time.*)

NARRATOR: Poor Kassim was forced to be a prisoner in the cave he had wanted to see. Shahriar became worried when he didn't come home and went to Ali Baba to tell him that Kassim was missing. Ali Baba thought his brother might be trapped in the cave, and so he returned there to check.

ALI BABA (*Entering*): Kassim must be here! I don't see any of the thieves, so I'll use the magic words to open the cave. (*Calls*) OPEN SESAME! (*Cave opens and* KASSIM *falls out into his arms.*)

KASSIM: Oh, thank you, dear brother, Ali Baba, for saving me!

ALI BABA: Quickly, Kassim! We must leave this place before any of the thieves return.

KASSIM: Yes, by all means! (*Greedily*) Just let me take a few jewels, first.

ALI BABA: No! The treasure is cursed. Don't touch any of it. We must be off. (*They race out.*)

ABDULLA (*Entering*): So! I was wise to keep guard over the cave. Now I will follow them and see where they live. (*Laughs*) Ha, ha! (*He exits quickly. Curtain*)

*　　　*　　　*

SCENE 5

SETTING: *Street scene in front of Ali Baba's house. Three or four houses are in a row. Ali Baba's house, at center, has a working door.*

AT RISE: ALI BABA *and* KASSIM *enter.*

NARRATOR: Ali Baba and Kassim arrived soon at Ali Baba's house, unaware that Abdulla had followed them.

ALI BABA (*Calling*): Wife! Morgana! We're home. (MORGANA *and* SHAHRIAR *come out.*) Kassim is safe!

SHAHRIAR (*Rushing to* KASSIM *and hugging him*): Oh, Kassim!

You are here at last. My poor husband, what did the thieves do to you?

KASSIM (*Wearily*): Let us go home, so I can rest, Shahriar. I'll tell you all about it there. (*They exit.*)

ALI BABA: We should go in, too, Morgana. I must tell you, also, about this adventure.

MORGANA: Right away, husband. Go in. I will join you in a minute. (*He enters the house and she goes to one side and hides behind tree.*)

ABDULLA (*Entering*): Aha. That house is where they live. Heh, heh! They can't fool Abdulla. I'll mark their front door with a large "X" and then bring Mustapha to see where the culprit lives. (*He puts a large "X" on* ALI BABA's *door, then exits.*)

MORGANA (*Coming out of hiding*): Just as I thought! Ali Baba and Kassim were followed. (*Pauses*) I know! I'll mark these other doors, too. The thieves will never know which door is the right one. (*She marks other doors onstage with an "X."*) There! Perfect. (*She enters her house and closes door behind her as* MUSTAPHA *and* ABDULLA *enter.*)

MUSTAPHA: Now, show me, Abdulla. Which door is theirs?

ABDULLA: I marked it. (*Points to a door*) It's this one. No! (*Turns to another*) This one.

MUSTAPHA: You fool! The peasants were smarter than you. They marked all the doors!

ABDULLA: Now we'll never know where the rascal lives who stole our treasure.

MUSTAPHA: I'm not so sure about that. Look! (*Points to floor*) A gold coin was dropped on the doorstep of that house. It must have been from our hoard. (*Laughs*) We found the right house after all!

ABDULLA: What luck we have!

MUSTAPHA: It is not luck, but good powers of observation.

Go now, and bring back all forty of our thieves. There are forty empty oil jars on the dock next to this house— tell the men to hide there. And, have an extra jar filled with oil, too. Now, hurry!

ABDULLA (*Excited*): Yes, yes, right away! We'll teach those peasants a lesson. (*Laughs*) Heh, heh, heh! (*Exits*)

MUSTAPHA: Now, to do my dirty work. (*He knocks on* ALI BABA's *door, and* ALI BABA *opens it.*) Good afternoon.

ALI BABA: Good afternoon, good merchant. How can I help you?

MUSTAPHA: Kind gentleman, I need a place to sleep tonight. I will pay you well if you let me stay here. I have forty jars of olive oil on the dock nearby.

ALI BABA: Why, certainly, you may stay here. I cannot refuse such a generous offer. (*Calls*) Morgana! Arrange a bed for this generous merchant. Tonight we will have a guest in our house. (*To* MUSTAPHA) Come in. Come in! (*They enter house. Curtain*)

*   *   *

SCENE 6

SETTING: *The dock. Part of Ali Baba's house and river are at rear. Several oil jars are onstage.*

AT RISE: MORGANA *enters.*

NARRATOR: Ali Baba did not recognize the merchant as Mustapha, the thief, and opened his house to him. But, Morgana was suspicious, and cautious as well. She went to the back of their house, which was on a dock overlooking a rushing river, and there she found forty large oil jars.

MORGANA: Look at all these oil containers! I wonder if they really contain oil. I will knock on one of them. (*She knocks on jar.*)

VOICE OF ABDULLA (*As if inside jar*): Yes, we're here, Master. Everything is ready for the attack. Is it time now for all forty of us to come out?

MORGANA (*Aside*): What is this? I must disguise my voice! (*In deep voice*) No, not yet. I will let you know.

VOICE OF ABDULLA: Good, Chief. We will wait for your signal.

MORGANA (*Aside*): These jars must be hiding the forty thieves that Ali Baba told me about. What will I do to save us? (*Pauses*) I know! I will seal the top of each jar, and then tip all of them into the river. (*She pushes jars backwards into river.*) By the time the thieves can get out of these, they'll be miles away from here—maybe even in the ocean.

NARRATOR: And so Morgana sealed each and every one of the jars, and pushed them into the rushing river. And for all we know, the thieves may still be sailing the high seas. (*Curtain*)

* * *

SCENE 7

SETTING: *Same as Scene 2.*

AT RISE: ALI BABA *and* MUSTAPHA *sit at a table, laughing and drinking.*

NARRATOR: Meanwhile, Ali Baba was entertaining Mustapha, the false merchant, in his home.

MUSTAPHA (*Laughing*): What a good table you set, Ali Baba! You must have inherited quite a fortune.

60

ALI BABA: I have only what truly belongs to me, kind merchant. I have been fortunate.

MUSTAPHA: I see. Such fortune can always be helped along. I will see what I can do.

ALI BABA: Why, that is kind of you. (MORGANA *enters with jar. She places jar at one side of stage.*) Here is my wife. She has come to dance for you.

MORGANA: For your pleasure, sir merchant. (*Music is played offstage, as she dances.*)

MUSTAPHA: Ahhh! So graceful! You are lucky to have such a wife, sir.

MORGANA (*Going to jar and picking it up*): This is called the olive oil dance. (*Dancing with jar*) Just pick up the jar, move about (*Turning jar upside down and placing it over* MUSTAPHA's *head*), then turn the jar upside down.

MUSTAPHA (*Struggling to get jar off; stunned*): What! Ugh! Ughhh! (*He falls over onto ground, unable to get jar off.*)

ALI BABA (*Shocked*): What are you doing, Morgana?

MORGANA: This man is not a merchant at all, husband, but the robber chief, Mustapha. Look! (*Points to* MUSTAPHA's *belt*) In his belt!

ALI BABA: A dagger! He meant to kill me.

MORGANA: And his men were hidden outside! They meant to kill us all, but they are already on their way again, now. They've decided to become sailors instead of thieves. (*She laughs.*)

ALI BABA: Sailors?

MORGANA: Yes! They are in their oil-jar boats, sailing away down to the sea.

ALI BABA: Morgana, you've outwitted Mustapha and his thieves—and saved our lives, too.

KASSIM (*Entering*): What has happened? Why is this man on the floor with a jar on his head?

ALI BABA: He is learning not to be greedy. And let that be a lesson to you as well, Kassim. My clever wife Morgana has saved us all!

KASSIM: Hurray for Morgana!

MORGANA: And so goes another one of the thousand and one Arabian nights. (*To audience*) Good night! (*She closes curtain.*)

THE END

Ali Baba and the Forty Thieves

PRODUCTION NOTES

Number of Puppets: 6 hand or rod puppets or marionettes.

Playing Time: 25 minutes.

Costumes: Traditional Arab dress, such as, full trousers or "harem pants" for men and women; veils for women; turbans for men. Use a fairy-tale book with good illustrations to get ideas for costumes. Mustapha must have a dagger in his belt.

Properties: Bags of gold for thieves and Ali Baba to carry; measuring cup on a wire for easy handling; gold piece (sewn or glued into Shahriar's hand); a number of large ceramic jars (should be flat on one side to lie on stage floor when Morgana pushes them); a large, full-dimensional jar on a wire for Scene 7.

Setting: An outside area, near a cave; interior of a humble house; richly-appointed house interior; street of houses; dock on a river. Sets should be simple, because five are needed; model them after illustrations in books, to create an Arabian flavor. In Scene 1, the cave front can be separate from the main set, or on hinges, and either moved to one side or opened, as indicated in text. In Scene 5, Ali Baba's house is center stage, and has a working door. Use a piece of chalk and mark X's on the doors, as indicated, or else "flip-over" squares on the doors with an X drawn on one side and released when the puppet "draws" the X.

Lighting: No special effects. The dock scene can be done in blue.

Sound: Live or recorded music for thieves' song, and dance, as indicated in text. "Scheherazade," or Arabian-sounding music, would be appropriate.

PUSS-IN-BOOTS

From the story by Charles Perrault

Characters

PETER, *a miller's son*
PUSS-IN-BOOTS
KING
COOK
PRINCESS
OGRE
LION
MOUSE

SCENE 1

TIME: *Long ago.*
SETTING: *In front of the mill that is Peter's home.*
AT RISE: PETER *is onstage, looking for his cat.*

PETER: Here, Puss! Here, kitty! Where can he have gone? And why did Papa leave me only a cat? I've probably lost that now. John got the mill and my brother George the donkey, but me.... just Puss. Oh, well. I should be grateful for that. He's such a nice cat. I wonder where he is? And what do you think he wanted with those coins? They were all I had.
PUSS: Hello, there, Master. (PUSS-IN-BOOTS, *a handsome cat, in fancy dress, enters.*)

PETER: Puss . . . Look at you! Where did you get all those fine clothes? A big red hat — a fancy blue cape — and those boots. What beautiful red boots! You didn't spend the last of my money on them, did you?

PUSS: Don't worry, Peter. You'll soon have plenty to eat, and you'll be dressed and treated like a king! (*He bows and curtsies.*) How do you do?

PETER: What are you doing?

PUSS: I'm practicing my manners.

PETER: Whatever for?

PUSS: To visit the King!

PETER: To visit the King? Did you say visit the King? But, why?

PUSS: Our King is very fond of partridge and rabbit, I understand.

PETER: Yes. That's true. But he complains that his hunters can't catch them. I hear that he seldom gets any to eat.

PUSS: And that is where I come in.

PETER: What do you mean?

PUSS: The King would pay a handsome price for a bagful, I dare say.

PETER: Most likely.

PUSS: I know a forest full of game. Have you ever seen a cat who wasn't a good hunter? Go home and I will meet you there later.

PETER: All right, Puss. Best of luck!

PUSS: Good luck to us both! (*They exit. Curtain.*)

*   *   *   *   *

SCENE 2

TIME: *A few hours later.*
SETTING: *The kitchen in the King's palace.*
AT RISE: KING *enters.*

KING: Oh, I'm so-o-o hungry! Where is that cook? I haven't had a rabbit or a partridge for so long! At night I dream of delicious cooked rabbit, fit for a king . . . that's me . . . all fixed with stuffing, and (*Rabbit on platter floats by.*) — what's that? I'm seeing things. Yum, yum! (*Tries to catch it*) Oh! (*It disappears.*) Where did it go? Fiddlesticks! Oh . . . just one little bite of a fancy roast partridge with figs and cherries. . . . I'd give anything if. ... . (*Partridge floats by.*) There's one! (*Tries to catch it, but it disappears, too*) I'm famished. I'm seeing things. They were both mirages. Where is that cook? I think I'm losing my mind. (*Calls*) Cook! Come here at once!

COOK (*Running in*): Yes, Your Majesty?

KING: Have my hunters returned from the fields?

COOK: Yes, Your Majesty.

KING: And what's for dinner?

COOK: Porridge, Your Majesty.

KING: Porridge! Now what kind of dish is that to set before a king? (*Aside*) Seems as if I've heard that line before. Porridge! I'm sick of porridge! What else do you have?

COOK: The hunters came back empty-handed. How about a nice roast cat?

KING: Cat?

COOK: Yes, one with red boots on just came to the back door. He says he wants to see you.

KING: A cat to see me? Send him in at once.

COOK: Yes, Your Majesty. (COOK *exits.*)

KING (*Shouting after him*): And no more porridge! If I have one more bowl of porridge or one more pie of blackbirds that keep squawking at me, I'll scream. Of course I don't mind those fiddlers playing while I eat, but that isn't very nourishing.

PUSS (*Entering with a bag of rabbits and partridges*): Your Majesty! My master, the Marquis of Carabas, sends you his humblest greetings and wishes to present to you this bag of rabbits and partridges. (*Lays bag before* KING)

KING: I accept his greetings and I am overjoyed with his gift. A whole bag of partridges and rabbits. Oh, joy! Goody, goody! (*To* PUSS) Thank the Marquis of. . . . What did you say his name was?

PUSS: The Marquis of Carabas.

KING: Yes, the Marquis of Carabas. Know him well! Thank him for me. What a wonderful gift! And give him this little token of my appreciation. Here is a bag of gold coins. (*Gets bag of coins and presents it to* PUSS)

PUSS (*Bowing*): Yes, Your Majesty. Thank you. Your Majesty is most generous. Good day, sir.

KING (*Calling*): Cook! Cook! (*To* PUSS) Oh, yes . . . Good day, Pussycat.

PUSS (*Aside, to audience*): Pussycat? Really! (*Exits with bag of coins.*)

KING: Cook! And now for a wonderful feast. (COOK *runs in.*) Look! (*Shows bag. Curtain.*)

*   *   *   *   *

SCENE 3

TIME: *A few minutes later.*
SETTING: *A spot by the side of a road, in front of a stream.*
AT RISE: PETER *is onstage.*

PETER: I wonder when Puss-in-Boots will return from the palace. Do you think he saw the King? I hope so.

PUSS (*Entering with bag*): Peter! Look what I have. A bag of gold! Here is the beginning of the fortune I promised you. (*Gives bag to* PETER.)

PETER: You did see the King. (*Looking into bag*) Hundreds of gold pieces. I can't believe it! You didn't steal these, did you?

PUSS: Oh, no. I just pleased the King with something for his stomach. You know, the way to a King's treasury is through his stomach.

PETER: Now I can get us a decent meal. And I can get a new suit . . . some fine clothes like yours, Puss. Then we can travel in style.

PUSS: No — wait. I have a plan to take care of that. This is only the beginning. Soon the King will be taking his daily ride by here. When you go for a swim, I'll hide your clothes, and when the King comes along. . . . Oh — I hear the coach. Go and get into the water.

PETER: What's going to happen?

PUSS: Do as I say.

PETER: All right. (PETER *exits.*)

PUSS: Oh, I'm so clever. Have you ever seen a cat as clever as I am? (*Suddenly alert*) Oh-oh. . . . Here come the King and his daughter now. (PUSS *exits.* KING'*s open coach comes in with* KING *and* PRINCESS *in it.*)

KING: Beautiful day for a ride, isn't it, my dear?

PRINCESS: Yes, Papa. Thank you for taking me out today. It is so lonely in that palace all by myself.

KING: One day you will find a handsome husband. We'll just keep looking.

PRINCESS: Oh, thank you, Papa.

PUSS (*Appearing, crying*): Boo-hoo. Boo-hoo.

KING: What's the matter, Pussycat?

PUSS: Oh, Your Majesty, my master, the Marquis of Carabas, has gone for a swim and some thieves have stolen his clothes. The Marquis can't come out of the water. Boo-hoo! He'll get sick if he stays in there any longer.

KING: I just happen to be coming back from the tailor, and I have a new suit that should fit the Marquis. Here. (*Hands box to* Puss) Take it to him ... so he can dress.

Puss: Oh, thank you, Your Majesty.

KING: Better hide your eyes, daughter.

PRINCESS: Oh, yes, Father. (*She covers her eyes.*)

KING: Oh, that poor boy. In that cold water. I hope he doesn't catch a chill.

PRINCESS: So do I, Papa. A marquis ... well! (Puss *holds cape as if to conceal* PETER *as he dresses.* NOTE: *Offstage, the original* PETER *in shabby clothes is exchanged for another* PETER, *dressed in a regal suit of clothes, made of rich fabrics, with gold trim.*)

Puss: The clothes are a perfect fit, Your Majesty. (*Takes down cape to reveal* PETER, *dressed as the Marquis, in his new finery.*)

KING: Perfect!

PRINCESS: I say!

PETER (*Bowing*): Your Majesty. These clothes are too good for me.

KING: Tut! Tut! Think nothing of it. I've many more where those came from. But do you think you might be able to get me another rabbit or partridge?

PETER: My friend, Puss-in-Boots, can get you more.

KING: What a clever cat!

PETER: So I find out.

KING: Oh, by the way ... This is my daughter, the Princess. Daughter — the Marquis of Carabas.

PRINCESS: How do you do!

PETER: My name is ...

Puss (*Interrupting*): Your Majesty, the Marquis wishes you to visit his castle down the road to the South.

PETER: What?

KING: A castle too! I knew it! Oh, by all means.

PUSS: Just follow this road and it will take you there. I'll run ahead.

KING: Off we go. . . . Come sit next to the Princess, young man. I'm sure she will like that.

PRINCESS (*Embarrassed*): Oh, Papa! (*The coach leaves, with* KING, PETER, *and* PRINCESS.)

PUSS: Now to visit the wicked Ogre who lives in that castle down the road. I had better get there before Peter and the King do. The Ogre thinks he is a great magician, but we will see who is smarter. It is about time someone did something about him. He is so wicked, he steals princesses away from their homes and devours them. Just see what I will do to him! Now to get a fine home for my Marquis of Carabas, and a princess, too. (*He exits. Curtain.*)

*   *   *   *   *

SCENE 4

SETTING: *Inside the Ogre's castle.*

AT RISE: OGRE *is onstage, trying to do magic tricks.*

OGRE (*Waving hands and humming a sinister tune*): Dum-da-dum-dum. . . . (*To audience*) Welcome to my beautiful castle, everyone. I suppose you have come to see me do magic tricks. I am very clever, and I can do any kind of magic I want. Just to show you. . . . (*Gets box and puts it center*) Here is my magic box. Let's see what I can bring out. (*Chants*)

> Here I conjure and here I weave . . . .
> Now spooky spider do I perceive.
> Appear and show yourself right now —
> I'll wave my hand in this way — *pow!*

(*Gestures; nothing happens*) What did I do wrong? I had no trouble getting that beautiful maiden to appear yesterday. Of course, that wasn't really magic. I stole her from a farm nearby. She was delicious. (*Suddenly a spider appears from the box when the* OGRE *isn't looking, scaring him.*) Yikes! Where did that come from? Let's try something bigger. How about a cat? (*Chants*)

> Here I conjure and here I weave . . . .
> Now pussycat do I perceive.
> One so tender and tasty, too —
> One I make into a stew.

(*Gestures; again nothing happens*) Now what did I do wrong this time? Maybe I have to wait awhile. I won't look. (*He hides his eyes, as* PUSS-IN-BOOTS *enters.*)

PUSS: Good day, Ogre.

OGRE (*Seeing* PUSS): It worked! It worked! I don't have to go hunting for someone to eat today! Come to me, kitty. Don't run away.

PUSS: Who's running?

OGRE: Aren't you afraid of me? I'm a terrible magician.

PUSS: You can say that again. Ha!

OGRE: I am! I am! I am!

PUSS: I might be afraid of you if you were a ferocious lion, but I'm not afraid of a stupid ogre who thinks he's a magician.

OGRE: Well, I am a magician. And just to prove it, I'll turn myself into a lion. It would probably be more fun to eat you then, anyway. (*He becomes a* LION. *See Production Notes*) Grr-r-r! Are you scared now?

PUSS: Humph! Any magician can turn himself into a lion. But it takes a really clever one to turn himself into something as small as a mouse. I know you can't do that.

OGRE (*As* LION): I can! I can! I can! Just watch! (LION *turns into a small* MOUSE.) Now, see? I'm a little gray mouse, and I'm just as good a magician as anyone else.

PUSS: But not as smart or as fast as I am! (*He chases* MOUSE.)

OGRE (*As* MOUSE): Help! Squeak! Squeak!

PUSS (*Pouncing on* MOUSE *and downing it with one gulp*): I've got you! Mm-m-m. . . . Delicious. I had better clean up this castle. I hear the King coming, with the Princess and Peter. (*Races about, tidying castle, removing box, and finishes just as* KING, PETER *and* PRINCESS *enter.*) Welcome to the castle of the Marquis of Carabas. (*Bows*)

PETER: Really?

PUSS: Shh-h!

KING: So this is your castle.

PETER: I guess so.

KING: He's very modest. Daughter, I think I've found the man for you.

PRINCESS: I think so, too.

KING: Will you take the hand of my daughter, good Marquis?

PETER: Sure! Sounds great to me.

PRINCESS: Me, too! (*Giggles*)

KING: With a castle like this, and with your title, the Marquis of Carabas, I'm sure you both will be very happy.

PETER: I hope so, Your Majesty.

KING: Now let us start the arrangements for the marriage. (KING *and* PRINCESS *exit.*)

PETER: Puss-in-Boots, you were the best gift of all the presents from Papa. Thank you very much. (PETER *exits*.)

PUSS (*To audience*): And so the Marquis of Carabas and the King's daughter were married, and they all, except the Ogre, lived happily ever after. As for me, I was made the royal prime minister. (*Bows regally as curtain closes.*)

THE END

Production Notes

Puss-in-Boots

Number of Puppets: 9 hand puppets or marionettes; 1 is costume-change puppet for Peter in a period suit made of rich-looking cloth, with gold trim. The first Peter is dressed in shabby clothes.

Playing Time: 15 minutes.

Description of Puppets: Rich-looking clothes for King, Princess, and Peter, as described above. Puss-in-Boots has high red boots, large red hat with a plume, blue cape, etc. Cook has white apron and high white hat. Appropriate animal puppets for Lion and Mouse. Ogre should be made to look as grotesque and frightening as possible.

Properties: Rabbit, partridge, on platters (use cut-outs); sack, for Puss; bag of coins, for King; suit box; open coach (use a cut-out); spider; black magician's box.

Setting: There are four sets, and each should be shown by a representative drawing or cut-out on the backdrop. Scene 1, in front of the mill; Scene 2, kitchen in the palace; Scene 3, a spot by the side of a road, near a stream; Scene 4, the Ogre's castle.

Lighting: No special effects.

SNOW WHITE AND THE SEVEN DWARFS

Adapted from Grimm's fairy tales

Characters

SNOW WHITE
QUEEN
PRINCE CHARMING
HUNTSMAN
MEANIE ⎫
MINEY ⎪
MOE ⎪
DEANIE ⎬ *The Seven Dwarfs*
DINEY ⎪
DOE ⎪
DUM DUM ⎭
RABBIT
DEER
VOICE OF MIRROR

Scene One

TIME: *Long ago.*

SETTING: *The throne room of the Queen's palace. There is a mirror on the wall, and a throne at one side.*

AT RISE: SNOW WHITE *is scrubbing the floor, with a rag and bucket, and singing.*

SNOW WHITE (*Singing to tune of "Twinkle, Twinkle, Little Star"*):

Such a day to wash and dust.
Please the Queen or else she'll bust.
Go outside and wash the stairs,
Stir the soup and mend the tears,
Hope it's time that she does say
I can go outside and play.

(*Speaks*) I've worked since sun-up. My stepmother the Queen does like a clean castle! I wish I had someone to help me clean all these rooms, though. I never worked so hard when Papa was alive. . . . Not that I object to work, but I seldom get to play. (QUEEN *enters.*)

QUEEN: Play, indeed! You are too old to play, and too ugly to let out of the castle. Snow White! My bed hasn't been made yet. Go to my room immediately and change the sheets and air the royal bedroom!

SNOW WHITE: Yes, Stepmother. (*She starts to go.*)

QUEEN: Don't call me Stepmother—I'm your queen. Go now and get busy. There's no time for play. (SNOW WHITE *exits. Mockingly*) "Skin as white as snow—cheeks as red as blood—hair as black as ebony." Ha! Snow White looks more like a skinny kitchen maid to me. Her mother—the first Queen—probably died of disappointment. Now I am Queen and easily the fairest in the land—or so my magic mirror says. But I'll ask it again today, just to be sure. (*She goes to mirror.*)

Mirror, mirror, on the wall
Who's the fairest one of all?

VOICE OF MIRROR:
Yesterday you were the fairest, O Queen,
But today, fairer than Snow White is nowhere seen.

QUEEN: You lie! How dare you! I'm furious! Well—we'll just see who the fairest is tomorrow. (*Calls*) Huntsman! Huntsman! (HUNTSMAN *enters.*)

HUNTSMAN: Yes, my Queen?

QUEEN: I've a small chore for you to do.

HUNTSMAN: Small or large, your wish is my command.

QUEEN: Take Snow White into the woods for a little outing, so she can play. Then when she is not looking—*kill her!*

HUNTSMAN: Oh, no! Sweet innocent Snow White! No! I beg of you—

QUEEN: If you wish to see your family again you *must* do as I say.

HUNTSMAN: I—I. . . .

QUEEN (*Calling*): Snow White! (SNOW WHITE *enters.*)

SNOW WHITE: Yes, Stepmother?

QUEEN: I've changed my mind. You may go out and play in the woods today. The Huntsman will go with you to protect you from harm.

SNOW WHITE: No animal would hurt me. They are all my friends.

QUEEN: Nevertheless, he shall accompany you.

HUNTSMAN: My queen, I—

QUEEN: How were your wife and your *dear* children when you left them this morning?

HUNTSMAN (*Glumly*): I'll take the fair princess to the woods.

QUEEN: Good! Goodbye, *sweet* Snow White. May you have a happy time.

SNOW WHITE: Goodbye—and thank you. (HUNTSMAN *and* SNOW WHITE *exit.*)

QUEEN: Now, magic mirror, we shall see who is the fairest in the land. (*She laughs. Curtain.*)

*   *   *

Scene Two

SETTING: *In the woods.*

AT RISE: RABBIT *hops across stage.* SNOW WHITE *and* HUNTSMAN *enter. He has a dagger in his hand.*

SNOW WHITE: Come along, good Huntsman. Don't dawdle. It's such a sunny warm day. All my little bird friends are singing to me and there's a little rabbit. I feel so good, not having to stay in that stuffy castle. Thank you for taking me out into the woods today.

HUNTSMAN: Have you no fear, my Snow White, for anything?

SNOW WHITE: Who would want to harm me, good Huntsman? (RABBIT *runs up to her.*) Oh, little rabbit. How sweet you are. Come! Let me pet you. Dear, sweet bunny. (*She pets* RABBIT.)

HUNTSMAN (*Lifting his dagger behind her*): I . . . my family . . . I must— (SNOW WHITE *turns and sees him.*)

SNOW WHITE: Oh! (RABBIT *runs away.*)

HUNTSMAN: I cannot. I can't hurt you, dear princess. (*He kneels.*)

SNOW WHITE: But tell me why you meant me harm!

HUNTSMAN: The Queen means to have you dead. I cannot harm my sweet Snow White.

SNOW WHITE: The Queen? But why?

HUNTSMAN: The magic mirror said that you were the fairest, and the Queen is so vain she wants no one to be more beautiful than she. The Queen must not find out. Run into the woods and do not return . . . or you shall die. Run, Snow White—*run!*

SNOW WHITE: Oh, no! What shall I do? What shall I do? Where can I go?

HUNTSMAN: Goodbye, sweet Snow White. May heaven protect you. (*He exits.*)

SNOW WHITE: Oh, where can I go? Who can help me? What shall I do? (*She begins to cry.* RABBIT *and* DEER *come in and nuzzle* SNOW WHITE. *She cries out in surprise.*) Oh! Oh, it's just a little deer. Hello, little one. Can you help me? Where can I go? (DEER *nudges her.*) Do you know a place? Please lead on. I will follow. (DEER *and* RABBIT *exit, followed by* SNOW WHITE. *Curtain.*)

*   *   *

Scene Three

SETTING: *Inside the Dwarfs' cottage. A window overlooking the woods is in the rear wall. At center, there is a table set for seven, with seven little chairs arranged around it.*

AT RISE: SNOW WHITE *enters, followed by* DEER *and* RABBIT.

SNOW WHITE: I wonder who lives here? Sweet little rabbit and deer, won't you stay? (*They exit.*) Don't run away! Oh, well—never mind. Perhaps they will come back. (*She looks around.*) Such a funny little house. There must be (*Counts dishes*)—one, two, three, four, five, six—seven little children living here. They certainly are tidy. Everything is so neat! The table is all set for dinner. Seven little loaves of bread with seven little glasses of wine. *Wine?* For children? (*Shakes head*) I'll just take a bite from one of the loaves of bread. (*She does.*) Mm-m-m. That's good. I wonder if they would allow me to stay here for a little while? I'm so tired. I'll just lie down for a moment until they get home. (*Yawns*) I wonder where they could be? (*Yawns again*) Seven little children! And no mommy. (*Goes to side of stage*) Here is the bedroom. (*She exits.*)

DWARFS (*Singing from offstage to the tune of "London Bridge Is Falling Down"*):
>Home we go from copper mine!
>Hard day's work—suits us fine.
>Seven dwarfs, not eight or nine—
>Hungry and tired.

MEANIE (*From offstage*): Wait, brothers. The door is open!

MINEY (*From offstage*): Is there a thief inside?

MOE (*Entering*): Come on in, men. We probably just forgot to lock the door and left it open this morning. (*The other Dwarfs—*MEANIE, MINEY, DEANIE, DINEY, DOE *and* DUM DUM—*enter.*)

DEANIE: Time for dinner. Everyone wash up!

DINEY: Bring in the wash tub, Dum Dum. (DUM DUM *goes out.*)

DOE: Am I hungry!

MOE: We all are starved from working all day in the copper mine. We should have enough copper to take to town soon. (DUM DUM *enters with a big wash tub.*)

DUM DUM: Here we are. Everyone clean up. (*Dwarfs crowd around tub.*)

DWARFS (*Singing to tune of "London Bridge"*):
>Scrub away the hard day's grime.
>Dinner's done—just in time.
>Bread and meat and cake and wine—
>Couldn't be better!

(*They all laugh and take the wash tub offstage, then go to table.*)

MEANIE: Ho, brothers! Part of my bread is missing. Someone has eaten it! There are crumbs about.

MINEY: Maybe they are still in the house!

DUM DUM: The bread crumbs?

MINEY: No, Dum Dum, the thieves!

MOE: They could be. Search every nook and cranny!

DEANIE: I'm scared!

MEANIE: Don't be a scaredy cat. You look in the bedroom and—

SNOW WHITE (*Yawning loudly, from offstage*): Ah-h-h!

DINEY: What was that? (DEANIE *exits into bedroom.*)

MINEY: It sounds like a ghost. (DEANIE *re-enters, running.*)

DEANIE: It is a ghost! It's—(*Breaks off as* SNOW WHITE *enters*)

SNOW WHITE: I slept so soundly. (*She sees Dwarfs.*) Oh! You are not little children at all!

MEANIE: No—of course not! We are seven dwarf brothers. (*Pointing*) This is Miney. That is Moe, Deanie, Diney, Doe, and Dum Dum, and I am Meanie.

DUM DUM: Who are you?

SNOW WHITE: I am Snow White.

DOE: Princess Snow White?

SNOW WHITE: Yes. I had to run away because the Queen wanted me to be killed. I can never return. (*She begins to cry.*)

DUM DUM: Don't cry. You can stay with us.

MEANIE: Well—I don't know about—

OTHERS (*Together*): Yes! She stays! She stays!

DINEY: We will protect you from the Queen.

SNOW WHITE: You are all too kind. Thank you very much. (*Yawns*) But I'm afraid I'm still tired.

DUM DUM: You just go back to the bedroom and sleep. We will sleep out here. And tomorrow we will build you a pretty bed.

SNOW WHITE: Oh, thank you. We shall all be so happy here!

DWARFS (*Singing to tune of "London Bridge"*):

Now we have a lady friend,
Sweet Snow White—we'll defend.
Just our luck the Queen did send
A lovely Princess.
(*Dwarfs dance about* Snow White *as curtain falls.*)

* * *

Scene Four

Setting: *The dungeon. The mirror is hanging on the wall. There is a bench at center with bottles and flasks on it.*
At Rise: Queen *rushes in.*

Queen: Mirror, mirror—Princess Snow White is dead. Now who is the fairest one of all? (*Cackles*)
Voice of Mirror:
  Fair indeed, are you, O Queen,
  But fairer than Snow White is nowhere seen.
  Happy she lives, beyond words to tell,
  Where the Dwarfs of the Copper Mountain dwell.
Queen: No! It is impossible! The Huntsman killed Snow White in the woods.
Voice of Mirror: Snow White lives with the good Seven Dwarfs this day.
Queen: I'll kill her myself. I will! First I'll drink a magic potion to turn myself into an ugly old woman. What are the magic words? Oh, yes. (*Recites*)
  Ugly see and ugly do.
  Let me look as few can do,
  Just long enough to kill my ward—
  That will be my sole reward.
(Queen *takes a bottle from bench and drinks from it.*)

Ah-h-h! (*She falls behind bench, then re-appears as an ugly old woman. She staggers to mirror.*) Mirror, mirror—now how do I look? (*She cackles.*)

VOICE OF MIRROR: Oh, Queen, I—

QUEEN: Never mind. I don't want to hear. I know how I look. But I'll only be this way long enough to kill Snow White. (*Laughs again*) And now for the apple. (*Holds up her hand, revealing bright red apple*) Here we are! A beautiful—red—*poisoned* apple! (*She exits, laughing evilly. Curtain.*)

*   *   *

Scene Five

SETTING: *Outside the Dwarfs' cottage.*

AT RISE: SNOW WHITE *enters from cottage.*

SNOW WHITE (*Calling*): Hurry, now. It's time for work. (*Dwarfs file out of cottage.*)

MINEY: We're off to work, Snow White.

MOE: You be careful today. If the Queen finds that you are alive, goodness knows what will happen to you.

DEANIE: She will try to kill Snow White!

DWARFS: Ooo!

DINEY: We had better stay at home.

SNOW WHITE: Nonsense! How could she know where I am? Now, off you go.

DUM DUM: Will you be all right?

SNOW WHITE: Yes—of course.

DOE: Don't let anyone in the house, Snow White.

MOE: And don't let anyone give you anything.

SNOW WHITE: I'll be all right. And careful too.

83

MEANIE: We had better go, men. The copper mine waits without.

SNOW WHITE: Without what?

MINEY: Without us to work in it! (*All laugh.*) Come on, brothers, off we go.

SNOW WHITE: Goodbye for now, boys.

DWARFS: Goodbye, Snow White. (*Dwarfs exit.*)

SNOW WHITE: Such sweet little dwarfs. I think I'm going to like it here. Now to bake them a delicious apple pie. Oh . . . I don't think there are any apples. I'll just go inside and see. (*She exits. QUEEN enters, in disguise of an ugly old woman. She carries an apple in her hand, and has a basket of apples over her arm.*)

QUEEN: Apples, indeed! (*She knocks on cottage door.*) Apples! Apples for sale! (*She cackles.*)

SNOW WHITE (*Opening door*): Did you say you had apples for sale?

QUEEN: Yes. Delicious red apples. And so reasonable.

SNOW WHITE: But I'm afraid I don't have any money. Are they good apples?

QUEEN: Good? Of course, my dear. Come—try one! They are so red—and delicious. (*Holds out apple in her hand.*)

SNOW WHITE: They do look good, old lady.

QUEEN: Just try one bite—to see how they taste.

SNOW WHITE: Well—maybe just a bite. (*She bites into apple, and gasps, then falls to ground and lies motionless.*)

QUEEN (*Laughing*): Ha ha! Now, mirror—who is the fairest? Snow White is dead and now I'm the fairest in the land. Well, at least I will be after this potion wears off. It should be gone now . . . now that Snow White is. . . . (*Worried*) Why doesn't the potion wear off? It's time, but—something is wrong! (*Pats her face*) My face! I'm still an ugly old woman. Oh, no! I'm still ugly! What will

I do? The potion has set in for ever. Now I'll never be beautiful again. What can I do? What can I do? Oh, no-o-o! (*She runs offstage. Curtain.*)

* * *

Scene Six

SETTING: *A hillside.*

AT RISE: SNOW WHITE *is lying motionless on a bed. Dwarfs are standing around her, crying.*

MOE: She was so beautiful. (*Sobs*)

DEANIE: We don't have the heart to bury her. How could we bury Snow White in the cold, dark ground?

DINEY: We should never have left her side.

DOE: She *is* still beautiful.

MINEY: Just as if she were sleeping.

MEANIE: What will we do without her?

DUM DUM: I miss our Snow White. (*He weeps and they all cry softly.* PRINCE CHARMING *comes in.*)

PRINCE: Dear Seven Dwarfs, who is this beautiful maiden that lies as if dead?

MOE: She is our beloved Snow White. The Queen came in the disguise of an ugly old woman and killed Snow White with a poisoned apple.

MEANIE: But one thing! The Queen cannot rid herself of that ugly face. *Just punishment.* Never again will she be beautiful.

MINEY: Nor will our Snow White. (*Sobs*)

PRINCE: Snow White will always be beautiful. (*He bends and kisses her.*)

85

Snow White (*Waking up*): Oh . . . What happened? Who are you?

Prince: Your devoted Prince Charming.

Snow White: And my seven little dwarfs?

Prince: Here they are—by your side.

Meanie: Look, men! Snow White is alive. Our Snow White is alive!

Dwarfs (*Ad lib*): Hurray! She's alive—our Snow White is alive! (*Etc.*)

Prince: Now, won't you come with me? I've been searching for a wife to complete my life.

Miney: Go with him, Snow White.

Moe: Be his bride!

Dwarfs: And be happy!

Snow White (*Rising*): Dear, dear little Dwarfs. I shall never forget you.

Prince: You must all come to our wedding.

Dum Dum: Will there be bread and wine?

Prince: Of course.

Dwarfs (*Together*): We'll be there!

Snow White: Goodbye, my friends.

Dwarfs: Goodbye, our dear Snow White. (Prince *and* Snow White *exit. Curtain.*)

THE END

Production Notes

SNOW WHITE AND THE SEVEN DWARFS

Number of Puppets: 14 hand puppets (or marionettes), and offstage Voice of Mirror. This show will take lots of puppeteers, so be sure to have a big stage with room for many people backstage.

Playing Time: 15 minutes.

Description of Puppets: The puppets can be designed after the Walt Disney movie, but try to be original and invent new costumes. Snow White is very pretty, with black hair, fair skin, and rosy cheeks. The Queen must be very beautiful, yet stern and vain. She wears lots of jewelry. Make a second puppet for the Queen when she changes herself into an ugly old woman: She should have an ugly face and wear dark clothes, with a shawl over her head. Sew an apple into her hand. The Huntsman is in browns and greens, with a dagger sewn to his hand. The Dwarfs are short, round, and have beards. They wear jackets and stocking caps. Prince Charming is handsome. He wears a cape and hat. If the stage is big enough, he might even ride a horse.

Properties: Wash tub (find one large enough for all the Dwarfs to wash in); bucket and cloth; apple basket.

Setting: Scene 1, the throne room—use a draped background, with a throne at one side (or painted on backdrop), and a mirror on wall. Scene 2, in the woods—a plain background with a few cut-out trees against it. Scene 3, inside the Dwarfs' cottage—a table set for seven, with seven chairs around it, is at center (or may be painted on backdrop). Backdrop also shows window overlooking woods. Scene 4, the dungeon—a dark background, with a workbench full of bottles and flasks at center (or painted on backdrop). Arches or hanging chains may be painted on backdrop. Scene 5, outside the cottage—cottage exterior is painted on backdrop (or else a cut-out of the cottage with an open window and door can be onstage). Scene 6, a hillside—show a flowery hillside and blue sky on the backdrop. There is a simple bed at center, for Snow White.

Lighting: No special effects.

THE EMPEROR'S NIGHTINGALE

Adapted from a story by Hans Christian Andersen

Characters

FISHERMAN
FIRST MINISTER
DOCTOR
LITTLE COOK
NIGHTINGALE
EMPEROR
JAPANESE COURIER
DEATH

SCENE 1

SETTING: *A small forest beside a river in China.*
AT RISE: FISHERMAN *appears in his boat and floats across stage.*

FISHERMAN (*Reciting*):
> Let me tell of the nightingale
> Who sang for the Emperor of China.
> Nowhere did any bird sing more beautifully or
>   finer.
> Watch closely now and let's unfold (*Throws out
>   net*)
> A wonderful tale, once again told,
> For grown-up and for minor.

(*Pulls in net and he and boat float off.* DOCTOR *and* FIRST MINISTER *come in.*)

DOCTOR: This is where we are to meet the little cook, here in the woods by the stream.

MINISTER: I know all about the world. I don't know why we have to ask a lowly cook.

DOCTOR: The Emperor wishes to hear the nightingale sing. Only this cook knows of the bird.

MINISTER: Here she comes now. (LITTLE COOK *enters and bows.*)

COOK: Good afternoon, Your Excellencies. You wish to hear the nightingale? Its song will bring tears to your eyes, it's so beautiful.

DOCTOR: Your Emperor wishes to hear its beautiful singing. Find the bird for us and you will have a permanent place in the Emperor's kitchen and permission to see the Emperor dine.

MINISTER: The bird is commanded to appear at court tonight. Quickly, point it out to us.

COOK: The nightingale lives right here in these woods. Now, listen carefully. (*Sound of cow mooing is heard.*)

MINISTER: That must be the nightingale. What remarkable power for such a small creature.

COOK: Oh, no. That's a cow mooing. (*Sound of frogs croaking is heard.*)

DOCTOR: How beautiful! It sounds just like the tinkling of temple bells.

COOK: No. Those are just frogs croaking. We shall soon hear the little bird. (*Melodious bird song is heard.*) Listen, listen! There it is. (NIGHTINGALE *flies in.*) See? There it is!

MINISTER: Is it possible? I should never have thought it would look like that. How common it looks. Seeing such important people as us must have frightened away all its colors.

COOK: Little nightingale, our gracious Emperor wishes you to sing for him tonight.

NIGHTINGALE: With the greatest of pleasure, sweet little cook.

MINISTER: Quickly, then. It's time we were at court. We mustn't keep His Majesty waiting.

DOCTOR: All at court are anxious to hear you sing, little nightingale.

NIGHTINGALE: My voice sounds best here among the trees, but I am willing to go with you if the Emperor commands it.

COOK: Fly ahead, sweet little bird. We will follow. (NIGHTINGALE *flies off, and others follow. Curtain*)

* * * * *

SCENE 2

SETTING: *The palace courtyard, decorated with chimes, bells and lighted lanterns. Throne and stand are at center.*

AT RISE: *If desired, there may be a procession across stage, ending with* MINISTER *and* DOCTOR *and finally,* EMPEROR, *who sits on throne.*

MINISTER: O Great Emperor, ruler of the sun, king of the moon, after much research and hardship I have accomplished what you commanded, and wish to tell you that . . .

EMPEROR: Get on with it. Have you found the nightingale?

MINISTER: Your Majesty, I have. I found him in . . .

DOCTOR (*Interrupting*): The little cook from the royal kitchens led us to the bird that sings so beautifully. She has the nightingale.

MINISTER: Humph! Really!

EMPEROR: Allow the little maid to enter. I wish to see her and this nightingale. (DOCTOR *signals, and* COOK *enters with* NIGHTINGALE *on her hand. She bows deeply.*) Little cook, have the nightingale sing for me.

COOK: My Emperor, the nightingale is anxious to sing for you. (*She sets* NIGHTINGALE *on stand and exits.*)

NIGHTINGALE: I sing my song to please you, great ruler, and to make all the people on this earth happy.

MINISTER: Much too good for them.

DOCTOR: Quiet, First Minister. Sh-h-h.

NIGHTINGALE: My song is of the night and day . . . of the spring and of the fall. Listen closely to my song. Think lovely thoughts. (*Bird song is heard.*)

EMPEROR (*Crying gently*): How beautiful. Why haven't I heard this nightingale before?

MINISTER: We have many birds in our forest.

DOCTOR: It has a fine warble, my Emperor.

EMPEROR (*Comes from throne, to* NIGHTINGALE): You sing so beautifully, my lovely little bird. (*Sniffs*) Thank you. Thank you! I award you the Medal of the Golden Slipper to wear round your neck.

NIGHTINGALE: I have been rewarded already. I see tears in the eyes of my Emperor. (*Sings again*)

EMPEROR: So beautiful! So beautiful! He will have a golden cage as well as twelve servants to wait on him beak and claw, and to walk him on a twenty-foot silken ribbon.

DOCTOR: How very delightful.

MINISTER: I can sing too . . . listen! (*He gargles. All laugh.*) Humph! (*He exits.* JAPANESE COURIER *enters carrying mechanical bird on a music box.*)

COURIER: O great Chinese Emperor, I come from the great Japanese Emperor, who wishes to present this magnificent mechanical bird. It is a present for his great friend. (*He sets it down.*)

EMPEROR: Thank you, Courier. Send my best regards to your Emperor. A valuable present will return with you for him. Now play the instrument. Turn the key and let us hear the jeweled bird sing. (COURIER *turns key and bird song is heard.*)

ALL (*Ad lib*): How wonderful! Beautiful! Magnificent! (*Etc.* NIGHTINGALE *flies away but no one notices.*)

EMPEROR: Now let us hear the nightingale and compare.

DOCTOR: The nightingale has flown away.

MINISTER: Just as well. That ungrateful bird. As First Minister I banish the nightingale from the castle gardens. (*To* EMPEROR) The mechanical bird is the best bird of all.

EMPEROR: Then let us hear the mechanical bird again. (*Bird is wound up and it sings.*) Beautiful! Beautiful to hear and to look upon. Place it next to my bed, and it will be played every night at bedtime. (*Procession enters and mechanical bird is carried off. All exit, then* COOK *enters.*)

COOK (*Calling*): Nightingale! My sweet nightingale! Where are you? Come back! (*Curtain*)

*   *   *   *   *

SCENE 3

BEFORE RISE: FISHERMAN *enters in front of curtain.*

FISHERMAN (*Reciting*):

    The Emperor now as time has passed
    Lies sick abed, and breathes his last.
    Nightingale, fly to his side and bring
    The song that only you can sing. (*Exits. Curtains open.*)

*   *   *

SETTING: *The Emperor's bedroom. Mechanical bird is beside bed.*

AT RISE: EMPEROR *lies on bed.* DEATH, *wearing crown and holding scepter, sits at back of bed.* DOCTOR *and* COOK *are talking.*

COOK: Doctor, is there no cure for our great Emperor?

DOCTOR: Do you not see? Death sits beside him. I am afraid his time has come to leave us forever.

EMPEROR (*Weakly*): Doctor, wind the mechanical bird once more. Its song eases my pain.

DOCTOR: Yes, my Emperor. (*He winds bird, and birdsong is heard, then bird breaks apart with jangling sound.*) Oh, dear! I'm afraid the jeweled bird will never sing again. It is worn out. (DOCTOR *carries out bird.*)

EMPEROR: Worn out, just like me. Little cook, if I could only hear my nightingale once more. Find him for me.

COOK: I will try. (*She exits.*)

EMPEROR: O Spirit of Death, do not sit so heavy upon my chest. I am weary.

DEATH: It is almost time for you to come with me. (*Bird song is heard.*)

EMPEROR (*Sitting up a little*): Listen!

DEATH: How beautiful! (NIGHTINGALE *flies in.*)

EMPEROR: My nightingale returns.

DEATH: Sing again, sweet bird.

NIGHTINGALE: Give the Emperor back his crown, and I will sing.

DEATH: Yes, yes. (*Gives crown to* EMPEROR) Now sing, nightingale. (*Bird song is heard.*) I've never heard anything so beautiful before. Not here in this world or any other.

NIGHTINGALE: Give back the scepter.

DEATH: Yes, yes, only sing again. (*Returns scepter and bird song is heard*) Beautiful! Sing again!

94

NIGHTINGALE: Only if you give our Emperor back to us.

DEATH: Yes, yes. Only sing again. (*Bird song is heard.*) Now I will go. One of your songs is worth more than anything. Rise, Great Emperor. I shall come back another time, many years from now. Goodbye, little nightingale. (*Exits*)

EMPEROR: Thank you, heavenly little bird. I banished you from my sight, and yet now you have charmed even Death away from me. How can I ever repay you?

NIGHTINGALE: You have rewarded me. I brought tears to your eyes the very first time I sang for you, and I shall never forget it. Those tears are the jewels that gladden the heart of a singer. (*Bird song is heard.*)

EMPEROR: Now you must stay with me always. You shall sing only when you wish.

NIGHTINGALE: I cannot build my nest and live in this palace, but let me come to you whenever I like. Then I will sit on the branch outside your window in the evening and sing to you. I will sing to cheer you and to make you thoughtful, too. I will sing about the good and about the evil which are kept hidden from you. Only you must tell no one a little bird told you so. (NIGHTINGALE *exits.* EMPEROR *goes behind bed and is hidden from view.* DOCTOR *and* COOK *enter.*)

COOK (*Crying*): Our poor, poor Emperor. What is to become of us?

DOCTOR: It must be his time, little cook. Death is gone and so is our Emperor. Our poor, poor Emperor. (*He cries.*)

EMPEROR (*Coming out wearing crown and carrying scepter*): Look! I'm well again. Good morning, everyone!

DOCTOR *and* COOK: Long live the Emperor! (*Curtain*)

THE END

Production Notes

THE EMPEROR'S NIGHTINGALE

Number of Puppets: 8 hand or rod puppets or marionettes.
Playing Time: 15 minutes.
Description of Puppets: Books of Chinese costumes will
  suggest costuming for Emperor and his court. They
  should have long brocade robes in bright colors and
  elaborate headdresses. Fisherman and Cook wear simple
  short coolie coats and trousers. Fisherman might wear a
  large flat straw hat. Death might be tall and thin, wearing black robe. Nightingale can be a small toy bird on a
  wire, worked either from above or below.
Properties: Net, jeweled mechanical bird on a fancy music
  box with large key, crown and scepter, small boat, either
  a flat cut-out or a three-dimensional one.
Setting: Scene 1: A forest of bamboo and fir trees beside a
  river. Scene 2: The palace courtyard, with a throne and
  stand for nightingale, and decorated with chimes, bells
  and lanterns. If desired, just a fancy curtain may be
  used. Scene 3: Emperor's bedroom with large bed sur-
  rounded by curtains.
Lighting: No special effects, although Scenes 1 and 3 may
  be dim and Scene 2 bright and colorful.
Sound: Cow mooing, frogs croaking, melodious bird song
  (either a sound effects record of bird calls or done live by
  someone who can whistle like a bird). The breaking of
  mechanical bird can be done by jumbling kitchen utensils together. If desired, recorded Chinese music may be
  used, or Stravinsky's "The Emperor and the Nightingale."

CINDERELLA

Characters

NARRATOR
CINDERELLA
LENA, *the skinny sister*
FATIMA, *the fat sister*
STEPMOTHER
OSCAR, *the page*
PRINCE CHARMING
FAIRY GODMOTHER

SCENE 1

SETTING: *The kitchen, with large fireplace.*
AT RISE: FATIMA *and* LENA *are rummaging through a trunk, tossing clothes about.*

NARRATOR: There were once three girls who lived with their stern mother in a little house not far from Prince Charming's castle. The oldest was Lena, who was too skinny and vain. The second was her sister, Fatima, who was too fat and clumsy. And the third was their stepsister, Cinderella. She was beautiful, good, and kind. Cinderella's father had remarried, bringing his new wife and her two daughters into the house, and no more than a year went by when he died. Cinderella's stepmother and stepsisters mistreated her and made her do all the nasty and heavy work in the house.

LENA: Where is Cinderella? I have work for her to do. There is a rumor that the Prince is having a ball tonight and all the beautiful girls of the town will be invited. I must get ready.

FATIMA: Why would he invite you? You are too skinny. He wouldn't look at you. He likes them well-rounded — like me!

LENA: Well-rounded? *Fat* is the word — *Fat*ima.

FATIMA: And you are nothing but skin and bones, Lena. You are ugly!

LENA: Ugly, am I? I'll make you eat your words!

FATIMA: You had better start eating something . . . skinny!

LENA: You fathead!

FATIMA: Skinny! (*They argue and fight.*)

STEPMOTHER (*Entering*): Girls, girls, shame on you! Arguing like that. You should act like ladies at all times. And set an example for your stepsister, Cinderella. Be gentle! (*Calls coarsely*) *Cinderella!*

CINDERELLA (*Entering*): Yes, ma'am.

STEPMOTHER: Come here at once. You haven't picked up after your sisters yet. Look at this mess!

FATIMA: What a lazy good-for-nothing!

CINDERELLA: But I've scrubbed all the floors, washed the breakfast dishes, made the beds and . . .

STEPMOTHER: Well, that's a start. But you had better hurry up and finish your morning chores. I've more for you to do.

LENA: And you must sew this tear in my sleeve.

FATIMA: And don't forget to bake those raspberry tarts! Yum, yum. (*There is a knock on door.*)

STEPMOTHER (*Annoyed*): Now who could that be?

LENA: The Prince has come to ask me to the ball.

FATIMA: No, to ask me!

LENA: No, me, you pig! (*They argue.* CINDERELLA *opens the door and* OSCAR *enters.*)

STEPMOTHER (*Warningly*): Girls! (*To* OSCAR) Ahhh! Welcome to our loving home, good page.

OSCAR: Good afternoon, ma'am. And good afternoon, ladies.

LENA *and* FATIMA: How do you do! (*Laughing*) Tee-hee! (LENA *and* FATIMA *stand in front of* CINDERELLA.)

OSCAR: His Highness, Prince Charming, has invited all the eligible young ladies of the countryside to a fancy dress ball tonight. All your daughters are invited, ma'am.

STEPMOTHER: They would love to come. Wouldn't you, girls?

FATIMA: Oh, yes.

LENA: Of course.

CINDERELLA: Oh, yes.

LENA (*To* CINDERELLA): *Not* you, stupid!

OSCAR: *All* eligible girls are invited.

STEPMOTHER: We understand, good page.

OSCAR: Well, goodbye, until tonight.

ALL: Goodbye! (*They curtsy and* OSCAR *exits.*)

LENA: I knew it. The Prince is anxious to meet me. I'm so glad I have a new dress for tonight. I'll start dressing now so that I'll be ready in time. I'll be so beautiful — in no time at all.

FATIMA: It will take longer than that to make *you* beautiful. Ha! More like a week! (*Laughs*)

LENA: A week? You will *never* get ready in time.

FATIMA: I'll start right away. Cinderella! Quick, get my dress — and my wig. Step on it!

LENA: Your wig won't look any better if she steps on it — not on *your* head. No, Cinderella, get my things first — my veils, my feathers.

CINDERELLA: I have nothing to wear. May I borrow . . . ?

STEPMOTHER: What? You don't think you are going, do you?

FATIMA (*Laughing*): Cinderella thinks she's going to the ball. The Prince certainly wouldn't look at her.

LENA: Not in those rags she wears.

STEPMOTHER: Someone must stay at home and watch the house. Besides, you won't have your chores done by tonight. Now, help your sisters get ready. (*She exits.*)

LENA: My veils, rouge and powder —

FATIMA: No, Cinderella. My comb —

CINDERELLA: Yes, sister.

LENA: No — me first!

FATIMA: Me first! (*They argue and rush about. Curtain*)

*   *   *   *   *

SCENE 2

SETTING: *The same as Scene 1.*

AT RISE: CINDERELLA *is sitting beside fireplace, sobbing.*

NARRATOR: And so the two vain sisters and their wicked mother got ready for the Prince's ball — with Cinderella's help. Cinderella was left sitting in the ashes and sobbing, because she was left behind.

CINDERELLA (*Crying*): But why couldn't I have gone? There are plenty of gowns in my stepsisters' closets that they never wear. Perhaps I *am* too plain — and the Prince would never look at me. But I would have liked to have gone anyway. (FAIRY GODMOTHER *appears.*)

GODMOTHER: Cinderella! Cinderella! Why do you cry? It sounds as if your heart would break.

CINDERELLA (*Startled*): Oh! Excuse me, but you startled me. How did you know my name?

100

GODMOTHER: I am your Fairy Godmother. I heard you crying. May I help you? What is wrong?

CINDERELLA: There is a ball tonight. The Prince has invited all the girls of the countryside, but I must stay at home and tend the house.

GODMOTHER: Nonsense! The house can tend itself. We'll see that you go.

CINDERELLA: But how? I've nothing to wear!

GODMOTHER: We'll fix that! (*She waves her magic wand and* CINDERELLA *is dressed in a beautiful gown. See Production Notes for change.*)

CINDERELLA: It's magic. This gown is so beautiful!

GODMOTHER (*Holding up clear slippers*): And here are your dancing slippers, made of glass.

CINDERELLA: Thank you, Fairy Godmother. But I've no way to get to the ball.

GODMOTHER (*Producing mice, lizards and pumpkin*): Here are some mice for horses, two lizards for coachmen and a pumpkin for the coach. Now watch! (*They are changed into coach, horses and coachmen. See Production Notes for change.*)

CINDERELLA: Oh, how can I thank you?

GODMOTHER: By promising to leave the ball before the clock strikes the hour of midnight. (CINDERELLA *gets into coach.*)

CINDERELLA: I promise. (*Waving*) Thank you! Thank you!

GODMOTHER: Have a good time. (*Curtain*)

*　　*　　*　　*　　*

SCENE 3

SETTING: *The courtyard in front of the castle, with steps leading to the castle door. A large clock face is on the wall.*

AT RISE: OSCAR *comes out of castle, then the* PRINCE.

NARRATOR: It was already late when Cinderella set out for the ball. At the castle, Oscar opened the doors for the dancing couples to cool themselves in the night air.

PRINCE: It's much cooler out here.

OSCAR: Are you having a good time at your ball, Prince?

PRINCE (*Half-heartedly*): I guess so. But it's just too stuffy in there.

OSCAR: Have you found a pretty maid among all your guests? One that might be your bride?

PRINCE: They are either too plain or too fussy. Too tall or too short. And there are two sisters with their mother, one *much* too skinny and the other *much* too fat. And all three are so vain! I'm sure that each thinks that she will be the next queen.

OSCAR: I remember them. I wonder where the third sister is? As I remember, she was most beautiful.

PRINCE: I haven't seen anyone like that.

OSCAR: I had better look after the guests. Please excuse me, Prince. (OSCAR *exits.*)

PRINCE: Surely there must be one for me among them. All the maidens of the neighboring towns were invited.

CINDERELLA (*Appearing*): Oh, excuse me, sir. I'm afraid I'm late.

PRINCE: I'm sure the Prince would welcome a beautiful lady such as you at any time. Let me take you inside. Won't you dance with me?

CINDERELLA: Oh, thank you, sir. I would be most delighted. (*They exit together. Stage is empty and music is heard.* LENA *and* FATIMA *enter, in ball gowns.*)

LENA: Did you see her? Who was that Princess dancing with the Prince?

FATIMA: Pretty dress, but *such* a plain girl. The Prince will never give her another look.

LENA: I didn't see him look at you a second time after you were introduced.

FATIMA: He barely said hello to you. Probably he could barely see you, you are so skinny, Lena!

LENA: Well, he would have no trouble seeing you, *Fatima*. (*They argue.*)

STEPMOTHER (*Appearing*): Girls! Girls! (*They stop arguing*) Don't fight until you get home. The Prince might get the wrong impression.

FATIMA: It seems the impressions are being made by that . . . that . . .

STEPMOTHER: She seems familiar. But no! Come back inside. We will put you girls in the front row again. Perhaps the Prince will ask one of you to dance.

LENA: *Me!*

FATIMA: No, *me!* (*They argue again as they exit. Music continues.* CINDERELLA *and* PRINCE *appear.*)

PRINCE: Please dance one more dance with me. I find you beautiful and charming.

CINDERELLA: I would love to. (*They start to dance. Clock hands move to midnight and clock begins to strike twelve.*) But no! I must go!

PRINCE: But you just got here. You mustn't . . .

CINDERELLA: The time! It's almost midnight.

PRINCE: But tonight is a special night.

CINDERELLA: I must go! Please!

PRINCE: You didn't tell me your name.

CINDERELLA: The time is almost up . . . oh! (*She starts off*)

PRINCE: Wait!

CINDERELLA: Goodbye, my prince. (*She runs off.*)

PRINCE (*Calling after her*): Princess! Oh, she's gone. But look! She left one of her glass slippers. (*Holds up glass slipper. Curtain*)

*   *   *   *   *

SCENE 4

SETTING: *Same as Scene 1.*
AT RISE: *Stage is empty.*

NARRATOR: Cinderella rushed back to the little house, as the coach disappeared and a pumpkin rolled into the gutter. The horses changed back to mice and scampered away. The coachmen turned back into lizards. When Cinderella got home, she was in her old tattered dress again. Lena and Fatima came home long after, still talking about the ball. (LENA *and* FATIMA *come in.*)

FATIMA: Wasn't the Prince handsome? He winked at me.

LENA: He probably had something in his eye. He brushed against my skirt as he danced by me.

FATIMA: I saw you stand in his way. (*They argue again.*)

STEPMOTHER (*Entering*): Girls! Girls! Not again. You'll never get a husband, let alone a prince, by arguing. Be sweet like me. (*Loud and demanding*) Cinderella! *Cinderella!* Get in here *at once!*

CINDERELLA (*Entering, in tattered dress*): I was just washing the attic windows.

STEPMOTHER: When I call you, I want you to come at once. Do you understand?

LENA: She's always late when we call her, too.

STEPMOTHER: Just what are you mooning about, girl? You'd think it was you who went to the ball last night, instead of my pretty girls.

FATIMA: Cinderella . . . at the ball? (*Laughs*)

LENA: She'd be a fine one at the Prince's ball. (*Laughs*) She's so clumsy.

STEPMOTHER: Cinderella, I have many things for you to do today. First, clean out the pigsty.

CINDERELLA: Yes, Stepmother. (*She exits.*)

FATIMA: You just have to start making her behave, Mother dear. (*There is a knock on the door*)

LENA: It's the Prince coming for me. I'll get it.

FATIMA: I'll get it. (*They push each other.*)

STEPMOTHER: I'll get it! (*She lets* OSCAR *in. He has glass slipper on a pillow.*)

OSCAR: His Highness, the Prince!

LENA *and* FATIMA: Oh-h-h!

STEPMOTHER: Girls, please. (PRINCE *enters*) Good day, Your Highness.

LENA: My Highness.

LENA *and* FATIMA: Our Highness. (*They curtsy.*)

STEPMOTHER: We must tell you how we enjoyed your ball.

PRINCE: I've come in search of a girl ... *the* girl for me. She dropped her glass slipper last night as she ran down the steps.

LENA (*Quickly*): I lost my slipper last night.

FATIMA (*Quickly*): So did I!

PRINCE: Whoever fits this shoe will be my bride.

LENA: I'm sure it's mine. Let me try it on.

STEPMOTHER: Yes. It looks like yours, dear. Page, over here. (OSCAR *kneels in front of* LENA) Now just slip your foot into that sweet little glass slipper, Lena. It does look like the one you lost.

FATIMA: Humph!

LENA: Yes, it does. (*She groans and grunts, trying to put shoe on. See Production Notes regarding trying on of shoe.*) My foot seems to have swelled a bit from last night.

FATIMA: Those clod hoppers couldn't get into that little shoe for anything — at any time!

OSCAR: The lady's foot does seem a bit too long.

FATIMA: Yes, about a foot too long. (*Laughs*)

PRINCE: Perhaps we had better ...

STEPMOTHER: Fatima! Didn't you say you had lost your slipper, too? Page, let the other girl try.

OSCAR: Yes, ma'am. (*He kneels in front of* FATIMA)

FATIMA: I'd recognize my shoe anywhere. Now to put it on.... (*She, too, grunts and groans trying to put shoe on.*)

LENA: If she gets one toe in, she's lucky.

STEPMOTHER: Lena, hush!

FATIMA: Ouch! Help me, Lena.

LENA: Why don't you try putting it on sideways?

OSCAR: I'm afraid the shoe might break, Your Highness.

PRINCE: We had better go on to the next house. (CINDER-ELLA *enters.*)

CINDERELLA: Stepmother, I've finished cleaning.

STEPMOTHER: Get out! *Get out!*

PRINCE: And who is this?

FATIMA: The scrub woman!

LENA: The maid!

STEPMOTHER: My stepdaughter. You are excused, Cinderella.

CINDERELLA: But that shoe is ...

STEPMOTHER: Get out!

PRINCE (*To* CINDERELLA): But you haven't tried on the glass slipper yet.

LENA: Cinderella? (*Laughs*)

STEPMOTHER: This one was home safe by the fireplace last night.

CINDERELLA: Let me try, Stepmother.

STEPMOTHER: Get out, girl!

GODMOTHER (*Appearing*): Let her try, my good woman!

STEPMOTHER: How dare you!

PRINCE (*To* CINDERELLA): Please try on the shoe, my dear. (OSCAR *kneels in front of* CINDERELLA. *She slips the shoe onto her foot.*)

SISTERS *and* STEPMOTHER: The slipper fits!

GODMOTHER: Yes. This *is* Cinderella's shoe. And Cinderella *did* attend the ball last night.

STEPMOTHER: Impossible!

GODMOTHER: You shall see! (*She waves her wand and* CIN-
DERELLA *magically changes into her beautiful ball gown
as in Scene 2.*)

LENA *and* FATIMA: Oh, no!

STEPMOTHER: It can't be!

PRINCE: It's the same girl. The girl for me! (*He goes to her*)
Will you marry me?

CINDERELLA: Yes. And love you with all my heart.

LENA *and* FATIMA: Oh-h-h! (*They faint.*)

NARRATOR: And so the Prince married Cinderella and they
all lived happily — except for Lena and Fatima — ever
after. (*Curtain*)

THE END

Production Notes

CINDERELLA

Number of Puppets: 10 hand or rod puppets or marionettes. (3 are costume-change puppets for Cinderella and
sisters.)
Characters: 1 male or female for Narrator.
Playing Time: 15 minutes.
Description of Puppets: Cinderella wears ragged clothes
and changes into ball gown (see Special Effects). Sisters
also change into ball gowns. Fatima should be fat and
Lena tall and thin. Godmother could be a half-size puppet with wings or an old lady with a pointed hat. Look at
illustrations in books of fairy tales for costume ideas, and
use your imagination.
Properties: Trunk with clothes, wand, glass slippers and
glass slipper attached to fancy pillow; mice, lizards and
pumpkin and coach, horses and coachmen, which can
be flat cut-outs.
Setting: Scenes 1, 2 and 4: The kitchen. There is a large
fireplace. Scene 3: The castle courtyard, with steps leading to the castle door. A large clock face, with hands
pointing nearly to midnight, is on the wall. The clock
might have hands that move toward midnight during
scene. Dancers might be visible through castle windows.
Lighting: Kitchen is bright for Scenes 1 and 4, and dim for
Scene 2. Courtyard is dim but with an offstage light il-
luminating the area.
Sound: Clock striking twelve, music (Prokofiev's *Cinderella*).

Special Effects: For magic change of Cinderella's clothes in a hand or rod puppet show, either have tattered dress over ball gown and quickly pull it off, or exchange puppets. In a marionette show, either exchange marionettes or use a "flip over" marionette with a head at each end, one long skirt ragged and the other fancy. For the magic change of pumpkin to coach, in hand or rod puppet show, use small pumpkin cut-out on a stick and exchange for large cut-out of coach and horses. For a marionette show, place the cut-out flat on the stage and bring up with strings (or it may be accordion-pleated so that it folds flat and can be attached to the front of the stage floor, where it is not seen until it is brought up with strings). When Cinderella loses her shoe in the courtyard, in a marionette show, either throw the shoe onstage, or release a shoe hidden under her skirt. In a hand or rod puppet show, simply have the Prince pick up the slipper from below for audience to see. To try on the shoe with hand or rod puppets, have Oscar hold the shoe and use a prop foot extended from under the skirt to try on shoe. In a marionette show, you can actually use the foot of the marionette. Cinderella can try on shoe without keeping it on her foot, since it is attached to the pillow.

ALADDIN, OR THE WONDERFUL LAMP

Characters

EVIL MAGICIAN
ALADDIN
PEDDLER
ALADDIN'S MOTHER
PRINCESS BUDDIR AL BUDDOOR
SULTAN
GENIE OF THE LAMP

SCENE 1

SETTING: *A street in Arabia, in front of Aladdin's house.*
AT RISE: EVIL MAGICIAN *is seated by a wall.*

PEDDLER (*Offstage*): Buy my baubles. Buy my wares. Who'll buy my strawberries?
MAGICIAN: All these poor peddlers and beggars scraping and bowing to each other. Ha! If they only knew of the riches in the magic cave...and of the wonderful lamp. But, alas, as clever and evil a magician as I am, I cannot enter the cave. Only an innocent youth may do so. Ah! To find a boy innocent enough to steal that magic lamp for me! (PEDDLER *enters, and* ALADDIN *comes in from the other side.*)
PEDDLER: Melons? Squash? Kumquats? Anyone to buy my wares? (ALADDIN *takes a melon and runs away.*) Come back here, thief! Thief! Bring that melon back! (MAGICIAN *stops* ALADDIN.)
ALADDIN: Let me go. Please! My mother and I are hungry.

111

PEDDLER: Give me back my melon.

MOTHER (*Entering*): Aladdin! What have you done? Shame! Please let my boy go. I am a poor widow, but Aladdin's a good boy. He's innocent. He did not mean any harm.

PEDDLER: *Thief!*

MAGICIAN: Let me pay for the melon.

MOTHER: Oh, sir...

MAGICIAN: 'Tis nothing. Here, peddler. A silver piece should do it. (*Hands him money*)

PEDDLER: The boy is still a thief!

MAGICIAN: Enough! Now be off. (PEDDLER *exits.*)

ALADDIN: Thank you, sir.

MOTHER: We are most grateful. Are you a stranger here?

MAGICIAN: Yes. I have come to find my nephew, my deceased brother's son. The boy's name is Aladdin and he lives with his mother somewhere on this street.

MOTHER: But he (*Indicates* ALADDIN) is the only boy here named Aladdin....

MAGICIAN (*Embracing them*): I knew it. My dear sister-in-law! My nephew! At last!

MOTHER: But my husband didn't have a brother...

MAGICIAN (*Interrupting*): I've found you at last. Please, nephew, you must help your old uncle find the jeweled caves. We will all be rich. Your mother will wear beautiful clothes and jewels and you will have plenty to eat.

MOTHER (*Aside*): Clothes? Jewels? (*To* MAGICIAN) Ah, you must be my husband's long-lost brother. Dear brother-in-law! Go with him, Aladdin. But come home soon.

ALADDIN: Goodbye, Mother. I'll return with armloads of jewels for you.

MOTHER: Goodbye, Aladdin. (ALADDIN *leaves with* MAGICIAN. *Curtain*)

*   *   *   *   *

SCENE 2

SETTING: *In front of walled-up cave. Cave should be able to open on cue.*

AT RISE: ALADDIN *and* MAGICIAN *enter.*

MAGICIAN: We go no farther. Here are the magic jeweled caves.

ALADDIN: But how do we get in?

MAGICIAN: You must say the magic words. Take this magic ring and read the inscription. It tells all. (ALADDIN *takes ring and reads.*)

ALADDIN:

Innocent lad, Aladdin I —

All evil curses, I defy.

Open caves, with jewels so rare.

A magic realm beyond compare. (*Cave opens with squeak.*) Let's go in now, Uncle.

MAGICIAN: No. You must go without me. Take all the jewels you can carry. And for me, bring only the little old lamp that sits at the base of the magic jewel tree.

ALADDIN: I'm on my way. (*He starts into cave.*)

MAGICIAN: Come right back.

ALADDIN: Right away, Uncle. (ALADDIN *exits into cave. Curtain*)

*   *   *   *   *

SCENE 3

SETTING: *Inside magic cave. An elaborate, jeweled tree is at center, with jewels and lamp at its base.*

AT RISE: ALADDIN *enters.*

ALADDIN (*Calling*): Uncle! It's dark in here. It's hard to see.

MAGICIAN (*Offstage*): Never mind. Don't dawdle. Do you see the jewel tree?

ALADDIN: Yes, there it is! It's beautiful!

MAGICIAN (*Offstage*): Pick up the lamp and hurry out.

ALADDIN: But I must pick up some jewels, too. (ALADDIN *picks up jewels and lamp.*)

MAGICIAN (*Offstage*): The time is short. Just hand me the lamp, and you can pick up all the jewels you want.

ALADDIN: I have the lamp and I'll bring it out with the jewels. Help me out, Uncle. (ALADDIN *goes to side.*)

MAGICIAN (*Offstage*): Give me the lamp first.

ALADDIN: I can't now, but I will as soon as I am outside.

MAGICIAN (*Offstage*): Unruly boy. Then stay in the caves — forever. (*Sound of rocks closing is heard.*)

ALADDIN: Uncle! Uncle! Here's the lamp. Oh, dear. The cave is shut. What will I do now? It won't do any good to cry or yell. No one can hear me. I'm all alone — trapped in these caves forever. What will happen to my poor mother? (*He sits down.*) I have these jewels for her and they won't do us any good. I wonder what that false uncle wanted with this lamp? It looks old and worn out. Perhaps if it were polished, it would look better. I'll just rub some of this grime away. (*He polishes lamp and* GENIE *appears*)

GENIE: What would you have, O Master? I am ready to obey you as your slave and the slave of all who may possess the magic lamp.

ALADDIN: Well, what do you know! No wonder he wanted this lamp. Genie of the Lamp! Take me and all these jewels home safely to my mother.

GENIE: At your command, O Master. (GENIE, ALADDIN, *lamp and jewels fly off. Curtain*)

* * * * *

SCENE 4

ALADDIN (*Calling*): Mother! Mother!

MOTHER (*Entering*): Ah, you're home, Aladdin.

ALADDIN: Look at all these jewels.

MOTHER: How marvelous. But where is your uncle?

ALADDIN: He was not my uncle, but an evil man who sealed me in the magic caves.

MOTHER: How did you get out?

ALADDIN: With the help of the magic lamp. The Genie of the Lamp is my slave and will do anything I ask him to. Let me show you. (ALADDIN *rubs the lamp and* GENIE *appears.*)

GENIE: What would you have, O Master?

MOTHER (*Frightened*): Praises be!

ALADDIN: Bring us food, for we are hungry!

GENIE: At your command. (*Food appears.*)

MOTHER: A miracle!

ALADDIN: And now, Genie, please take my mother, these jewels, and me to the Sultan's palace.

MOTHER: What are you saying, Aladdin?

ALADDIN: Please, Mother. I love the Princess Buddir al Buddoor and wish to marry her.

MOTHER: But we are in rags.

ALADDIN: That will be arranged. Genie! Off we go!

GENIE: Yes, O Master! (ALADDIN, MOTHER, GENIE *and jewels are whisked offstage. Curtain*)

*   *   *   *   *

SETTING: *The Sultan's throne room.*
AT RISE: SULTAN *is sitting on throne.* PRINCESS *enters.*

PRINCESS: Did you call for me, Father?
SULTAN: Dear Princess Buddir al Buddoor, it's high time for you to marry.
PRINCESS: Yes, dear Father. But there is no one I love.
SULTAN: Today we will receive princes for you to meet. There is one here already with his mother awaiting our interview. Show them in. (PRINCESS *walks to side of stage and brings in* MOTHER, *who is now beautifully dressed. She holds a platter of jewels.*)
PRINCESS: Good woman, please enter.
MOTHER: O Sultan, my son, Aladdin, wishes to present this small token as a gift to our great Sultan and ruler. He humbly wishes to be considered as the husband of the fair Princess.
SULTAN: Thank you, good woman. Have the Prince Aladdin come in. (MOTHER *exits.*) He must be a wealthy Prince to give such a great sum of jewels. (MOTHER *returns with* ALADDIN, *now dressed in elegant clothes.*)
ALADDIN: Thank you for receiving us, O great Sultan.
SULTAN: So you wish to marry my daughter. Do you have a palace fine enough for her?
ALADDIN: Look, my ruler! (*Back curtains are pulled aside and a beautiful jeweled palace appears.*)
SULTAN: Beautiful! More beautiful than my own.
PRINCESS: He is so handsome, Father.
SULTAN: You are, indeed, a wealthy Prince and will be a good provider for my daughter. (*To* PRINCESS) Go with him, Princess, and be happy. (SULTAN *and* PRINCESS *embrace, then* ALADDIN *and* PRINCESS *exit. Curtain*)

*　　*　　*　　*　　*

Scene 6

SETTING: *Aladdin's palace. There are many fancy lamps hanging from ceiling, and a fancy couch is at one side.*
AT RISE: ALADDIN, *carrying lamp, and* PRINCESS *enter.*

ALADDIN: And here we are, my sweet Princess Buddir al Buddoor.
PRINCESS: I am so happy. Your palace is beautiful.
ALADDIN: Now I must leave for a few hours to look after my mother's needs, but I will return to my bride's side in a short time.
PRINCESS: I shall wait for you forever, my Aladdin. (ALAD-DIN *puts down lamp and exits.*) He is such a good man. I am most fortunate.
MAGICIAN (*Offstage*): Lamps for sale! Lamps to trade! (MAGICIAN *enters with a basket of fancy lamps.*) Ah, Princess Buddir al Buddoor. Is the Prince at home?
PRINCESS: My husband, Prince Aladdin, is away.
MAGICIAN: But perhaps you have an old lamp you would like to trade for a new one?
PRINCESS: Not I!
MAGICIAN: Surely of all these lamps there is one that mars the beauty of this palace.
PRINCESS: Why, yes. There is an old one, but . . .
MAGICIAN: Exchange it for one of these beautiful new lamps. Won't Prince Aladdin be pleased by your cleverness?
PRINCESS: Yes. Oh, yes! They are handsome. Here is the old one. (*She gives him magic lamp.*) I'll take that golden one, there! (*He gives her new lamp.*)
MAGICIAN: Clever, indeed! Let us see if this is the right one. (*He rubs lamp and* GENIE *appears.*)
GENIE: I am the Genie of the Lamp.

PRINCESS: Oh!

GENIE: What would you have, O Master?

MAGICIAN: Ah ... it works! *It works!* (*Laughs evilly*)

PRINCESS: What have I done?

MAGICIAN: Genie of the Lamp, take this palace, Princess Buddir al Buddoor, and me to deepest Africa. (*To PRINCESS*) Now, Princess, you and this magic lamp are mine.

PRINCESS: Oh-h-h!

MAGICIAN (*Laughing evilly*): Ha, ha, ha. (*Curtain*)

*   *   *   *   *

SCENE 7

SETTING: *The same as Scene 6, except that an African jungle scene is visible at rear.*

AT RISE: MAGICIAN *and* PRINCESS *are on stage.*

MAGICIAN (*Evilly*): Happy, my little Princess? (*Laughs*) You'll never see your Aladdin again. We have been here in Africa for several months, and he has probably forgotten you by this time. Be satisfied with your lot.

PRINCESS: Never. Aladdin will search until he finds me.

MAGICIAN: He'll never find us here ... in the middle of Africa. (*ALADDIN appears at back and only PRINCESS sees him.*)

PRINCESS: Oh! (*ALADDIN hides behind curtain.*)

MAGICIAN: What is it? (*He looks around.*)

PRINCESS: Nothing. It's nothing.

MAGICIAN: Now to get my magic lamp. (*He exits. ALADDIN appears again.*)

PRINCESS: Aladdin, how did you find me?

ALADDIN: Sh-h-h. I asked the magic ring the evil magician gave me when we first met. We must be careful he doesn't know I am here. Take this goblet and see that he drinks

118

all of this potion. It will make him sleep and give us a chance to escape. (*He hands her goblet.*)

PRINCESS: All right. Oh, I hear him returning.

ALADDIN: Be sure he drinks it all.

PRINCESS: Yes, Aladdin. (ALADDIN *hides again.* MAGICIAN *enters with lamp.*)

MAGICIAN: Princess Buddir al Buddoor, what do you have there?

PRINCESS: I was about to quench my thirst from this hot African sun with a delicious drink of peach nectar.

MAGICIAN: Give that to me. I am the Master and should be satisfied first.

PRINCESS: But ...

MAGICIAN: Hush. The drink is mine. (*He takes it from her.*)

PRINCESS: Yes, O Master.

MAGICIAN (*Drinking down contents of goblet*): Mm-m-m! Delicious!

PRINCESS: Is there none left for me?

MAGICIAN: No! I was very thirsty. And now I am tired. The sun does make me sleepy as well. Ho-hum. (MAGICIAN *lies down on couch*) I'll just sleep a little while. (*He snores.*)

PRINCESS (*To* MAGICIAN): Master! Oh, *Master!* (*She sees that he is asleep, then runs to* ALADDIN's *hiding place.*) Aladdin! Quickly! (ALADDIN *appears.*) He sleeps. And here is your magic lamp. (*Hands it to him*) I am sorry.

ALADDIN: How could you have known? All is forgiven. But we must go back. And now for the lamp. (*He rubs it.*) Genie, appear!

GENIE (*Appearing*): I am the Genie of the ...

ALADDIN: Oh, let's get on with it.

GENIE: What will you have, young Master?

ALADDIN: Return the Princess, the palace and me back home.

PRINCESS: What will we do with the evil magician?

ALADDIN: I know. We'll put him into the magic cave. No. Better still — let's put him on the moon. Genie, take this evil man and fly him to the moon.

GENIE: Yes, Master. (GENIE *and the* MAGICIAN *fly off.*)

ALADDIN: Now we have sent him where he can do no more harm.

GENIE (*Returning*): It is done, Master.

ALADDIN: Good. And now for home!

GENIE: At your command, Aladdin. (GENIE, ALADDIN *and* PRINCESS *exit. Curtain*)

*   *   *   *   *

SCENE 8

SETTING: *The same as Scene 7, except jungle scene is removed.*

AT RISE: ALADDIN, PRINCESS *and* GENIE *enter from one side,* SULTAN *and* MOTHER *from other.*

MOTHER: Aladdin, where have you been?

SULTAN: And you, my daughter? We have been so worried since you vanished as if by magic.

ALADDIN: It's a long story, but we are home now, safe and happy.

PRINCESS: And never again will I trade my husband's lamp, and I will obey him always, may it do him ease. (*Curtain*)

THE END

Production Notes

ALADDIN, OR THE WONDERFUL LAMP

Number of Puppets: 7 hand puppets.

Playing Time: 10 minutes.

Description of Puppets: Aladdin is dressed first in ragged clothes — baggy trousers, loose shirt and vest. He wears fez. Later he wears rich-looking pants, sash, jacket and turban. Mother first wears ragged dress and scarf. She later wears beautiful dress and scarf. Sultan, who may be fat, wears full pants and turban, jacket. Magician wears similar outfit. Princess wears colorful outfit, full pants, jeweled blouse and veil. Genie might have pointed ears and wear a full caftan or have a gauze body.

Properties: Fruit in basket, including melon, ring, coins, jewels and old lamp, tray of food, basket of fancy lamps, goblet.

Setting: Scenes 1 and 4: A street in Arabia. Scene 2: Outside magic cave. Exterior of cave may be painted on a curtain that parts so Aladdin can enter. Scene 3: Inside cave. A jeweled tree is at center. Scene 5: Sultan's palace. Throne may be represented by pile of cushions. Scenes 6, 7 and 8: Aladdin's palace. Fancy lamps hang from ceiling, and there is a couch on one side. There may be curtains and cushions in room. In scenes 6 and 8, outside of palace at back, towers and minarets are visible. In scene 7, an African jungle scene is visible.

Lighting: Scene 3 may be dim to indicate inside of cave.

Sound: Squeaking and crashing as cave opens and closes. Sound effects may be used when Genie appears.

SLEEPING BEAUTY

Characters

NARRATOR
QUEEN
KING
HEDGEHOG
BRIAR ROSE
FAIRY VIOLET
FAIRY RUBY
FAIRY GOLDEN
FAIRY GRUNDELL
PRINCE
BLACK CAT
DRAGON

SCENE 1

BEFORE RISE: NARRATOR *comes out and addresses audience.*

NARRATOR: Once upon a time, there lived a King and Queen in their happy kingdom. They were good and kind to their subjects and were well loved by all. There was only one thing missing from their happy lives — they didn't have any children.... (*Exits as curtains open*)

*　　*　　*

SETTING: *The castle garden.*
AT RISE: KING *and* QUEEN *enter.*

KING: It's such a nice day, my dear. Why do you look so glum?

QUEEN: Don't mind me, good husband. We've been married many years and still we do not have a sweet child to play with.

KING: Life has been good to us otherwise. Perhaps one day we will have an heir to inherit our kingdom and brighten our days.

QUEEN: I do hope so.

KING: I must leave you to attend to business of the court. Enjoy the garden, my dear.

QUEEN: Until later, dear husband. (*He exits.*) I'm sure he wants a baby too — a little one to play by our side.

HEDGEHOG (*Entering*): Hello, there.

QUEEN: It's a little hedgehog.

HEDGEHOG: I could not help but hear what you said, my Queen. I live here in your garden. Your wish will come true.

QUEEN: And do you know what the wish of my heart is?

HEDGEHOG: It is to have a little child of your own.

QUEEN: That is true — a beautiful little baby.

HEDGEHOG: You must wait one year and then you will have a baby girl.

QUEEN: Thank you for your wonderful news, Master Hedgehog.

HEDGEHOG: Goodbye, my Queen ... and good luck.

QUEEN: Goodbye, little friend. (HEDGEHOG *exits.*) Husband! Husband! Listen!

KING (*Entering*): What is it? Is anything wrong?

QUEEN: Wrong? No — a good omen. A hedgehog just told me we are to have a baby.

KING: A hedgehog? (*Comforting her*) Yes, dear ... yes, dear. It's best you come in now, out of the sun.

QUEEN: A baby — just for us. (*They exit. Curtain*)

*　　*　　*　　*　　*

SCENE 2

BEFORE RISE: NARRATOR *addresses audience.*

NARRATOR: The Hedgehog's words came true. The Queen had a little girl and she was named Briar Rose for the beautiful briar roses that grew row by row in the garden. On her christening day the King and Queen gave a party and invited all but one of the thirteen fairies in the kingdom. (*Exits. Curtains open.*)

*　　*　　*

SETTING: *The throne room.*

AT RISE: FAIRY VIOLET, FAIRY RUBY *and* FAIRY GOLDEN *are at left.* KING *and* QUEEN *stand near baby's crib.*

KING: It is so good to have you all here at the christening of our little girl. Welcome! Welcome!

QUEEN: Isn't she a sweet baby? We are so proud. Our first child, you know. A hedgehog once told me . . .

KING (*Interrupting* QUEEN): Please continue with your gifts, good fairies.

FAIRIES (*Singing to tune of "London Bridge Is Falling Down"*):
> Join us here in wishes true.
> Place them here, they are due.
> Take them all, we love her, too,
> Our sweet Princess.
> Take them all and don't despair,
> Give them out with loving care.

124

Thoughtful gifts, you'll see, so rare,
For our Princess.

QUEEN: Lovely ... lovely ...

FAIRY VIOLET: Nine of our sisters have presented their gifts to the new princess, My Queen. There are but three of us left. My gift to the child is that she be beautiful and kind all her life.

QUEEN: Thank you, Fairy Violet. We hope that she will be.

FAIRY VIOLET: Goodbye, my friends. Now I must go prepare the flowers for spring.

QUEEN: Have a pretty spring!

ALL: Goodbye. (*She exits.*)

FAIRY RUBY (*To* FAIRY GOLDEN): Did you notice that Fairy Grundell wasn't invited? If she finds out about the party she will be furious.

FAIRY GOLDEN: I understand there were only twelve golden plates for our supper. That must be the reason. Nearly all twelve of us have left. Just you and I are here to protect the sweet little child. I will look out for Fairy Grundell. She may be on the castle grounds. (*She exits.*)

FAIRY RUBY: And as next to the last good fairy, I, Fairy Ruby, present Princess Briar Rose with the gift of dance. (FAIRY RUBY *dances and all applaud.*)

KING: Thank you, dear Fairy Ruby. (*She exits.*)

FAIRY GRUNDELL (*Offstage*): Stand aside! Stand aside, or I'll turn you into a lizard! (*She enters.*) So-o-o — it's true. Everyone was invited but me. Ah-h-h ... to celebrate a new princess. And gifts — a ball, a crown, good tidings and wishes. I think I should give a gift, too. Let me see, what shall it be?

KING: I don't think we need any gifts from you, Fairy Grundell.

FAIRY GRUNDELL: But a gift she shall receive. When Princess Briar Rose reaches the age of sixteen she shall prick her finger on a spindle and die. (*She laughs evilly.*)

125

ALL (*Ad lib*): No! You can't do that!

KING: Grundell, you evil fairy. You are to leave this kingdom and never return again. Go!

FAIRY GRUNDELL: That will not save her. Remember, when she is sixteen ... (*Laughing, she exits.*)

QUEEN (*Crying*): Oh, husband. What shall we do? My poor baby.

HEDGEHOG (*Entering*): My King and Queen. Do not lose heart. Listen ...

QUEEN: There's my little hedgehog.

KING: How did he get in here?

QUEEN: You once told me of my baby's birth. Do you have more good news?

HEDGEHOG: You have forgotten Fairy Golden. She can help to save Princess Briar Rose.

FAIRY GOLDEN (*Entering*): I cannot remove the curse, but I have not given my gift yet. (*Crossing to baby's crib*) Sweet Briar Rose, should Fairy Grundell's spell fall on you, I pledge you will not die, but will sleep one hundred years until a handsome prince kisses you. Then you and all in the castle will awake.

QUEEN: Dear Fairy Golden, we are eternally grateful to you.

KING: And to the hedgehog, as well.

HEDGEHOG: My good wishes too. I will be nearby. (HEDGEHOG *exits.*)

FAIRY GOLDEN: Goodbye for now.

ALL: Goodbye. (FAIRY GOLDEN *exits. Curtain.*)

*   *   *   *   *

SCENE 3

BEFORE RISE: NARRATOR *addresses audience.*

NARRATOR: The King, fearing for Briar Rose's safety, had all spinning wheels, shuttles and bobbins in the palace and nearby towns destroyed. Yarns and threads had to be brought in from other cities and boroughs for clothes and soft goods. Meanwhile, Briar Rose grew into a charming, beautiful, kind girl. (*Exits. Curtains open.*)

*   *   *

SETTING: *Same as Scene 1, sixteen years later.*
AT RISE: KING *and* QUEEN *enter.*

QUEEN: Tomorrow is Briar Rose's sixteenth birthday. We must be sure to warn her to stay in the castle until the sun sets.

KING: But we must not alarm her. She's grown into such a sweet young thing. All the fairies' wishes and gifts have come true. Let's hope Fairy Grundell's evil wish doesn't come to pass.

QUEEN: Hush ... here comes our daughter now.

BRIAR ROSE (*Entering*): Good morning, Mother and Father.

QUEEN: Good morning, Briar Rose.

KING: You look so pretty today. And tomorrow you will be sixteen. Stay in the garden and close to the castle today, dear. (*To* QUEEN) Come, my dear, let's prepare for the celebration.

QUEEN: Come in soon, dear.

BRIAR ROSE: I will. (KING *and* QUEEN *exit.*) I wonder why they were so concerned?

HEDGEHOG (*Appearing*): Good morning.

BRIAR ROSE: Why, it's a dear little hedgehog. Aren't you cute!

HEDGEHOG: Listen carefully, Princess. I am your friend. Beware of evil fairies, at least until after tomorrow.

BRIAR ROSE: I don't understand.

HEDGEHOG: I don't mean to alarm you, but be careful. Goodbye for now — until we meet again.

BRIAR ROSE: Goodbye, friend. (*He exits.* BLACK CAT *enters from opposite side of stage.*) Oh, look at that beautiful kitty. Here, kitty!

BLACK CAT: Meow ... Good morning, Princess.

BRIAR ROSE: You can talk! What a strange garden this is!

CAT: Come and play with me. Meow-w-w.

BRIAR ROSE: What shall we do?

CAT: Let's explore the castle's towers.

BRIAR ROSE: What a delightful idea! Lead on, kitty. (*They exit. Curtain*)

* * * * *

SCENE 4

BEFORE RISE: NARRATOR *addresses audience.*

NARRATOR: And so the black cat led Briar Rose into the topmost tower of the castle. (*Exits. Curtain opens.*)

* * * * *

SETTING: *The interior of old tower.*

AT RISE: FAIRY GRUNDELL *stands by window. Spinning wheel and bed are at right.* CAT *enters.*

FAIRY GRUNDELL: Cat! Sixteen years have passed and the King and Queen still think their precious princess is safe from harm. (*Singing to tune of "Pop! Goes the Weasel"*)
Sixteen years have hurried by
It's time for her to perish.
All she has to do then is die.
Spin, spinning wheel.

128

(*Spinning wheel turns by itself.*)

> Just to touch this poisoned pin,
> That's all she has to do.
> So hurry on, dear Briar Rose.
> Spin, spinning wheel.

(*She cackles as spinning wheel turns.*)

CAT: Meow-w-w.

FAIRY GRUNDELL: Come over to me, cat. Little do they know I'm here and have the last remaining spinning wheel after all these years.

BRIAR ROSE (*Offstage*): Here, kitty. Where are you?

FAIRY GRUNDELL: Ah! I hear the Princess outside the door. Good work, cat! (*She sits on bed and spins.* BRIAR ROSE *enters.*)

BRIAR ROSE: Oh. There you are, kitty. Oh! (*Sees* FAIRY GRUNDELL) Excuse me. I didn't know anyone was up here.

FAIRY GRUNDELL (*Sweetly*): Come in, my dear.

BRIAR ROSE: I thought I knew everyone who worked here, but I don't think I've met you.

FAIRY GRUNDELL: I am just a flax maid for the Queen and this is where I work. Do not stop me because I must spin this whole basket of flax by the end of the day. (*She sighs and continues to spin.*)

BRIAR ROSE: Please, let me help you, you poor old soul. You must be very tired. Show me how and I'll spin for you. I've never seen a spinning wheel before.

FAIRY GRUNDELL: As you wish, my dear. It's very simple. All you have to do is turn the wheel and twist the flax on this point.

BRIAR ROSE (*Sitting at wheel*): Like this? (*She turns wheel.*)

FAIRY GRUNDELL: And one hand on the spindle.

BRIAR ROSE: Oh, I see. (*She pricks her finger.*) Oh! I stuck my finger! Oh, my goodness. I'm so sleepy. I ... (*She falls asleep on bed.*)

FAIRY GRUNDELL (*Laughing wildly*): Princess Briar Rose is dead! This will teach them not to overlook Fairy Grundell. (*She goes to window.*) Look, cat! They are preparing for her sixteenth birthday. Wait until they find her. (*She laughs.*)

CAT: Meow-w-w ...

FAIRY GOLDEN (*Entering*): Evil Fairy Grundell. Be off with you!

FAIRY GRUNDELL: Fairy Golden! What are you doing here?

FAIRY GOLDEN: Briar Rose hasn't died, but only sleeps. I will surround the palace with a high briar hedge and after one hundred years the Princess will be awakened by the kiss of a handsome Prince. All the members of the court will also sleep and awaken at the same time.

FAIRY GRUNDELL: Just to make things interesting for this Prince, I will turn myself into a horrible dragon to keep him out. (*She laughs and exits with* CAT.)

FAIRY GOLDEN: Sleep, fair Princess, and await your true Prince. Goodbye! (*Curtain*)

*　　*　　*　　*　　*

SCENE 5

BEFORE RISE: NARRATOR *addresses audience.*

NARRATOR: Everyone in the palace fell fast asleep. Round the castle a hedge of briar grew. It grew so high that one could see only the topmost towers. Fairy Grundell turned herself into an ugly dragon and roamed about the hedge keeping young princes away. When one hundred years passed, a handsome Prince, who had heard the legend of the beautiful Sleeping Beauty, came to see if he could find her. (*Exits. Curtain opens.*)

*　　*　　*　　*　　*

SETTING: *Same as Scenes 1 and 3, except there is tall hedge of briar roses covering back of stage.*
AT RISE: DRAGON *enters.*

DRAGON: Beware, all strangers. Beware! One hundred years have passed. One hundred years! Sss-s-s-s. (*Exits*)

PRINCE (*Entering*): This must be the castle where a princess is supposed to sleep, though I can hardly see the roof or towers. This briar hedge grows so high. (*He touches the hedge.*) Those thorns are very sharp. I shall have to cut them away with my sword. (DRAGON *roars loudly offstage.*)

PRINCE: What was that?

DRAGON (*Offstage*): Go away, stranger, lest you lose your life.

PRINCE: Who threatens me?

DRAGON (*Offstage*): Go away and leave us in peace.

PRINCE: Whoever speaks, show yourself. I intend to wake Sleeping Beauty.

DRAGON (*Offstage*): So-o-o . . . another victim for the briar hedge — take care. (*The* DRAGON *enters and noisy battle takes place, with much clashing and moaning. The* PRINCE *kills* DRAGON.)

DRAGON (*Moaning*): Oh-h-h, fair Prince. You have won. The one hundred years have passed . . . and Fairy Grundell . . . is . . . no . . . more. (*Makes hissing sound, then expires.*)

PRINCE: The dragon is dead, but how will I ever get through this thick briar hedge?

HEDGEHOG (*Entering*): Good Prince, follow me. This briar patch has been my home and I know a way through to the castle.

PRINCE: Lead on, Sir Hedgehog. (*They exit. If desired,*

hedge may be lowered as curtains close. See Production Notes.)

*   *   *   *   *

SCENE 6

BEFORE RISE: NARRATOR *addresses audience.*

NARRATOR: The Prince entered the castle and saw the horses and hounds lying asleep in the courtyard. All the members of the court were asleep as well, in the same position they had taken when the spell was first placed upon them one hundred years before. The Prince roamed the castle halls until at last he reached the tower. He opened the door into the little room where Briar Rose slept.

*   *   *

SETTING: *Same as Scene 4.*

AT RISE: BRIAR ROSE *is still asleep on bed near window.* PRINCE *enters.*

PRINCE: This is the last room of the castle. Everyone and everything asleep. The Princess must be here somewhere. (*He sees her.*) Another sleeper yet. How beautiful . . . this must be Sleeping Beauty. (*He kisses her.*)

BRIAR ROSE (*Waking up*): I must have dozed off for a moment. (*Yawns*) Excuse me. Do you work here in the palace too?

PRINCE: One hundred years have passed since you and the others in the castle fell asleep. I have come to awaken you.

BRIAR ROSE: Thank you, dear Prince. (*Looking out window*) Look! Everyone else was asleep. But now they're awake as well. (KING *and* QUEEN *enter.*)

QUEEN: Dear Briar Rose, my child. Are you all right?

KING: The spell is broken. Thank you, good Prince.

QUEEN: What if Fairy Grundell returns?

PRINCE: She turned herself into a dragon and I killed her. She won't bother you anymore.

KING: Our Princess has been saved. (*To* PRINCE) Now for the marriage of you, good Prince, and you, dear daughter.

NARRATOR: So the handsome Prince saved the Princess from the evil spell. On the next day all was made ready for the grand marriage of Prince Charming and Briar Rose, our Sleeping Beauty. (*All puppets may appear, including* HEDGEHOG, *in tableau of wedding, as curtain closes.*)

THE END

Production Notes

SLEEPING BEAUTY

Number of Puppets: 11 hand or rod puppets or marionettes.

Characters: 1 male or female for Narrator.

Playing Time: 15 minutes.

Description of Puppets: Use your imagination for the puppets. Fairy tale books will give you costume ideas. Queen
is beautiful and the King handsome. He might have a
short beard so that he looks older than Prince. Briar
Rose is pretty and wears an attractive gown. Good fairies
wear gowns colored according to their names. Grundell
is an old woman and wears a dark gown. Dragon should
be fierce and menacing.

Properties: None required.

Setting: Scenes 1 and 3: The castle garden. Background
shows flowers, statues, part of castle. Scene 2: The
throne room, with baby crib, thrones. Scenes 4 and 6:
The tower, a dark room with a single window, a simple
bed, and spinning wheel, baskets of flax (white yarn).
Scene 5: The castle garden, with high hedge across back
of stage, hiding corner of castle.

Lighting: No special effects.

Sound: Music from Tchaikovsky's "Sleeping Beauty" may
be used.

Special Effects: The hedge wall may be drawn on soft
material and lowered at the end of Scene 5 when Dragon
dies. Put the wall on a long rod across top of stage and
lower it on two strings. The spinning wheel should turn
by itself. You can wind a long cord around the side of the
wheel and pull from below or above, or you can make a
treadmill cord on a handle from above or below.

THE FROG PRINCE

Adapted from Grimm's fairy tales

Characters

GWENDOLYN, *a spoiled little princess*
MIZARD THE WIZARD
KING GOODFELLOW, *Gwendolyn's father*
PRINCE TAD
FROG
FROG WIZARD

Scene One

SETTING: *The garden of the palace. There is a well just off center stage. A few weeping willow trees are at back. Math book is on bench at side.*

AT RISE: GWENDOLYN *is playing in the garden, bouncing her golden ball.* NOTE: *Put golden rubber ball at end of a piece of straight black coat-hanger wire, and control ball from below or above the stage.*

GWENDOLYN (*In a sing-song fashion*): Bouncy, bouncy, bally. (*Speaks*) It's such a beautiful day. I don't want to study my school work. I'd much rather play bouncy bally. (*Sing-song*) Bouncy, bouncy, bally. (*She throws ball in the air.*)

MIZARD (*Entering*): Oh, there you are, Gwendolyn. Playing bouncy bally? Aren't you learning your arithmetic as your father wants you to?

GWENDOLYN: No! I'd much rather play in the garden.

MIZARD: That's right, Princess. Don't you do anything you don't want to do.

GWENDOLYN: I won't. (*She bounces ball again.*) Bouncy, bouncy, bally.

KING (*From offstage*): Gwendolyn! Oh, Gwendolyn, my child!

MIZARD: Your father's coming. You'd better hide that golden ball and pretend you're studying. Here's your arithmetic book. (*He hands it to her.*)

GWENDOLYN: I'll put this golden ball behind the well. He'll never see it there. (*She hides ball behind well.*)

MIZARD: Here's the book. (*She takes it.*) Heh-heh! (*To himself*) She has it upside down. (*He exits.* KING *enters from other side of stage.*)

GWENDOLYN (*Reading from book*): Two plus two equals . . . seven. Three plus two equals . . . nine.

KING (*To himself*): Oh, isn't that sweet! Gwendolyn is studying her new math. I never could understand those figures myself. She is such a good girl. (KING *turns away and* GWENDOLYN *sticks her tongue out at him.*)

GWENDOLYN (*Jeering*): Yah-h-h!

KING (*Turning*): What did you say, dear?

GWENDOLYN: Oh, I was just stretching, Papa. I'm so tired from studying so hard.

KING: That's my good girl. Oh, by the way—did you see a golden ball? There seems to be one missing from the treasury.

GWENDOLYN: Oh, no, Daddy. What would I be doing with a golden ball?

KING: Well, I just thought I'd ask. Now, don't be late for supper.

GWENDOLYN: I won't, Daddy. (KING *exits.*) I won't study

my books. (*She throws book into well.*) That's for you, Mr. Arithmetic. I won't read any book, except maybe a comic book.

MIZARD (*Re-entering*): Has the King gone yet?

GWENDOLYN: Yes.

MIZARD: Fine. Now—what'll we do today?

GWENDOLYN: Let's play ball. (*She gets golden ball from behind well.*)

MIZARD: Play ball? (*Laughs*) Ho ho! I haven't played ball since I was knee-high to a toad. How do you play that?

GWENDOLYN: It's easy. Just stand over there. (*Points to well*)

MIZARD: Over here? (*He moves backward to the edge of the well.*)

GWENDOLYN: That's good. Now catch! (*She throws ball to him. It knocks him backward into well. Ball lands on stage and not in well.*)

MIZARD (*From well*): Help! Hel-l-l-p! I'm drowning. Help! Save me!

GWENDOLYN (*Picking up ball*): Oh, dear, my golden ball almost fell into the well.

MIZARD (*From well*): Hel-l-l-p!

GWENDOLYN (*In a sing-song fashion*):
>Mizard's in the well.
>Who pushed him in?
>Little Tommy Tin.
>Who'll pull him out?
>Not me! (*She laughs.*)
>Bouncy, bouncy, bally . . .
>(*She exits, singing and bouncing ball.*)

MIZARD (*From well*): Help! Someone! Anybody! Get me out of here! (PRINCE *enters.*)

PRINCE: Did I hear somebody yell for help? Where are you?

MIZARD (*From well*): In the well. Get me out!

PRINCE (*Rushing to well*): Here! Give me your hand! Now —up you come! (PRINCE *reaches into well and with much effort pulls* MIZARD *out.* MIZARD's *robe is wet and it has shrunk.*)

MIZARD (*Coughing*): I'm half drowned. Who are you, anyway?

PRINCE: I'm Prince Tad. (*Laughs*) Look at your clothes! They've shrunk.

MIZARD: Why did you come here?

PRINCE: I've come to meet Princess Gwendolyn. I hope to make her my wife one day.

MIZARD: Meet the Princess, huh? Laugh at me, huh? You'll meet the Princess, all right. But not like that. I'm going to turn you into a frog.

PRINCE: Keep away from me, you old fake. (PRINCE *backs behind well.*)

MIZARD: A fake, am I? I'll fix you! (*Chants*)
> Flip, flop, from the top,
> Into a frog you cannot stop.
> Until she does good deeds three,
> You, an ugly frog shall be.

(PRINCE *sinks behind well and* FROG *appears on well.*)

FROG: Grr-up! Grr-up!

MIZARD (*Throwing* FROG *into well*): Now stay down there in the well where you belong. (*He laughs.*)

GWENDOLYN (*Entering, bouncing her ball*): Bouncy, bouncy, bally. Bouncy, bouncy—Mizard! How did you get out of the well?

MIZARD: I'm a wizard and so I wished myself out—that's how.

GWENDOLYN: Play ball with me again.

MIZARD: Oh, play ball with the frogs in the well. (*He exits.*)

138

GWENDOLYN (*Calling after him*): You come back here! (*Shrugs*) Well—I'll just play ball by myself, then. Bouncy, bouncy, bally. (*Throws ball up and catches it*) Bouncy, bouncy, bally. Bouncy, bouncy— (*Ball falls into well.*) Oh! My beautiful golden ball. It fell into the well. Oh, no! How am I going to get it out? My poor beautiful ball. (*She cries.*) Boo hoo! I wish there were someone who would get my ball for me. (*She hides her face in her hands, crying, as* FROG *appears on edge of well.*)

FROG: Princess Gwendolyn!

GWENDOLYN (*Looking up*): Who said that?

FROG: It's your froggie, Gwendolyn.

GWENDOLYN: You're not my froggie! Get back in the well. (*She pushes him in. To herself*) Oh—now maybe he could get my golden ball for me. (*Calls into well, sweetly*) Yoo-hoo! Froggie, dear! Oh, Froggie!

FROG (*Appearing*): Yes, my Gwendolyn?

GWENDOLYN: I seem to have dropped my beautiful golden ball down your well and I can't get it out. Would you get it for me, Froggie?

FROG: I am eager to do your bidding—but first you must do three favors for me.

GWENDOLYN: What are the three favors I must do?

FROG: Well—come closer—first you must let me eat from your golden plate.

GWENDOLYN: Well, really!

FROG: Second—come a little closer—you must let me sleep at the foot of your bed tonight.

GWENDOLYN: Well, I never!

FROG: Third—come still closer—you must give me a kiss.

GWENDOLYN: Well, of all the nerve! Never!

FROG: Then I can't help you get your ball. (*He disappears again.*)

GWENDOLYN (*Calling*): Yoo-hoo! Froggie! All right. I'll do it.

FROG (*Appearing*): Then I'll get your ball for you. (*He goes back into well.*)

GWENDOLYN: Well! If he thinks I'm going to do those things for him, he has another guess coming. It would be all right if he were a handsome prince, but a frog? Never!

FROG (*Appearing with ball*): Here's your golden ball, Gwendolyn. Now don't forget your promises.

GWENDOLYN: If you think I'm going to keep my promises to an ugly old frog, you are wrong. (*She pushes him back into well.*) Now stay down there where you belong. Kiss a frog? *Never!* (*She exits, singing*) Bouncy, bouncy, bally! (*Curtain.*)

* * *

Scene Two

TIME: *Later that day.*

SETTING: *Dining room in the palace. There is a fancy table set for two with delicious-looking food on it. King's throne has been pulled up to the table. There is a little fancy chair for Gwendolyn.*

AT RISE: GWENDOLYN *enters, still bouncing her golden ball.*

GWENDOLYN: Bouncy, bouncy, bally! Bouncy, bouncy, bally. Oh—look at that terrible table and all those awful things to eat. Filet mignon—asparagus—and raspberry mousse. Ugh! I just won't eat, that's all. I won't eat anything! I don't want to.

KING (*Entering*): Oh, there you are, Gwendolyn, my sweet

little girl. It's time for supper. Doesn't that look delicious? (*He sits at table.*)

GWENDOLYN: No! It looks awful! I hate all that old food.

KING: But, Gwendolyn, it's good for you.

GWENDOLYN: I know what's good for me. I want candy, cake, cookies, and ice cream.

KING: But, Gwendolyn. . . . (*There is a knock on door offstage.*) There seems to be someone at the front door of the castle.

GWENDOLYN: I don't hear anyone, Papa.

KING: I'm sure I heard a knocking. (*Gets up, starts off*)

GWENDOLYN (*Holding his cape as he tries to walk*): There's no one there, Papa.

KING (*Breaking away*): I'll just go see who it is. (*He exits.*)

GWENDOLYN: It's probably that terrible frog. Ugh! I'll just pretend I don't know him. (*She turns away.*)

KING (*Re-entering with* FROG): Well, lookee here! It's a little froggie, Gwendolyn! He says he knows you.

GWENDOLYN: I've never seen him before in my whole life.

KING: And he says you promised him he could eat from your golden plate.

GWENDOLYN: He's a big, fat liar!

KING (*Shocked*): Now Gwendolyn! Frogs that talk don't usually tell fibs, now do they? We will just put him in my chair . . . (*Places* FROG *on throne*) Now he can reach your plate. Can't you, Mr. Frog?

FROG: Did you forget your promise, Gwendolyn?

KING: I'll go get him a napkin. (KING *exits.*)

FROG (*Jumping on table and beginning to eat*): Oh, Princess, this is delicious.

GWENDOLYN: Well, if you like it so much—eat it all. (*She upsets plate on top of* FROG's *head.*)

FROG (*Coughing and spluttering*): Hm-m-m-m—delicious.

KING (*Entering*): Here's his napkin—Oh! I see he is done.

FROG: Don't forget tonight, Princess.

KING: What's happening tonight? Is there going to be a party? I just *love* parties.

GWENDOLYN: He's done now, Papa. I'll show the sweet little froggie to the door. (*She drags* FROG *from table and exits quickly with him.*)

KING (*To audience*): Isn't she sweet? She just loves animals. (*He exits. Loud noise of door slamming is heard from offstage.*)

GWENDOLYN (*From offstage; shouting*): And stay out! (*She enters.*) Well! If he thinks I'm going to let him sleep in my bedroom tonight, he has another think coming. Sleep near a frog? Never! (*She exits. Curtain.*)

* * *

Scene Three

SETTING: *Gwendolyn's bedroom. There is a large open window center stage. The bed is down left.*

AT RISE: GWENDOLYN *is in bed, wearing a nightgown, tossing golden ball in air.*

GWENDOLYN (*In a tired voice*): Bouncy, bouncy, bally! (*Yawns*) Bouncy, bouncy, bally—(*Yawns again*) Oh, I just know that I'll dream of slimy things like snakes and frogs tonight. But one good thing! I've locked all the doors so he can't get in. (*She yawns and falls asleep.*)

FROG (*Calling from offstage*): Gwendolyn! My Gwendolyn!

GWENDOLYN (*Sitting up*): What was that?

FROG (*Appearing at window*): Gwendolyn! It's your frog-gie, Gwendolyn!

GWENDOLYN: He's come back!

FROG (*Jumping in and jumping onto foot of bed*): Did you forget your second promise?

GWENDOLYN: Get out of here! Help! Help! Someone help me! (*She jumps out of bed and runs to window.*) Hel-l-l-p!

KING (*Entering, in his nightshirt*): Gwendolyn, what's wrong?

GWENDOLYN: He's back, Daddy!

KING: Who? (*He sees* FROG.) Oh, hello, Froggie! Gwendo-lyn, here's your froggie again!

GWENDOLYN: Ugh!

KING: You didn't promise him something else, did you?

GWENDOLYN: No!

KING: Now, Gwendolyn. It isn't character-building if we don't keep our promises.

GWENDOLYN: Well—I said he could sleep at the foot of my bed tonight, but . . .

KING: Then sleep here he will. It's only for one night. Now back to bed with you. You will catch your death of cold. (*He ushers her back to bed.*) Now sleep tight. (*He kisses her on forehead.*) And good night to you, Mr. Froggie. (*Pats him on head*) Strange . . . very strange . . . (*He exits.*)

GWENDOLYN: Just you wait, Mr. Slimy. Just—you—wait! (*Curtain*)

*　　*　　*

Scene Four

SETTING: *The palace garden, the same as Scene 1.*

AT RISE: FROG *jumps out of well and hides behind it, just as* MIZARD *enters, carrying a metal lid. He covers well with lid.*

MIZARD: The Prince won't meet the Princess now! (*Cackles*)

GWENDOLYN (*Entering*): Mizard, what are you doing?

MIZARD: Your frog won't get out this time. I've put a heavy metal lid on the well. Now I'll get a big stone and put it on the lid to hold it down. (*He exits.*)

GWENDOLYN: Happy day! (*Sings to tune of "London Bridge Is Falling Down"*)

              Now we're rid of Mister Frog,

              Mister Frog, Mister Frog,

              Now I'll do just as I please,

              I'm free of him.

(*Speaks*) I'm free! Hooray!

FROG (*Jumping out from behind well*): Gwendolyn! My sweet Gwendolyn!

GWENDOLYN: Who said that? (*Turns and sees* FROG *behind her*) Oh, no! (*Runs around stage with* FROG *chasing her*) Get away from me! Get away!

FROG: Did you forget your last promise, Gwendolyn?

GWENDOLYN: Help! Help! (*She falls.*) Ooops! I tripped.

FROG: Gwendolyn! (*He gives her a big kiss.*)

GWENDOLYN: Ecch! Ecch! Help! I've been kissed by a frog! (*FROG goes behind well.*) Help! (*She runs offstage.*)

FROG (*From behind well*): Come back, Gwendolyn! (*PRINCE TAD steps out from behind well.*)

PRINCE: Come back, Gwendolyn! (*He discovers that he is*

no longer a frog.) Why, look at me! I'm no longer a frog. I'm a prince again!

MIZARD (*Entering*): Oh! You've broken the spell, have you? We'll see about that. I'll put you under another spell. (*Thinks a moment*) Now how does it go? Flop, flip? (*While* MIZARD *is thinking and reciting,* PRINCE *takes lid from well and holds it like a shield in front of himself.* MIZARD, *still mumbling, crosses to stand behind well.*) Now I remember! (*Recites*)

> Flip, flop, from the top,
> Into a frog, you cannot stop.
> So turn into a frog once more,
> And remain a frog forevermore.

Oh, no! What have I done? My reflection—in the lid— I've cast the spell upon myself! Oh, no! (*He falls down behind well, and in an instant* FROG WIZARD *leaps out from behind well.*)

FROG WIZARD: Brr-up! Brr-up!

PRINCE: Mizard the Wizard turned himself into a frog! Well, what do you know?

GWENDOLYN (*Re-entering*): Mizard, where are you? (*She sees* PRINCE TAD) Oh! Who are you?

PRINCE: I was the frog who ate from your golden plate, slept at the foot of your bed, and gave you a kiss a moment ago. Evil Mizard the Wizard put me under a spell, and turned me into a frog. Only you could free me from the spell. I am really Prince Tad, and I have come to make you my wife.

GWENDOLYN: Well, I think I should have something to say about that. But I'm glad you're not a frog anymore. By the way, where is Mizard the Wizard?

PRINCE: There he is, on the well. (*Points to* FROG WIZARD)

GWENDOLYN: That doesn't look like Mizard—it looks like an awful old frog, and I'm sick of them. (*She picks up* FROG WIZARD *and drops him into well, then calls after him.*) Stay there and don't come up again, do you hear? (*To* PRINCE) Now, if you were a proper prince, you would have brought me a present. All true princes bring princesses presents. You should give me what I deserve.

PRINCE: I have a present for you. I have brought you what you deserve. Come here, Gwendolyn.

GWENDOLYN (*Curiously; approaching him*): What is it? Let me have it!

PRINCE: Here it is. (*He puts her over well and spanks her.*) A good spanking!

GWENDOLYN: Stop! Help! (*She wails.*) Oh-h-h-h!

PRINCE: You will learn your spelling, your arithmetic, be good to your papa, and be good to others, too. (*Spanks her again*)

GWENDOLYN: Yes! I'll be good. (*Wails again*) Oh-h-h! Yes, my prince!

PRINCE: Your Prince Tad, forevermore. (*He stops spanking her.*)

GWENDOLYN (*Standing*): My Prince Tad forevermore.

PRINCE: We will be happy together and rule wisely, won't we?

GWENDOLYN: Yes—yes! I'll be good, my prince—my Frog Prince! (*They kiss and exit together. Curtain*)

THE END

THE FROG PRINCE

Number of Puppets: 6 hand puppets or marionettes.

Playing Time: 20 minutes.

Description of Puppets: Gwendolyn wears a long gown, and a small crown on top of her hair (which may be made of gold fringe). Mizard the Wizard wears a turban and long robes. He has an earring in one ear. After he falls into well, he wears a shorter robe made of shiny fabric to look as if it is wet and has shrunk. King Goodfellow is chubby. He wears an elegant crown, and a cape. Prince Tad wears a beret with a feather, and a jacket with a short cape. Frog may have crossed eyes. Frog Wizard has a small turban and earring to look like Mizard.

Properties: Golden ball on the end of heavy wire; math book; dishes of food; plates; napkin; lid for well.

Setting: Scenes 1 and 4: Palace garden. Well is just off center stage. A few weeping willow trees are at back. Bench is at one side. Scene 2: The dining room of the palace. There is a fancy table set for two at center, with King's throne at one end and small chair for Gwendolyn at other. Scene 3: Gwendolyn's bedroom. A large open window is at center stage. Bed is down left.

Lighting: No special effects.

THE GINGERBREAD BOY

A folk tale of old England

Characters

THE LITTLE OLD WOMAN
THE LITTLE OLD MAN
THE GINGERBREAD BOY
COW
CHICKS
HORSE
FARMER JONES
RED HEN
FOX
NARRATOR

SCENE 1

SETTING: *The kitchen of The Little Old Woman, with a window, center stage and stove at left.*

AT RISE: THE LITTLE OLD WOMAN *is looking out the window.* THE LITTLE OLD MAN *enters.*

NARRATOR: Once upon a time there lived a little old woman and a little old man. They hadn't any little boy or girl of their own, so they lived in a little old house all alone.

OLD MAN: Good morning, wife. It is such a beautiful day!

OLD WOMAN: It is a nice day, dear husband, but I feel sad.

OLD MAN: What's wrong, dear? I would think you would be happy when the sun shines like this.

OLD WOMAN: I don't have any little boy or girl to take care of, and that makes me unhappy and lonesome.

OLD MAN: Why don't you busy yourself with baking? You love to bake!

OLD WOMAN: What a good idea! (*Suddenly*) I know! I will bake a gingerbread boy.

OLD MAN (*Teasing*): Wouldn't it be a surprise if he came to life?

OLD WOMAN (*Earnestly*): Do you think it could happen? (*Laughs*) Oh, don't talk nonsense.

OLD MAN (*Laughing*): You never can tell what will happen. I'm going to read my paper. I'll be nearby if you need me.

OLD WOMAN: Good. I will start baking right away. I'll call you when I'm done. (OLD MAN *exits, laughing.*) Now I'll get ready to bake. (*She goes to table.*) Here's the cookie dough. First I must roll it out. (*Gets rolling pin*) Hm-m-m. (*She hums as she moves rolling pin.*) Now I'll cut it into the shape of a gingerbread boy. (*Hums again, gets cookie cutter*) Oh, how cute! Good! Here are currants for buttons. (*Pretends to put decorations on cookie*) One! Two! Three! Four! Five! Then two fat raisins for eyes. One! Two! Why, they twinkle! I'll make him a mouth of pink frosting. (*Gets tube of icing*) And a little peaked cap of white frosting. There! Now I'll pinch his little gingerbread nose and ears into shape. (*She bends over table.*) All done! (GINGERBREAD BOY *appears and she holds it up.*) Now we'll have a little gingerbread boy all our own. (*She opens door to oven.*) I'll pop him into the oven, like this. It won't be long till he's done. (*She puts* GINGERBREAD BOY *into oven, closes door, and cleans the table as she sings "London Bridge," or another merry tune, and she continues to hum this melody as she finishes cleaning up.*)

NARRATOR: And while the old woman cleaned her house the Gingerbread Boy baked until he was nice and brown. Then he grew hot! Oh, so hot!

GINGERBREAD BOY (*From inside oven*): Let me out! Let me out, Old Woman!

OLD WOMAN: Goodness gracious! Who is that? (*Sniffs*) It smells as if the Gingerbread Boy is done. I'd better take him out. (*Calls*) Husband! It's time! (OLD MAN *enters.*)

OLD MAN: Is the Gingerbread Boy ready?

OLD WOMAN (*Opening the oven door*): Look! (GINGERBREAD BOY *appears as she pretends to take him out of oven.*)

OLD MAN: Isn't he a nice one!

GINGERBREAD BOY: Nice one! I'm a nice one! Ha, ha!

OLD WOMAN: Why, he's alive! He's moving. Hold still, Gingerbread Boy. (*He jumps out of her hands and runs around the room.*)

OLD MAN: Come back, Gingerbread Boy! (OLD MAN *and* OLD WOMAN *chase* GINGERBREAD BOY *around the room.*)

GINGERBREAD BOY:
>Run! Run! Run! As fast as you can!
>You can't catch me. I'm the Gingerbread Man.

(*Exits*)

OLD MAN *and* OLD WOMAN (*Together*): Come back! Come back! (*They exit after him, on the run. Curtain*)

* * *

SCENE 2

SETTING: *A pasture.*

AT RISE: COW *is grazing, and* GINGERBREAD BOY *runs in.*

150

NARRATOR: And they couldn't catch him. So the Gingerbread Boy ran on and on. Soon he came to a cow in a pasture.

COW (*Sniffing*): Um! Um! (*Sniffs*) Stop, little Gingerbread Boy! I would like to eat you. Mooooo!

GINGERBREAD BOY:

> I've run away from a little old woman;
> I've run away from a little old man;
> And I can run away from you, I can.

(COW *chases* GINGERBREAD BOY.)

COW: Come here! Come here!

GINGERBREAD BOY:

> Run! Run! Run! As fast as you can!
> You can't catch me. I'm the Gingerbread Man. I am! I am!

COW (*Out of breath*): Oh, dear . . . I'd better stop, or all my milk will turn to butter. (*Calls out*) You're a naughty boy to run away from your parents! You'll be sorry! (COW *exits*.)

NARRATOR: And so the little Gingerbread Boy ran on and on. Soon he came to a horse. (HORSE *enters*.)

HORSE: Hi there, Gingerbread Boy.

GINGERBREAD BOY: No time! I'm in a hurry!

HORSE: Please stop, little Gingerbread Boy. You look very good to eat.

GINGERBREAD BOY:

> I've run away from a little old woman;
> I've run away from a little old man;
> I've run away from a cow;
> And I can run away from you, I can.

HORSE: I'm as fast as the wind, so I'll catch you. (HORSE *chases* GINGERBREAD BOY.)

NARRATOR: So the horse ran after him. They both ran as fast as the wind, but the Gingerbread Boy was faster.

151

GINGERBREAD BOY:

> Run! Run! Run! As fast as you can!
> You can't catch me. I'm the Gingerbread
> Man. I am! I am!

HORSE: Neighhhh! You are right. (*Out of breath*) I can't catch you! I must be getting old. Oh, well. I'll go back to my oats. (HORSE *exits. Curtain*)

* * *

SCENE 3

SETTING: *A farm, with a barn, center stage, and a haystack.*
AT RISE: FARMER *is pitching hay.*

NARRATOR: By and by the Gingerbread Boy came to a barn where a farmer was pitching his hay.
FARMER (*Singing to the tune of "London Bridge"*):

> Pitch the hay and store the wheat,
> Pile it high, nice and neat,
> Milk the cows and mow the field,
> Like a farmer!

(*Speaks*) I've worked hard, and I'm hungry. (*Sees* GINGERBREAD BOY *run in*) There's a delicious-looking gingerbread boy! Yum, yum! He smells good! (*Calls to* GINGERBREAD BOY) Don't run so fast, little Gingerbread Boy! Gingerbread boys are made to eat!
GINGERBREAD BOY (*Laughing*):

> I've run away from a little old woman;
> I've run away from a little old man;
> I've run away from a cow;
> I've run away from a horse;
> And I can run away from you, I can, I can!

152

FARMER: I'll catch you with my pitchfork! (FARMER *chases*
GINGERBREAD BOY.)

GINGERBREAD BOY:

>Run! Run! Run! As fast as you can!
>You can't catch me. I'm the Gingerbread
>Man. I am! I am!

FARMER: Come back. Come back! (*Stops to catch his breath*)
He's too fast for me. Guess I'll go back to my hay!
Maybe my wife will have gingerbread for dessert
tonight! (*He exits.*)

GINGERBREAD BOY: Ha, ha! (*Laughs, runs around the stage,
and exits.*)

HEN (*Entering*): Cluck! Cluck! Farmer! Farmer! Where's
my corn? I'm hungry! Cluck! Cluck! I am so hungry I
could eat anything! (*She pecks around the stage and clucks.*
GINGERBREAD BOY *enters.*)

GINGERBREAD BOY: Ha, ha!

HEN: Gingerbread Boy! Stand still a minute. I want to
peck and nibble you. You look good, oh, so good to eat!

GINGERBREAD BOY:

>I've run away from a little old woman;
>I've run away from a little old man;
>I've run away from a cow;
>I've run away from a horse;
>I've run away from the farmer;
>And I can run away from you, I can, I can!

HEN: I'll catch you and feed you to my chicks. (HEN *chases*
GINGERBREAD BOY, *clucking.* GINGERBREAD BOY *runs off
and exits.* HEN *stops, out of breath.*) I'd better stop. I won't
be able to lay any eggs. Cluck! Cluck! I'd better call my
chicks and gather them together. Here, chick, chick,
chick! (CHICKS *come running in.*)

CHICKS: Peep, peep!

HEN: We'll have nothing but chicken feed for dinner, I fear. Come along, now. (HEN *and* CHICKS *exit with much peeping and clucking. Curtain*)

*   *   *

SCENE 4

SETTING: *The river.*

AT RISE: *The* FOX *is on the bank.*

FOX: They say that I am a sly old fox. You can't keep me out of your chicken coops with any old fences or locks. I steal and lie and you can't trust me. You'll see that I am always on the hunt for something to eat. Watch your step and don't come too close. (*Laughs*) Ha, ha . . . I'm a hungry fox!

GINGERBREAD BOY (*Entering; alarmed*): Oh, oh! There's a fox. (*Calls out*)
> Run! Run! Run! Catch me if you can!
> You can't catch me. I'm the Gingerbread Man. I am! I am!

FOX: Hi, there, little Gingerbread Boy.

GINGERBREAD BOY:
> I've run away from a little old woman;
> I've run away from a little old man;
> I've run away from a cow;
> I've run away from a horse;
> I've run away from a farmer;
> I've run away from a hen;
> And I can run away from you, I can, I can!

FOX (*Bored*): Why, I wouldn't catch you if I could.

GINGERBREAD BOY (*Surprised*): You wouldn't?

Fox (*Slyly*): Oh, no! I don't like gingerbread.

GINGERBREAD BOY: Then maybe you can help me. I've got to cross this river. Everyone is chasing me. If I swam this river I would melt away, frosting cap and all.

Fox: Jump on my tail and I will take you across.

GINGERBREAD BOY: That's good of you. (*He jumps on* Fox's *tail and* Fox *pretends to swim behind the cut-out of the waves.* NOTE: *Use circular as well as up-and-down movements of the puppet. Hold the* GINGERBREAD BOY *on top of the* FOX *at the various places as mentioned in the following dialogue.*)

Fox: I think you had better get on my back or you may fall off.

GINGERBREAD BOY: Yes, I will! (*Moves to* Fox's *back*)

Fox: The water is deeper. You may get wet where you are. Jump on my neck.

GINGERBREAD BOY: All right! (*Jumps to* Fox's *neck*)

Fox: The water grows deeper still. Jump on my nose! Jump on my nose!

GINGERBREAD BOY: Sure enough! (*Moves to sit on nose of* Fox)

Fox (*Slyly*): Soon you'll be inside me, for now, I am going to eat you up!

GINGERBREAD BOY: Why, I thought you didn't like gingerbread boys.

Fox: You shouldn't believe everything you hear—especially from a fox!

GINGERBREAD BOY: Well, you won't eat me if I can help it. I'll tickle your nose. Tickle, tickle! (*Tickles nose of* Fox)

Fox: Stop! Don't do that! I'm going to sneeze if you do. I can't help it. Ah—ah—choo! (GINGERBREAD BOY *flies up into air and lands on the shore.*)

GINGERBREAD BOY: I'm safe on the shore.

FOX (*Floundering in the water*): Come back! Come back!

GINGERBREAD BOY: I've run away from everyone and I can run away from you. You can't catch me. And you won't eat me!

FOX (*Climbing onto the shore*): Come back! (FOX *chases* GINGERBREAD BOY.)

NARRATOR: But the little Gingerbread Boy ran all the way home. (GINGERBREAD BOY *exits with* FOX *in pursuit. Curtain.*)

*   *   *

SCENE 5

SETTING: *Same as Scene 1.*

AT RISE: OLD WOMAN *and* OLD MAN *are onstage.*

OLD WOMAN: My little Gingerbread Boy has run away. Poor thing! (*Weeps*)

OLD MAN: Don't be sad. You can bake another gingerbread boy.

OLD WOMAN: No, it wouldn't be the same.

GINGERBREAD BOY (*Running in*): Look! I've come home!

OLD WOMAN: My little Gingerbread Boy! (OLD WOMAN *embraces* GINGERBREAD BOY.)

NARRATOR: And so the Gingerbread Boy learned his lesson . . . as all good little boys and girls should . . . and he never ran away from home again. (*Curtain*)

THE END

The Gingerbread Boy

Number of Puppets: 8 hand or rod puppets or marionettes; several chicks (as many as desired) on multiple controls.

Playing Time: 15 minutes.

Costumes: The Little Old Woman wears a dress and an apron and has a mobcap on her head. The Little Old Man can be in his shirtsleeves with suspenders holding up his pants. The Farmer is in overalls with a plaid shirt and straw hat. The animals should be large, and constructed to move well. The Gingerbread Boy may be made with hinged joints, like a jumping jack, so that his arms and legs fold out. Paint a broad smile on his face.

Properties: Stove, with a swinging door; rolling pin; cookie cutter; tube of icing; newspaper (attached to the Little Old Man's hand); pitchfork (Farmer holds this in both hands).

Setting: Kitchen, a painted set on a drop, or, a cut-out, placed in front of the pasture drop. The farmyard scene shows the barn, and the haystack, painted on the drop (or make the haystack separately and put it in front of the stage). Show the river using a cut-out of waves, with an indication of shore on either end.

Lighting: No special effects.

Sound: No special effects; background music may be traditional English melodies, such as, "Country Gardens."

SNOW WHITE AND ROSE RED

Characters

NARRATOR
MOTHER
SNOW WHITE
ROSE RED
BEAR
PRINCE
DWARF
BIRD

SCENE 1

BEFORE RISE: NARRATOR *speaks to audience.*

NARRATOR: Once upon a time, there lived a poor widow with two young daughters. The girls were as fresh and lovely as the red and white flowers that bloomed in the enchanted forest near the inn which the widow ran. The mother named her lovely daughters Snow White and Rose Red, and they loved each other so dearly, they never wanted to be separated. One day, as the three were all sitting comfortably around the fire on their hearth — well, I won't tell you any more. Let's see what happened that day... (*Curtains open.*)

*   *   *

SETTING: *The interior of the inn. There is a table at center. A door is up left and a large fireplace is up right.*

AT RISE: MOTHER, SNOW WHITE *and* ROSE RED *are sitting beside fireplace.*

MOTHER: Oh, my! I'm afraid we aren't going to have much of a meal again today, girls. The snowdrifts have covered all the roads and no one has ridden past our inn for several weeks.

SNOW WHITE: Don't worry, Mother. We still have some bread and cheese left from last week.

ROSE RED: Yes, and there's that plum pie in the pantry.

MOTHER: I hoped we could share that plum pie with guests. It looks so delicious. Perhaps one of you girls could go out and get more firewood to keep us warm at least.

SNOW WHITE: I'll go look, Mother.

ROSE RED: No, we'll both go. You know how we hate to be separated, Mother. We shall never leave one another. Never, never, never.

MOTHER: Yes, dear, I know.

SNOW WHITE *and* ROSE RED (*Reciting*):
We're Laurel and Hardy. We're pepper and salt.
When one of us is tardy, we're both of us at fault.
Some call us Punch and Judy. At work or at play
We follow one another, like night follows day.
We're mistletoe and holly, we're butter and bread.

SNOW WHITE: Snow White is what my name is.

ROSE RED: And I am Rose Red.

MOTHER (*Laughing*): Yes, yes. Now be off with you before it gets dark.

SNOW WHITE: The darkness doesn't frighten us, Mother!

ROSE RED: Not when we're together.

MOTHER: Surely you girls have a guardian angel watching over you. You're always so happy together and you've made this such a cheerful home, even though we have so little.

SNOW WHITE: What more could we want, Mother?

ROSE RED: We have each other, a roof over our heads, a warm fire in the fireplace, and all the flowers we can pick from the enchanted forest nearby.

MOTHER: True enough! Although I do worry about having enough food for you sometimes.

SNOW WHITE: Why, if we had too much to eat, you would have two fat, lazy daughters on your hands.

MOTHER (*Laughing*): Oh, tee-hee. (*Knock on door is heard.*) Quickly, girls. See who is at the door. Perhaps there is a tired traveler outside seeking shelter for the night. (*They go to door and open it.* BEAR *stands in doorway.*)

SNOW WHITE *and* ROSE RED (*Afraid*): Oh! (*Both run to* MOTHER. BEAR *enters.*)

BEAR: Please don't be afraid. I won't harm you. I am half-frozen and only wish to come in and warm myself by your fire.

MOTHER: Poor bear! I never saw a bear look more frozen than you. Come in and lie down by the fire, but be careful not to lie too close, or you might burn that pretty coat of yours.

BEAR: You are most kind. And who are these two charming girls?

MOTHER: My daughters. This is Snow White and this is Rose Red. Do not be afraid, girls. The bear will not harm you. Somehow I feel certain that he means well.

SNOW WHITE: We're not afraid, Mother.

ROSE RED: It was just a surprise to see a bear at the door.

SNOW WHITE: Here, let me wipe the snow off your coat. (*Does so*)

ROSE RED: And I will dry your feet. (*Does so*)

BEAR: You are all too kind. After I have warmed myself and rested a bit, perhaps you would allow me to repay your hospitality. I know several magic tricks I could perform for you.

SNOW WHITE: How exciting!

ROSE RED: I love magic!

SNOW WHITE: And can you sing, too?

ROSE RED: And dance?

SNOW WHITE: And tell us stories of the enchanted forest?

MOTHER: Girls! Can't you see how tired he looks? Snow White, you help me set the table, and Rose Red, you fetch the plum pie. Now we have a special guest with whom we can share the pie.

ROSE RED: Yes, Mother. (*She exits*)

BEAR: You mustn't go to all this trouble for me. I will be rested soon and will return to the forest.

MOTHER: I wouldn't hear of such a thing. You would surely freeze to death. You must stay here with us until spring.

SNOW WHITE: Oh, yes. Please do. (ROSE RED *returns with pie.*)

ROSE RED: Yes, please stay.

BEAR: Very well. But you must let me perform one of my tricks for you. Hide your eyes! (*They cover their eyes.*) You're not peeking?

MOTHER: No.

SNOW WHITE: Not I!

ROSE RED: Nor I!

BEAR: Then — Abba dabba dabba! (*Food appears on table. See Production Notes.*) You may look now.

SNOW WHITE: Oh, Mother. Look at all the food!

ROSE RED: Yes. And it smells good, too. Yum, yum.

MOTHER: How wonderful! Now we have company and enough food to get us through the winter. (SNOW WHITE *and* ROSE RED *dance with* BEAR. *Curtain*)

*　　*　　*　　*　　*

SCENE 2

BEFORE RISE: NARRATOR *speaks to audience.*

NARRATOR: And so the months passed happily. The two girls played with the bear, listened to his stories, and ate from a table that was always filled with food. Then, one day.... (*Curtains open.*)

*   *   *

SETTING: *The magic forest. There is a log at one side and a rose bush nearby.*

AT RISE: BEAR *and* SNOW WHITE *and* ROSE RED *are standing at edge of forest.*

BEAR: It is time for me to leave you now. I must return to guard the treasures of the enchanted forest from the evil dwarfs.

SNOW WHITE: Oh, you mustn't go.

ROSE RED: We would miss you so.

BEAR: I'm afraid I must. You see, in the winter, when the ground is hard and covered with snow, the wicked dwarfs are obliged to stay in their lairs. But now, since spring has come and the sun has warmed the earth, the dwarfs roam about freely and steal all they can find. The treasure means nothing to me, but the dwarfs use it to wage war with each other and for other evil purposes. So you see, it is my duty to keep the treasure from them.

SNOW WHITE: We understand!

ROSE RED: Farewell, then. But don't forget to return next winter. We shall miss you deeply.

BEAR: Farewell. (BEAR *leaves. As he goes, he brushes past rose bush*)

SNOW WHITE: Look, Rose Red. Did you notice as Bear passed that bush, a piece of his furry coat was pulled off?

ROSE RED: Yes. And I thought for a minute that I saw the glittering of gold through the hole in his coat.

SNOW WHITE: We must have been imagining things!

ROSE RED: Yes. How silly we are. But come. Let's see if we can find some mushrooms for supper.

SNOW WHITE: There are usually some under that old log.

ROSE RED: Oh! Did you see something white bobbing up and down behind this log?

SNOW WHITE: My! We really are seeing things today, aren't we?

DWARF (*Appearing from behind log*): Well, don't just stand there, you ninnies. Are you going to pass me by without offering any help?

ROSE RED: Look! It's a little man with a long white beard.

SNOW WHITE: And his beard seems to be caught in the log.

DWARF: Will you stop wagging those tongues of yours and get me out of here?

SNOW WHITE: What happened, little man?

DWARF: What happened? You blind goose! Stop rolling your eyes and use them. What do you think happened?

SNOW WHITE: Well, I . . .

DWARF: I was going to split this log for firewood. I drove the wedge in properly, but it was too smooth and flew out. The log snapped shut so suddenly that I couldn't draw out my bee-autiful white beard. So here it sticks, and so here stick I.

ROSE RED: Oh, how funny! (*Laughs*) Tee-hee!

DWARF: Don't you laugh, you stupid creatures. Ugh! How ugly you both are!

SNOW WHITE: Ugly, are we? Well, maybe we'll just wait for an apology before we give you our assistance.

DWARF: Oowwww — you horrid creatures!

ROSE RED: Horrid, did you call us? Well!

DWARF: All right, all right. Let's just say you're unusual.

SNOW WHITE: I guess that's a little better. Here, Rose Red, you pull that way, and I'll pull this way. (*They both pull on* DWARF.) Oh, dear! It's caught too tight.

ROSE RED: I'll run and get some help.

DWARF: You scatterbrains! Why call other people? There are already two of you, and that's too many for me. Can't you think of anything better?

SNOW WHITE: Don't be so impatient. Wait! I have an idea. (*She takes out scissors and cuts off the end of his beard. See Production Notes.*) There!

DWARF (*Rushing about*): Oh, oh, oh! Look what you've done! You stupid, stupid girls. You've cut off my bee-autiful beard. It will take me ten years to grow it back the way it was. Bad luck to you! (*Shaking fist*) Bad luck! Now go away and leave me alone so I can do some fishing. (*Picks up fishing pole and drops line at back of stage.*)

ROSE RED: Come on, Snow White. (*They start to leave.*) My, he looked so funny caught in that log.

SNOW WHITE (*Looking back at* DWARF): And look what he's doing now. What's left of his beard is getting tangled up in his fishing line. Careful, little man. If a fish bites, you'll fall into the water. (*Line is pulled from below, and* DWARF *is dragged along.*)

DWARF: Help! A stupid fish is pulling me into the water! Don't just stand there! Do something! (SNOW WHITE *and* ROSE RED *run to his side and hold him.*)

SNOW WHITE: I'll hold onto him and you try to untangle his beard and the line.

ROSE RED (*Working on line*): It certainly is a mess. Let's see. This knot belongs here and this string goes here. No, that's not right. Oh, it's no use. Only one thing left to do. Snow White, give me your scissors.

DWARF: Quick — my feet are getting wet!

SNOW WHITE (*Cutting off beard*): There! Now you're free!

DWARF: Oh, you donkey. You've done it again. You've cut off more of my bee-autiful beard! Look at me. I won't be able to face anyone for thirty years looking like this. The shame, the shame! (DWARF *picks up large filled sack from behind log and exits.*)

SNOW WHITE (*Laughing*): He'll probably make a lot of people happy by *not* facing them. Tee-hee.

ROSE RED (*Laughing*): Such a funny little man. And so rude.

SNOW WHITE: I wonder what he had in that big sack he was carrying?

ROSE RED: He certainly didn't offer to let us see, did he?

SNOW WHITE: Let's go home. I'm hungry after all that exercise.

ROSE RED: I wonder if there's any raisin beard — I mean, *bread* — left?

SNOW WHITE: If there isn't, we can go to town and buy some. (*They exit. Curtain*)

* * * * *

SCENE 3

SETTING: *Another part of the forest. Castle is visible above and through the trees.*

AT RISE: SNOW WHITE *and* ROSE RED *skip in, carrying a large shopping basket.*

SNOW WHITE *and* ROSE RED (*Chanting*):

    To town we go, to town we go
    To buy some ribbons and see a show.
    We'll look in windows and visit the wharf.
    We certainly hope, though,
    We don't meet that dwarf.

(*They laugh.*)

Snow White: Oh, Rose Red, look at that big bird circling overhead. What do you suppose he's looking for?

Rose Red: Probably something to eat, or maybe some twigs for his nest.

Snow White: Look! He's swooping down on something!

Dwarf (*Offstage*): Help! Help!

Rose Red: Oh, not again.

Dwarf (*Offstage*): Help! Save me! I'm a goner! (*Huge* Bird *appears with* Dwarf *in his claws.* Dwarf *is carrying sack.*)

Snow White: It's that same little dwarf, Rose Red! Just look at his clipped beard.

Rose Red: So it is! Well, I suppose we had better help.

Snow White: Shoo, shoo, you nasty old buzzard.

Dwarf: Oh! He's pulling me away. Help! (Bird *carries* Dwarf *toward exit.*)

Rose Red: Grab him, quickly! (Snow White *grabs him.*)

Snow White: I've got his foot.

Rose Red: Oh, dear! Now the bird has his claws around what's left of his beard! Quick, Snow White, the scissors again.

Dwarf: HELLLLLP! (Snow White *cuts the rest of the* Dwarf's *beard off*)

Snow White: There! (Bird *drops* Dwarf *and flies away.*)

Bird: Caw... Caw... Caw... (*Exits*)

Dwarf: Ooooooh! Now I have no beard at all. I'm bare! Oh, you meddling rubbish. Why didn't you cut off the bird's claws instead of my precious beard?

Rose Red: Oh — we never thought of that.

Dwarf (*Angry*): Dizzy, dizzy, dumb dumb.

Snow White: My, such language!

Rose Red (*Picking up sack*): Here's your bag, little man. You must have dropped it.

DWARF: My bag — gimme! What are you trying to do, rob me?

ROSE RED: Careful. It's heavy! Oops! (DWARF *pulls it from her hand and he spills jewels all over a nearby rock formation. See Production Notes.*)

DWARF: Look what you've done. You've spilled it! Oh, my jewels... my precious jewels all over the place!

SNOW WHITE: Did you ever see such pretty colors?

ROSE RED: Where did you ever find such pretty stones?

DWARF: Don't just stand there gawking and gaping. Put them in my bag, idiots. Stupid creatures, ugly fools! (*He is quickly putting stones back into the bag. Girls help him. A loud growling noise is heard.*)

ROSE RED: What was that?

SNOW WHITE: Oh, I hope it wasn't thunder. (*She looks at the sky*)

DWARF: Oowwww — it's that horrid bear. Give me my bag so I can run...

ROSE RED (*Frightened*): Oh look, Snow White! (BEAR *enters and takes hold of* DWARF.)

DWARF: Spare me! Spare me, my dear lord bear. I will give you back all your treasures. Here — only spare my life. (*Hands him sack*) I am only a weak little fellow. Hardly a mouthful. Here, take these two wicked girls! They will make a nice meal for you! They are as fat as young lambs! Don't they look appetizing? Eat them! Eat them!

BEAR (*Growling*): Gr-r-r. (BEAR *picks up* DWARF *and throws him offstage.*)

DWARF (*Offstage*): Ahhhhhh! (*Girls back away from* BEAR)

BEAR: Don't go, Rose Red and Snow White. Fear not!

SNOW WHITE: That voice! It is *our* bear, Rose Red.

ROSE RED: Look, Snow White! (BEAR *changes into a handsome* PRINCE *all dressed in gold. See Production Notes.*)

SNOW WHITE: Who are you? What have you done with our bear?

PRINCE: I was your bear, sweet Snow White.

ROSE RED: But who are you?

PRINCE: I am the King's son. I was enchanted by that wicked dwarf and had to wander around the forest for many years in the form of a bear until the dwarf's death freed me. He had stolen all of my father's treasures, but now he has received his well-deserved punishment.

SNOW WHITE: But what prevented you from slaying him sooner, dear Prince?

PRINCE: He had magical power in his beard, and only after his beard was completely cut off, did he lose his magic.

ROSE RED: Oh, my! No wonder he hated to part with his beard.

PRINCE: But I must return to the palace now and to my father and my twin brother, Prince Charming. I am sure that he will come to love you, Snow White, just as much as I now love Rose Red. Rose Red, say you'll be mine and come with me to the palace to be my wife.

ROSE RED: Oh yes. Yes, my sweet prince. I will gladly go with you. (*They start off*) Farewell, Snow White. Farewell!

SNOW WHITE: But Rose Red — you said that we'd never part. Oh, never mind — (ROSE RED *and* PRINCE *exit.* SNOW WHITE *sings a few bars of the song, "Someday, My Prince Will Come," then exits.*)

NARRATOR: But that's another story, children — and one I'm sure you all know well. (*Curtain*)

THE END

Production Notes

SNOW WHITE AND ROSE RED

Number of Puppets: 7 hand puppets.

Characters: 1 male or female for Narrator.

Playing Time: 15 minutes.

Description of Puppets: Snow White and Rose Red are sweet young girls. Each wears the appropriate color. Mother wears an apron over her dark dress and a baker's hat on her head. Bear, while large and bulky, should not look too fierce. Dwarf is short and dressed in dark green. He should look cross. His long white beard is in three sections, attached to each other and his face with velcro tape or large snaps. When it is "cut off" one section at a time is pulled off. Prince is a standard, handsome fairy-tale prince, dressed in gold. Bird may be flat cardboard for lightness.

Properties: Pie, large fake scissors, fishing pole with a line (a large fish could be attached to the end of the line), shopping basket, sack of jewels.

Setting: Scene 1: Interior of the Inn. Table is at center, with door up left and large fireplace up right. Scene 2: Edge of the magic forest, with a large log and a rose-bush. A stream may be indicated on one side. Scene 3: Another part of the forest, with castle visible through trees. There is a flat rock formation.

Lighting: No special effects.

Special Effects: Table should have a false flip-over top with all food attached. The false top is on the upstage side and is tipped up quickly to reveal food. When Bear turns into Prince, simply exchange one puppet for the other.

169

The flat rock in Scene 3 has a duplicate underneath with glass jewels attached. When bag of jewels spills, flip down the plain front rock to reveal jeweled duplicate. Formation may be flat cardboard.

THE RELUCTANT DRAGON

Adapted from a story by Kenneth Grahame

Characters

ROBERT, *a boy*
ROBERT'S MOTHER
SHEPHERD
DRAGON
MRS. SMYTHE
ST. GEORGE

Scene One

TIME: *Long ago.*
SETTING: *A kitchen interior, in an English cottage.*
AT RISE: ROBERT *is on the floor, reading a large book.*
ROBERT'S MOTHER *is cooking, holding a bowl and spoon.*

MOTHER: Robert! Put your book away now. It's nearly time
for supper.
ROBERT: Just let me finish this one story. It's all about dragons, giants, and dwarfs.
MOTHER: All right, child. (*Thoughtfully*) I've often won-
dered if there really are such things as dragons, giants and
dwarfs.
ROBERT: Oh, there surely are, Mother. It says so in these
wonderful books I've borrowed.
MOTHER: Oh? Perhaps, book learning is useful, in spite of

171

what the neighbors say. (*Sound of pounding on door is heard.*)

SHEPHERD (*From offstage*): It's all up! Help! It's all up for us. Open up! (ROBERT *opens door and* SHEPHERD *runs in.*)

MOTHER: What's wrong, Shepherd?

SHEPHERD: I'll never go up on the Downs again!

MOTHER: Now, don't you carry on. Tell us all about it.

SHEPHERD: You know that cave up there? Well . . . for some time sounds have been coming from that cave. Heavy sighs with grunts mixed up in them. And sometimes snoring, too.

MOTHER: What is it?

SHEPHERD: I'm coming to that. Tonight I crept by the cave and I saw him! As plain as I see you.

MOTHER: Saw whom?

SHEPHERD: Why, *him*, I tell you. He was sitting halfway out of his cave. He was as big as a whale and all covered with scales. He seemed to be daydreaming or something, not raging or snorting.

ROBERT: Scales, did you say?

SHEPHERD: Yes—and claws and a long scaly tail.

ROBERT (*Yawning*): It's all right, Shepherd. Don't worry. It's only a dragon.

MOTHER *and* SHEPHERD (*Shocked*): Only a dragon?

SHEPHERD: How do you know?

MOTHER: Robert knows a great deal about creatures from reading books.

ROBERT: I always said that cave up there was a dragon cave. I would have been surprised if you'd told me it *didn't* have a dragon in it.

SHEPHERD (*Shrieking*): *Do something!*

ROBERT: Tomorrow morning, if I'm free, I'll go up there and have a talk with him. Now, please don't worry. You don't understand dragons—they're very sensitive, you know.

MOTHER: Robert's quite right. Now you go home, Shepherd, and everything will be all right. Won't it, Robert?

ROBERT: Yes, Mother.

SHEPHERD: Oh, me—oh, my. . . . (*He exits. Curtain.*)

* * *

Scene Two

TIME: *The next day.*

SETTING: *Up on the Downs. The opening of the cave is at right. There is a group of rocks at center, with a book of poems on it.*

AT RISE: ROBERT *enters and calls.*

ROBERT (*Calling*): Dra-a-a-gon! Oh, Mr. Dragon!

DRAGON (*From offstage; mildly*): Someone come to call? (DRAGON *enters.*)

ROBERT: I'm only a boy from the nearby town.

DRAGON: Now don't you throw stones or anything. You must never do that. I'm very sensitive.

ROBERT: I won't. (*He sits down on rock, center stage.*)

DRAGON: Oh—all right.

ROBERT: I've simply come to meet you and ask how you are, but if I'm bothering you I'll go.

DRAGON: No—no, don't. Really, I'm happy up here, but it is a bit dull at times.

ROBERT: Going to stay here long?

DRAGON: I just don't know. To tell you the truth, I'm lazy. Other dragons are so active—always raging and scourging the countryside, digesting damsels, running after knights

173

and all—but I like to eat my meals on time, then sleep a bit. I like this country and I'd like to live here.

ROBERT: What do you think about up here by yourself?

DRAGON: Well, I guess it's all right to tell you. (*Shyly*) Did you ever—just for fun—try to write poetry?

ROBERT: Sure I have. Some of it pretty good, too. Only there's no one who'll listen to it.

DRAGON: That's the way it is with me. I'd like to read some of my poems for you and your friends sometime. Listen to this one (*Recites*):

> The pretty clouds go drifting by,
> Up in yonder pale blue sky.
> The warm sun shines on daffodils,
> Giving me such pleasant thrills.

I can dance, too. Watch this. (DRAGON *does a funny dance, finishing with his end in the air.*)

ROBERT: Very interesting—but you don't quite realize your position. (DRAGON *sees his position and straightens up.*)

DRAGON (*Laughing awkwardly*): Oh!

ROBERT: You're an enemy of the people, you see.

DRAGON: Nonsense! Haven't got an enemy in the world.

ROBERT: Oh, dear. I wish you'd try to understand. They'll come after you with sharp sticks and swords. According to them you're a terrible monster.

DRAGON: Not a word of truth to it.

ROBERT: Well, try to be sensible. And do try to act more fearful, the way a dragon should, or you'll find yourself in a terrible situation. (*Standing*) Goodbye for now.

DRAGON: Do come again. I'll miss your company. (ROBERT *exits. Curtain.*)

* * *

Scene Three

SETTING: *The village street.*

AT RISE: MRS. SMYTHE, *the town gossip, is talking to* MOTHER.

MRS. SMYTHE: Oh, it's terrible! The Shepherd told me all about that horrible, dreadful creature up on the Downs. We'll all be eaten alive.

MOTHER: Well, my son went up there this morning, and—

MRS. SMYTHE: You'll never see him again. He's lost forever! Oh, you poor woman. My heart goes out to you . . . but none of us are safe.

ROBERT (*Entering*): Good morning, Mrs. Smythe.

MRS. SMYTHE: Robert! You didn't go up there, did you? Thank heavens.

ROBERT: Up where? Up on the Downs? Sure.

MRS. SMYTHE: And was the monster asleep?

ROBERT: He's no monster. He's a nice fellow, that dragon.

MRS. SMYTHE: A *dragon!* (*She screams and faints on the street.*)

MOTHER: Was he really, Robert? That's nice. Did you have a talk with him?

ROBERT: Yes. He'd like to read us some of his poetry soon.

MRS. SMYTHE (*Sitting up, then standing*): A dragon! I thought it might be. Well, thank heavens I sent the Shepherd to find St. George, the dragon killer, and bring him to this town. We'll be saved.

ROBERT: You don't understand. This dragon likes poetry.

MRS. SMYTHE (*Ignoring him*): He must be exterminated right away.

MOTHER: I had better get dinner started. (*She exits.*)

MRS. SMYTHE: St. George will soon be here to free our suffering village and win fame and renown.

ROBERT: But our village is not suffering! (*Music is heard from offstage*) In fact—

SHEPHERD (*Running in*): Mrs. Smythe! St. George is approaching!

MRS. SMYTHE: Oh, dear. And the streets aren't decorated. Quickly. Let's get the flags and banners out. Robert! Don't just stand there! *Do something!* (MRS. SMYTHE *and* SHEPHERD *exit.*)

ROBERT: Guess I'll go back up on the Downs and warn my friend. (*He exits. Music grows louder. Banners and flags are lowered over stage. One banner reads* WELCOME ST. GEORGE. MRS. SMYTHE, SHEPHERD *and* MOTHER *enter. Cheers and crowd noises are heard from offstage, and* ST. GEORGE *enters on his horse.*)

ST. GEORGE: Friends, Romans, countrymen! No—not that one. (*Pauses, then brightly*) Ah! Four score and twenty years ago . . . No. Er . . . 'twas the night before Christmas and all through the house. Hm-m-m? (*Looks about*)

MRS. SMYTHE: Welcome to our town, most respected St. George. Save us from a most despicable scourge! There is a terrible dragon up on our Downs.

ST. GEORGE: Have no hear. That's why I'm fear. (*Shakes head*) No, that's not right. A dragon, huh? Just my business. Be glad he's not down on your ups. (*Laughs*) Heh, heh!

SHEPHERD: He's living in a cave. I'll take you to the edge of town and point the way.

ST. GEORGE: Well . . . there's no pime like the tresent. Ah. . . . No time like the present. I'll go up there right away and look into this little matter.

MRS. SMYTHE: Our hero!

176

MOTHER: While you're up there, please tell my son, Robert, to come home for lunch.

ST. GEORGE: Right-o. Well, off I go.

SHEPHERD: Have faith and courage.

MRS. SMYTHE: Godspeed.

ALL: Goodbye! Goodbye! (ST. GEORGE *exits on his horse. Curtain.*)

*   *   *

Scene Four

SETTING: *The same as Scene 2.*

AT RISE: DRAGON *is onstage.*

DRAGON: I must try this poem before I recite it for the boy and his friends. (*Reads from book*)

> Flowers bright, tasteful sight,
> Blooming in the sun's strong light.
> Red and ocher, blue and white,
> They fade away into the night.

That's not bad—although I've written better. (ROBERT *runs in.*)

ROBERT: Dragon! Now you're in for it. He's coming. You'll have to get ready and *do* something.

DRAGON: Don't be so excited, boy. Sit down and get your breath and then perhaps you'll tell me who's coming.

ROBERT: It's *only* St. George, the dragon killer, that's who.

DRAGON: Oh, dear me! This is dreadful. I won't talk to him, and that's that. You must tell him not to come. Say he can send a note, but I won't see him.

ROBERT: Now, Dragon. Don't be stubborn. You've got to

fight him some time or other. Better do it now and then we can get on with our poems.

DRAGON: My dear boy, try to understand. I won't fight. I've never fought and I'm not going to start now.

ROBERT: But if you don't, he'll kill you!

DRAGON: Oh, I don't think so. You'll arrange something, I'm sure. I leave it up to you. (DRAGON *exits into cave.*)

ROBERT (*To himself*): What do I do now? (ST. GEORGE *enters.*)

ST. GEORGE: Hello there, young fellow. Have you seen a dragon about?

ROBERT: He's over in that cave, but he's not about to come out.

ST. GEORGE: Won't come out?

ROBERT: No. You see, St. George, he's a *perfect* dragon.

ST. GEORGE: I quite understand. A villain worthy of my sword.

ROBERT: No! He's not bad. He's a kind, loving sort of dragon. A real gentleman.

ST. GEORGE: Oh? Perhaps I've misjudged him. Just tell him I'd like to talk to him, then. I promise him no harm. Just want to discuss matters.

ROBERT: Well—I'll try. (*Calls into cave*) Dragon! Yoo-hoo!

DRAGON (*From offstage*): I'm busy. Another time.

ROBERT (*To* ST. GEORGE): Perhaps you'd better go away.

ST. GEORGE: Quite impossible! It's against the rules.

ROBERT: Well—let's try to talk to him. (ROBERT *goes to cave again and calls.*) Dragon! Please come out! St. George and I would like to talk to you. (DRAGON *enters from cave.*)

DRAGON (*Speaking quickly*): So glad to meet you, St. George. Perhaps sometime when you can stay longer I can recite for you. Good day. (*He starts to leave.*)

St. George: I think we'd better try to settle this little affair right away and wight it fout—er . . . fight it out.

Robert: Yes—do! It'll save such a lot of bother.

Dragon: My young friend, you stay out of this. The whole thing is nonsense. I'm not going to fight and that's that!

St. George: But this would be a beautiful place to fight. Your beautiful scales rippling and my shining armor glittering in the sun.

Dragon: Now you're trying to get to me through my artistic senses. (*Thoughtfully*) Not that it wouldn't make a pretty picture.

Robert: Good—we seem to be getting down to business.

St. George: The fight can be fixed. I could stab you so that it wouldn't hurt you a bit. How about here? (*He touches* Dragon *on his chest with sword.*)

Dragon (*Laughing*): I'm ticklish. No, not there. I'm bound to laugh.

St. George: How about under the neck—here! (*Touches him under neck.*)

Dragon: That's a good place. Are you sure you can do it right?

St. George: Sure—just leave it to me.

Dragon: All right. Your plan seems like a good one. Let's do it.

Robert: St. George, just what is the Dragon going to get out of this?

St. George: Well—I'm supposed to lead him down the street in triumph.

Robert: And then?

St. George: There'll be shouting and speeches.

Robert: And then what?

Dragon (*Interrupting*): A lovely banquet! Yes, I'll go

through with it. This means I'll be recognized by society at last.

ST. GEORGE: Can you ramp and breathe fire and rage?

DRAGON: I know I can ramp and rage, but I'm a bit out of practice as far as fire-breathing is concerned. I'll do my best.

ST. GEORGE: Good. There has to be a princess—terror-stricken and chained to a rock and all that sort of thing.

ROBERT: Mother will surely help us out. Now I must go home, or Mother will worry. (*To* DRAGON) It's all arranged. First thing in the morning.

DRAGON: Not too early. I'm not my best in the morning. I must get my sleep. Goodbye, Robert. And goodbye, St. George.

ST. GEORGE: 'Bye 'bye. . . . (ROBERT *and* ST. GEORGE *start out.*)

DRAGON (*Calling after them*): And may the best man win! (*Laughs and re-enters cave as curtains close.*)

*   *   *

Scene Five

SETTING: *The same as Scene 2.*

AT RISE: DRAGON *is vocalizing and polishing scales on his chest with his paw.* ROBERT *and his* MOTHER *enter.*

ROBERT: Good morning, Dragon.

DRAGON: Good morning, boy. How do I look? I've been polishing my scales.

ROBERT: Beautiful. Just beautiful. This is my mother.

DRAGON: And a good good morning to you, ma'am.

MOTHER: I hope I can be of service.

DRAGON: Oh, you'll do just fine. Not too dramatic, now. Be realistic—like this (*He overacts*)—HELP! HELP ME! OOOO! SAVE ME FROM THE DRAGON! OOOO!

MOTHER: I get the general idea.

DRAGON: Good. Oh, I hear them coming. I'll go into the cave. (*To himself*) Oh, dear . . . and without a rehearsal! I hope the fight goes well. (*Exits into cave*)

MOTHER (*To* ROBERT): I must say he is a different sort of dragon, dear. I'll stand over here and look distressed. (*She stands near cave. Crowd noises are heard from offstage. Mrs. SMYTHE and the SHEPHERD enter and stand center, behind rocks.*)

MRS. SMYTHE: Oooh! How exciting! We will finally rid ourselves of this terrible monster. Stay near me, Shepherd, and protect me.

SHEPHERD (*Shaking with fright*): Y-y-yes, Mrs. Smythe. I'll pro-pro-protect you. (*He hides behind her. ST. GEORGE rides in on his horse. Cheering is heard from offstage.*)

ROBERT (*To himself*): I hope this goes right. Maybe we should have had a run-through. (*DRAGON re-enters, snorting and carrying on furiously. All gasp.*) It looks as if he's as good an actor as he is a poet. (*DRAGON and ST. GEORGE begin to fight. There is much shouting and snorting.*)

DRAGON (*Ad lib*): Ramp, ramp! Rage, rage! Snort, snort! Scourge, scourge! (*Etc.*)

ST. GEORGE (*Fiercely*): That'll teach you. Take that! (*Swings at DRAGON with sword. DRAGON falls to ground in an emotional dying scene. He moans, groans, thrashes about, and at last gives a loud hiss and lies still. All cheer.*)

MRS. SMYTHE *and* SHEPHERD (*Together*): Hooray!

SHEPHERD: Aren't you going to cut his head off?

ST. GEORGE: I think not. Let's all go down to the town and celebrate instead. I'm sure he'll be a very good dragon from now on. The maiden is saved.

MOTHER (*Very casually*): I'm saved.

ST. GEORGE: The town is saved.

MRS. SMYTHE: We're all saved. Hail to St. George!

ALL: Hail to St. George! Hip hip, hoorah! (MOTHER, MRS. SMYTHE *and* SHEPHERD *exit.*)

ROBERT: You can get up now, Dragon. (DRAGON *gets up.*)

DRAGON: I'm a bit dusty and sore.

ST. GEORGE: That was a fine job of fighting. Some of the most beautiful action I've ever seen out of a dragon.

DRAGON: Do you really think so? Perhaps I should go into acting.

ROBERT: Well, we had better get down to the village.

ST. GEORGE: Ah, yes. We must hear the speeches!

DRAGON: I'll recite a poem I've written for the occasion:

> St. George and the Dragon
> Fought up on the Downs.
> People came to see
> From villages and towns.
>
> The fight was a fair one,
> As all could tell.
> Here's fame to St. George.
> All's well that ends well.

(*They all exit together as curtain closes.*)

THE END

Production Notes

The Reluctant Dragon

Puppets: 6 hand puppets or marionettes.

Costumes: The Dragon can be a hand puppet with a moving mouth, or a sock puppet. He can have one large hand to help him emote (the puppeteer's other hand in a matching glove), and a long tail to flick about. If he is a marionette, make him big and funny-looking. For a fire-breathing effect, put a rubber tube or straw in his mouth and blow talcum powder through it. St. George should be short and dumpy, with a big walrus moustache and armor. He carries a sword in his hand at all times. His horse can be modeled after a theatrical hobbyhorse and worn over his hips. If it is a marionette show, build a full marionette horse for St. George to ride.

Properties: Book; bowl and spoon for Mother.

Setting: Scene 1, a kitchen interior in an English cottage, is a simple painted backdrop. Scenes 2, 4, and 5: Up on the Downs: backdrop shows rolling hills. There are several rocks, at center, and a cave entrance (a cut-out) at right. Scene 3: The village street. Half-timbered buildings and shops are painted on backdrop. Banners are suspended from above stage, including one reading WELCOME ST. GEORGE.

Lighting: No special effects.

Sound: Crowd noises and cheering, as indicated in text.

KING MIDAS AND THE GOLDEN TOUCH

Characters

NARRATOR
KING MIDAS
MARIGOLD, *his daughter*
JOHANNA, *her nurse*
JONATHAN, *a manservant*
ORO, *the Spirit of Gold*
GOLDIE, *the cat*

SCENE 1

SETTING: *King Midas's throne room, with a beautiful garden alive with flowers at one side. The sun is shining.*
AT RISE: KING MIDAS *and* JONATHAN *enter.*

NARRATOR: There once lived a king called Midas. He had more gold than any other king or rich man anywhere in the world, yet King Midas was not content. He always wished for more and more gold.
MIDAS: I don't want to think about the country's problems. I don't have time. I have to find new ways to get gold.
JONATHAN: But there are papers to sign. And your fields need planting. We must buy seeds for your farmers to sow.
MIDAS: But that costs money. I have no gold to spare.
JONATHAN: Your people are waiting in the hall to speak to you. Some have been waiting for many days. There are problems to be solved.
MIDAS: Well, they will just have to wait. It's time to count my gold.

(*Sings to the tune of "Three Blind Mice"*)
        Duties tend — know I should.
        What I like — if I could
        Is counting gold and by the score.
        Any other work is a bore,
        For gold is what I do adore.
        I love gold!
(*He does a little dance.*)
        Better none — than yellow gold.
        None so rare — so I'm told.
        So please excuse me if I stray
        From my chores this very day.
        Listen to what I have to say —
        I love gold!

JONATHAN: But, Your Majesty ...

MARIGOLD (*Entering with her cat,* GOLDIE): Good morning, Daddy.

MIDAS: Good morning, Marigold. Isn't she the sweetest child you've ever seen, Jonathan?

JONATHAN: Yes, she certainly is, King Midas.

MIDAS: I'm so lucky to have such a good little girl. (MARIGOLD *is playing with* GOLDIE) Come over to me, my sweet, and give Papa a kiss.

MARIGOLD (*Coming over*): For the dearest Daddy in the world. (*Kisses him*)

MIDAS: That's my girl.

MARIGOLD: Look at Goldie, Papa. See how she plays. (GOLDIE *romps around*)

MIDAS: Yes, she is a good companion, isn't she?

MARIGOLD: But I'd rather you played with me, Papa. Come to the garden and see my pretty flowers. They are all the colors of the rainbow. Aren't they beautiful? (*Sings to the tune of "London Bridge Is Falling Down"*)

Look, my flowers, see how nice,
Smell them too, once or twice,
Smell their fragrance, to entice
My dear Daddy.
Marigold and roses, too,
Daffodils, violets blue,
Come and see my daisy too —
My dear Daddy.

MIDAS: Not now, dear. I have to go with Jonathan to the treasure room and count gold.

MARIGOLD: But you just counted your gold yesterday morning. It's surely still there.

MIDAS: Now, Marigold, your father knows best. Run along and play with Goldie.

MARIGOLD (*Disappointed*): Yes, Father. Come along, Goldie. Let's play in the garden. (MARIGOLD *and* GOLDIE *exit into garden.*)

MIDAS: Jonathan, come along to the treasure room.

JONATHAN: Yes, Your Majesty. (*They exit. Curtain*)

*   *   *   *   *

SCENE 2

SETTING: *The treasure room, dark and foreboding. Only one shaft of light enters room, at center. There is a candlestick at one side. Room is filled with chests and bags of gold.*

AT RISE: MIDAS *and* JONATHAN *enter.*

MIDAS: Now, where did we leave off? Oh, yes, with this bag. Do you have the accounting book, Jonathan?

JONATHAN: Yes, Your Majesty. Call out the numbers and I'll mark them off. (*Opens book*)

MIDAS: Good idea! Now, let's see. (*Counting*) Two million, twenty-five ...

JONATHAN: Two million, twenty-five. Yes.

MIDAS: Two million, twenty-six. Two million, twenty-seven. Two million, twenty-eight!

JONATHAN: Got it, Your Majesty. Wait! I must go and get another candle. I'll be right back. (*He exits.*)

MIDAS: All this gold. They say I am the richest man in the world, but that can't be right. Surely there must be some other way to get more gold. ... Tax the people? No, that wouldn't be fair. I'm fond of my subjects and they like me. Wage war on a nearby country and take their gold? No, I'm a gentle person and wouldn't want to do that. If there were just some way ... Hm-m-m. I just love to touch all my beautiful gold. Better than any other thing in the world, except my beautiful, sweet daughter, Marigold. Touch... touch ... that's it. I wish I had the Golden Touch. I wish ... I wish that whatever I touch would turn to gold. (*There is a mysterious sound of bells and a golden figure, ORO, comes from the beam of light.*) What's this? A golden man ... in that shaft of light. Who are you?

ORO (*Chanting*):

> Oro is my name, the Spirit of Gold.
> I can also bring you riches untold.
> I can grant the wish you want so much —
> That is, if you want the golden touch.
>
> Then now, think twice before you say
> What is on your mind. It's best to weigh
> What you wish to have. Just let me know
> And I promise that I'll make it so.

MIDAS: The Golden Touch. Oh, yes! How wonderful. What must I do?

ORO: Just wait until the sun rises tomorrow morning and

187

then your wish will come true. Goodbye, King Midas. And I hope you will be happy with your new power.

MIDAS: Thank you, Oro, Spirit of Gold. Thank you. How wonderful! The Golden Touch! (ORO *exits.*) Oh! He is gone!

JONATHAN (*Offstage*): Your Majesty . . .

MIDAS: I'd better not tell anyone. I'm sure they wouldn't believe me anyway. I'll just wait until it happens. (*He snickers.*)

JONATHAN (*Entering*): Did I hear you talking to someone?

MIDAS: Me? Talking to someone? (*Laughs*) No, no. Don't be silly. I was just talking . . . er . . . counting to myself.

JONATHAN: Shall we get back to the accounts?

MIDAS: No, let's take the rest of the day off. Perhaps I'll see my subjects now. And here is some gold to buy seed for the farmers to plant. (*Hands* JONATHAN *a bag of gold*) I feel quite generous today. (*He laughs as they exit. Curtain*)

* * * * *

SCENE 3

TIME: *The next day, before dawn.*
SETTING: *The same as Scene 1.*
AT RISE: MIDAS *runs in.*

MIDAS: Oh, my. Today is the day! Where is Jonathan? Where is Johanna? Let's get things started today. (*He pulls cord and sound of bell is heard.* JOHANNA *runs in.*)

JOHANNA: Your Majesty. Up so early? Usually you sleep until noon.

MIDAS: Well, I . . .

JONATHAN (*Running in*): King Midas? Up so early? Usually you . . .

MIDAS: Sleep till noon. Yes, I know, but today is a special day.

JONATHAN: It is? Is it your birthday?

MIDAS: No. . . . (*Laughs*)

JOHANNA: Is it the princess's birthday?

MIDAS: No, but watch. (*He touches curtains and nothing happens.*)

JOHANNA: Would you like the curtains down, Your Majesty?

MIDAS: What happened? Why aren't they gold?

JOHANNA: I can change them to gold-colored ones, Your Majesty.

MIDAS: No, you don't understand.

JONATHAN: We will lower them when the sun rises.

MIDAS: When the sun rises . . . that's it. The sun isn't up yet.

JOHANNA: But the sun is just rising now. See what a pretty day it will be!

MARIGOLD (*Entering*): Good morning, Papa. Come out into the garden and play with me.

MIDAS: Another time, dear. Johanna, take Marigold for a walk. Today is my special day.

MARIGOLD: But Papa. You promised.

JOHANNA: Come along, child. Your father is busy.

MARIGOLD: Yes, Johanna. Perhaps we can pick some of my beautiful flowers. I'm so happy when I'm in the garden. Goodbye, Papa.

MIDAS: Goodbye, dear. Have a good time. (MARIGOLD *and* JOHANNA *exit.*) Ah, now! Now for the wonderful surprise. The sun has risen — now look! (*He touches curtains and they turn to gold. See Production Notes for changing objects to gold.*) Ha-ha!

JONATHAN: Amazing. How did you do that?

MIDAS: Now watch this. (*He touches his throne and it turns to gold. He laughs.*) Isn't this wonderful?

JONATHAN: Well, I say . . .

MIDAS: I have the Golden Touch! Whatever I touch turns to gold. Don't you think I'm lucky?

JONATHAN: I guess so, Your Majesty. But all that counting! We will never finish this way. We will have to build a new treasury to hold all this.

MIDAS (*Laughing*): Everything will be so beautiful. Solid gold. But I'm so hungry. Have you my breakfast?

JONATHAN: Right here. (*He gets a tray that holds bread and eggs.*)

MIDAS: Hm-m-m. Looks delicious. I'm famished. I haven't had anything to eat since supper last night. Let's see! Think I'll open my egg first. It looks so good and I love eggs. (*He touches egg and it turns to gold.*) Oh! My egg is solid gold. Oh, dear! I'll try a piece of bread. (*It turns to gold*) Oh, no!

JONATHAN: What is wrong?

MIDAS: My food. My food turns to gold. I'll have to be fed. That's ridiculous!

JONATHAN: Yes, Your Majesty.

MIDAS: What?

JONATHAN: How wonderful to have the Golden Touch.

MIDAS: Yes, it . . . is, isn't it? Marigold will be so pleased. I know, I'll touch all her flowers so they will be presents of solid gold.

JONATHAN: But, Your Majesty . . . (MIDAS *goes to garden and touches flowers. They turn to gold.*)

MIDAS: Look! Look! Aren't they beautiful now? Come, Jonathan. Let's see what else we can turn to gold.

JONATHAN: Yes, King Midas. (*They exit, and* MARIGOLD *and* JOHANNA *enter.*)

MARIGOLD: Such a pretty day. Thank you, Johanna, for taking me for my walk.

JOHANNA: Don't you think you should take a nap, dear Marigold?

MARIGOLD: In a minute. I just want to see and smell my pretty flowers again. (*She turns and sees them.*) Oh, no! My pretty flowers. What happened to them? They are all hard and brittle. And they have lost their beautiful perfume. (*She cries.*)

MIDAS (*Entering*): What's wrong, dear sweet daughter? Why do you cry so? Johanna, get Marigold a handkerchief for her tears.

JOHANNA: Yes, Your Majesty. (*She exits.*)

MARIGOLD: My pretty flowers. They've all died and have turned to stone. (*Cries*)

MIDAS: Stone? No, dear ... that's gold. Solid gold!

MARIGOLD: But I loved them as they were. Oh, what will I do without my rainbow garden? (*She cries harder.*)

MIDAS: Now, don't cry. I can't bear to see you cry. Here ... come to Papa and let me kiss your tears away. (*He kisses her and she turns to golden statue.*) Marigold! Marigold ... what have I done? What *have* I done? (*Calls*) Oro! Spirit of Gold ... come back!

ORO (*Appearing*): King Midas, is something wrong? How do you like your Golden Touch?

MIDAS: Please, please, save my little girl. I don't want the Golden Touch. Take it away. Give me back my child.

ORO: Greed is a misery. Count your blessings for what you already have. Never again will you have the Golden Touch. Share your great wealth with your people.

MIDAS: Anything. ... Only return Marigold to me.

ORO: Soon a magical snow will fall. Place Marigold among her flowers. Then promise that never again will you want more than your fair share on this earth. Be kind to your subjects and be happy with what you have.

MIDAS: Yes, oh, yes. Thank you, Oro, Spirit of Gold. I swear! I have learned my lesson. (*It starts to snow. See Production Notes.*)

191

ORO: Look! The snow is here. Quickly!

MIDAS: Oh, yes! (MIDAS *picks up statue of his daughter and puts it among the flowers.*)

ORO: Goodbye, King Midas.

MIDAS: Goodbye . . . and thank you again. (ORO *exits. The snow continues to fall. The flowers change back.*) Look! Marigold's flowers are back. Please bring my daughter back to me! Never again will I be greedy. I promise I will be thoughtful of others. My poor little girl! (*He puts his face in his hands. Statue turns to* MARIGOLD. *Snow stops.*)

MARIGOLD: Look, Papa! My flowers are real again. How good they smell.

MIDAS (*Looking up*): Marigold, you are back. (*He runs to her.*)

MARIGOLD: My garden is more beautiful than ever. And the soft snow makes the flowers fresh and pretty. (JONATHAN *and* JOHANNA *enter.*)

MIDAS: Look, everyone. Marigold is back!

JOHANNA: Back from our walk? But Your Majesty, we weren't gone long.

JONATHAN: The walk has brought fresh beauty to little Marigold.

MIDAS: Jonathan, get 100 bags of gold to give to my people.

JONATHAN: What did you say, King Midas?

MIDAS: You heard me. One hundred bags of gold. Hurry now . . .

JONATHAN: Yes, Your Majesty. (*He exits.*)

MIDAS: Johanna, dress Marigold in her best, for today we visit our people. It is time to share! It is time for giving! It is time for love! (MIDAS *embraces* MARIGOLD *and she then runs off with* JOHANNA. MIDAS *goes into the garden among the flowers. Curtain.*)

THE END

Production Notes

KING MIDAS AND THE GOLDEN TOUCH

Number of Puppets: 6 hand or rod puppets or marionettes.
Characters: 1 male or female for Narrator.
Playing Time: 15 minutes.
Description of Puppets: King Midas is kindly and gray-haired. Marigold is a little girl with blonde hair. Jonathan and Johanna are middle-aged and kindly. The cat is yellow. Oro can be an old elf or a handsome youth dressed in gold with yellow hair. The play can take place at any time, but Grecian costumes would be nice. Costume or fairy-tale books will give you ideas.
Properties: Book, bags of gold, tray with bread and eggs.
Setting: Scenes 1 and 3: throne room and flower garden. There is a throne at one side. On wall are curtained window and bell cord. Scene 2: treasure room, with bags of gold and candlestick.
Lighting: Scene 1 is bright and sunny, Scene 2 is dark with only a single shaft of light from above, and Scene 3 is dim at beginning and brightens.
Sound: Sound of bells when Oro enters.
Special Effects: For turning objects into gold: either use the flip-down prop that covers the original with a golden version, or quickly exchange original object with a golden one. Use a turn-about throne, golden on one side. The curtains that turn to gold can be any color and, when pulled down, have top section of gold. Marigold, when turned to gold, is a golden statue version of the puppet. The flowers can be painted with a flip-down version in gold or else exchanged quickly with another identical set painted gold.

To make it snow, make a trough of muslin and two pieces of wood and cut slits diagonally all along the muslin. Suspend this from the top of your stage and fill with artificial snow made of bits of plastic or white paper. When jiggled from below by an attached cord, the trough will allow the snow to fall softly on the scene at the back of the stage. Oro should always appear from above or below, never from the side of the stage.

RUMPELSTILTSKIN

Characters

Hunter
Miller
King
Sarah, *the Miller's daughter*
Rumpelstiltskin
Baby

Scene 1

Setting: *The throne room in the palace. There is a throne at center, and there are banners and a tapestry decorating the stone walls.*

At Rise: Miller *enters, carrying basket of pumpernickel bread.*

Miller: Where could the King be? Ah . . . here comes someone now. (Hunter *enters with gun and some rabbits.*) Oh — it's only a hunter. (*To* Hunter) Good day, sir. Why have *you* come to see the King?

Hunter: To give him a present, Miller. And why are you here?

Miller: I also have a gift for the King. I see you have some rabbits. Did you catch them yourself?

Hunter: Yes. I am the finest hunter in the land.

Miller: Oh, you are, are you?

Hunter: Yes. I can catch as many as five hundred rabbits in one day. These are only a few I caught this morning.

MILLER: My, that is a lot of rabbits. But that doesn't compare to the amount of flour I mill in one day. Milling 500 sacks of flour is but a start for me. See here! (*Holds out basket*) I have brought a delicious loaf of bread made from my wheat.

HUNTER: Let me have a slice.

MILLER: Oh, no! I have brought this bread for the King. (*He exits.*)

HUNTER: Humph! Five hundred sacks of flour in one day.... Impossible! These rabbits are getting heavy. I do wish the King would appear so that I can give them to him. I want him to appoint me Royal Hunter for the castle. (KING enters.) Good day, Your Majesty. (*He bows deeply.*)

KING: Good day, Hunter. You wish to see me?

HUNTER: I wish to present the rabbits that I caught for you. (*Gives rabbits to KING*)

KING: Why, thank you! There are many rabbits here. You must be a good hunter.

HUNTER: Yes, I am. I can offer you anything in the woods — a deer, a unicorn, or perhaps a questing beast. Just name it and I will hunt it down. I can also find any lost pet animals for you, because I know the forest so well.

KING: I hope you are not lying, for there has been too much bragging and too much fibbing recently. You may stay on and be Royal Hunter for the castle, but you must prove your trustworthiness.

HUNTER: Oh, thank you, Your Majesty. (*He exits.*)

KING: Unicorn! Questing beast! Really! Some people do carry on so. I must do something about all this falsehood going about. Such fabrications. But what? Someone must pay the penalty and serve as an example. (MILLER enters.)

MILLER: Your Majesty (*Bows*) — Your Majesty (*Bows*) — Your Majesty (*Bows*) —

KING: Yes, Miller. May I help you?

MILLER: I, your humble servant, have come to present to you this loaf of pumpernickel bread. I have milled the flour, and my daughter, Sarah, has baked it especially for you.

KING (*Taking basket*): Thank you, good Miller. (*Tastes bread*) Hm-m-m. This is delicious. I do wish I had a wife who could bake like this. And one that could spin cloth, for my weavers are all so clumsy. I would make her my queen.

MILLER: Oh, my daughter is very clever. Not only can she bake, but she can spin straw into gold.

KING: Did you say your daughter could spin straw into gold?

MILLER (*To audience*): I think I said the wrong thing. (*To KING*) Ah . . . yes!

KING: If your daughter can spin straw into gold as well as she can bake pumpernickel bread, I will marry her. But if she cannot, I will throw you into my dungeons to punish you for lying.

MILLER: But, Your Majesty . . .

KING: Be off with you. Bring your daughter here tomorrow.

MILLER: Good day, Your Majesty. Good day! (*To himself*) Oh, what did I say? (*Exits*)

KING: A girl that spins straw into gold? We shall see. We shall see. (*Curtain*)

* * * * *

SCENE 2

SETTING: *The royal treasury. There is a spinning wheel at one side of stage, with pile of straw beside it.*

AT RISE: MILLER *enters with* SARAH, *his daughter.*

SARAH: But, Papa, I can't spin straw into gold. No one can.

MILLER: If you do, you will be Queen. You must try, dear. I will be sent to the dungeons if you don't.

SARAH: I will try, Papa.

MILLER: The King is coming. I had better leave you. Do the best you can. Goodbye, dear.

SARAH: Goodbye, Papa. (MILLER *exits.*) What will I say? What will I do? I must save poor Papa. I'm sure he must have meant well. (KING *enters.*)

KING: Good day, pretty child. You must be Sarah, the Miller's daughter.

SARAH: Good day, Your Majesty. Yes, I am Sarah.

KING: Thank you for the delicious bread you baked for me yesterday.

SARAH: For your pleasure, Your Majesty.

KING: Your father tells me you can spin.

SARAH: Yes, I can spin.

KING: He tells me you can spin straw into gold. You have been brought here to prove that what your father claims is true. (*Points to straw*) Here is a bundle of straw. Spin this into gold.

SARAH: But, Your Majesty . . .

KING: Yes? Did you wish to tell me something?

SARAH: Ah . . . no, sir.

KING: I will leave you now, but I will be back soon. If you have accomplished the deed when I return, you will be my wife and Queen. If you have not, I'm afraid your father will be thrown into my dungeons for fibbing. (*He exits.*)

SARAH: What shall I do? I'll try. (SARAH *begins to spin.*) Just put the straw to the spinning wheel. . . . (*Tries again*) Oh, dear. Nothing happens. Poor Papa! What will I do? (*She breaks down and cries.*) Boo-hoo. (RUMPELSTILTSKIN *enters.*)

RUMPELSTILTSKIN: Good day, girl.

SARAH (*Surprised*): Oh! Who are you?

RUMPELSTILTSKIN: Never mind who I am. I know who you are and I know you have a problem.

SARAH: Yes. I must spin —

RUMPELSTILTSKIN: Straw into gold. I know all about it. And your father will suffer if you do not. Tsk, tsk! What some people get themselves into. Hm-m-m. Perhaps I can help you.

SARAH: Can you? But how? No one can spin straw into gold!

RUMPELSTILTSKIN: *I* can. But you must give me something precious for my services.

SARAH: I have so little. Now, what can I give you? Would you take my necklace?

RUMPELSTILTSKIN: Well — yes! It is a pretty thing. I can wrap it about my waist.

SARAH (*Taking off necklace*): Here it is. Take it. (*He takes necklace.*)

RUMPELSTILTSKIN: Now I'll get to work. Close your eyes and no peeking. (*She covers her face with her hands, and he spins.*)

> Whirl, whirl, here we go,
> Just so fast and not too slow.
> All this gold, see it glow.

(*Draws length of golden cord from straw.*) You can look now.

SARAH (*Uncovering her eyes and seeing gold*): Oh, how wonderful! You did do it! My papa is safe now. Thank you so much, Mr. — what did you say your name was?

RUMPELSTILTSKIN: I didn't say. (*Laughs*) Goodbye. (*Disappears*)

SARAH: What a funny little man. He must be a magician.

KING (*From offstage*): Sarah! Have you finished spinning? May I come in?

SARAH: Come in, Your Majesty. (KING *enters.*)

KING: Why, you *have* turned the straw into gold! There is enough to buy you a beautiful wedding dress — for we are to be married.

SARAH: And Papa won't be thrown into the dungeons?

KING: That's right. He will be Royal Miller instead.

SARAH (*Bowing*): Thank you, Your Majesty.

KING: But I wonder . . . would you spin some more straw, so that we could have a wonderful wedding feast for the entire court? (*Brings out straw*) Here is more straw. We must have a proper party.

SARAH: I could bake some more pumpernickel bread.

KING: It was delicious, but we must have cookies, cake, ice cream and spaghetti. Now get to work. I'll be right back. (*Exits*)

SARAH: Oh, dear! (*Beginning to cry*) Now what will I do? I do wish that little man would come back.

RUMPELSTILTSKIN (*Entering*): Here I am. I heard your call. What's wrong this time?

SARAH: The King has brought more straw — much more — so that we can have enough gold for a wedding feast.

RUMPELSTILTSKIN: And you want me to spin this straw into gold, too? (*She nods.*) What do you have to give me this time?

SARAH: Now, let me see . . . (*Looks about, then at her hand*) All I have left of value is this ring my mother gave to me.

RUMPELSTILTSKIN: That will do. Give it to me! (*She gives ring to him.*) Now turn around and hide your eyes. (*He spins*)

> Spin, spin, thick and thin,
> To help the maiden and her kin,
> Someday Sarah the King will win.

(*Draws out more gold from straw.*) You can look now!

SARAH: Wonderful! Thank you again. I will always be grateful to you.

RUMPELSTILTSKIN: Yes, my dear, you will be grateful! (*Laughs and exits.*)

SARAH: It's amazing how he does it. I just hope that was the last time I need to call him. I have nothing left to give him. (KING *enters.*)

KING: Well, my dear, that didn't take you long. We shall have a magnificent feast with this much gold. But there is still one thing lacking, and that is a new wedding coach for us. I'm sure you won't mind spinning a bit more straw. Here is a pile that should only take you a moment. (*He brings in large bundle of straw.*) Call me when you are done. (*He exits.*)

SARAH: Oh, my! Now what shall I do? (RUMPELSTILTSKIN *appears.*)

RUMPELSTILTSKIN: Well, here we are again. Still in trouble, eh?

SARAH: This is the last time, little man. Please help me again.

RUMPELSTILTSKIN: What do you have to offer this time?

SARAH: I've given you all my precious possessions. Surely you will still help me. It takes you so little time.

RUMPELSTILTSKIN: You must pay for know-how, my dear. If you have nothing to offer, I will leave. Goodbye!

SARAH: Wait! There must be something — (*Searches*) What will I do? (*Weeps*)

RUMPELSTILTSKIN: Maybe we can figure something out. Now, let's see. You are going to marry the King?

SARAH: Yes . . .

RUMPELSTILTSKIN: And be Queen?

SARAH: Yes . . .

RUMPELSTILTSKIN: And after a year or so have a little child?

SARAH: Oh, I hope so!

RUMPELSTILTSKIN: Fine! Then as payment for the gold you must promise to give me your first-born child.

SARAH: Oh, no! I beg of you. Take anything else — my crown, my jewels, my —

RUMPELSTILTSKIN: Your first child — nothing more or less. Come now. I'm in a hurry. Your answer?

SARAH: All right. I agree. (*She covers her face and he spins.*)

RUMPELSTILTSKIN:

> Roll, roll, gold so fine,
> Sarah's goodness is a sign
> That her first child will be mine.

(*Draws very long length of golden cord from straw, then cackles wickedly and exits*)

SARAH (*Uncovering her eyes*): My first child — to be taken from me. Oh, no! I must protect my baby! (KING *enters.*)

KING: Sarah! (*Sees gold*) Why, this is more gold than I ever expected. We have enough for a new castle. I don't want to be greedy, so I promise you will never have to spin gold again. And we will be so happy ...

SARAH: Yes (*Sadly*) ... so happy ... (*They exit. Curtain.*)

* * * * *

SCENE 3

SETTING: *Nursery. Cradle, with canopy of rich-looking cloth over it, is at center.*

AT RISE: SARAH, *now in royal robe and crown, holds* BABY. KING *enters.*

KING: Oh, there you are, my dear Queen Sarah ... and my new little baby girl. She's just as pretty as her mother. I am going to arrange a christening party for her. Take care of our little princess, Sarah. We wouldn't want anything to happen to her. (KING *exits.*)

SARAH: My sweet little girl. We are so lucky to have you.
(BABY *coos.*) Go to sleep. (*Sings*)

> My sweet little dear,
> I'll sing you to sleep,
> With all our love, for you to keep.
> Here's all we can give you.
> What more can I say?

(RUMPELSTILTSKIN *enters.*)

RUMPELSTILTSKIN: Now I've come to take her away. (*Laughs*)

SARAH: You've come back! Leave this castle at once!

RUMPELSTILTSKIN: I've come for my payment. Have you forgotten? Give me the child!

SARAH: Oh, no. Not my baby. Take anything — there's gold, my crown, jewels, anything — but don't take my baby!

RUMPELSTILTSKIN: I don't want your jewels. I am lonesome in the woods and I want someone to play with. I must have the child.

SARAH: You are cruel and mean! She is a princess, and she should stay here with us. (SARAH *cries and* BABY *cries.*)

RUMPELSTILTSKIN: Oh, I hate to see women cry! Don't cry. I ... well ... I'll give you another chance.

SARAH: Oh, would you? Please?

RUMPELSTILTSKIN: If you can guess my name within twenty-four hours, you can keep the child, and I won't bother you again. If not, you must give me your crown, your jewels, and all the gold in the castle ... and the baby as well.

SARAH: Yes — yes, little man! Is your name Paul? Is it Peter? Is it —

RUMPELSTILTSKIN (*Laughing*): Ha-ha! Remember, twenty-four hours and then the little princess will be mine. (*Laughs*) Ha-ha! (*Exits*)

SARAH: His name? Surely it won't be so difficult to find out his name. I know. I'll call the Hunter. Perhaps he can find out. (*Calls*) Hunter! (HUNTER *enters.*)

HUNTER: Did you call, O Queen?

SARAH: There was a little man here, just a moment ago. I must know his name, or he will take the baby.

HUNTER: Take the baby? Oh, no!

SARAH: Search the land — through the woods, the hills and mountains, the forest. We have but twenty-four hours. We *must* know his name.

HUNTER: What did he look like?

SARAH: He is very short and has a big bushy beard. He wears a stocking cap and pointed shoes. He couldn't be far from the castle yet — see if you can catch him.

HUNTER: Yes, Your Majesty. I'll hurry. (*Exits*)

SARAH (*Calling*): Yes, do. Hurry! (*Curtain*)

* * * * *

SCENE 4

SETTING: *The woods. This scene may be played before curtain.*

AT RISE: RUMPELSTILTSKIN *is skipping around stage. He does not see* HUNTER, *who is hiding behind trees, peering out, then ducking as* RUMPELSTILTSKIN *comes near.*

RUMPELSTILTSKIN (*Singing*):
>It won't be long, if my luck is good,
>I'll have a playmate in the wood.
>The Queen will help me win the game —
>She can't guess Rumpelstiltskin is my name.

(*Laughs*) A playmate! Ha-ha! A princess! (*Shouts*) Rumpelstiltskin — oops! Sh-h-h! (*Softly*) Rumpelstiltskin is my name. (*To audience*) Now, don't you tell anyone! (*Laughs and exits.* HUNTER *comes out of hiding.*)

HUNTER: So that's it! His name is Rumpelstiltskin! (*Runs off. Curtain.*)

*   *   *   *   *

SCENE 5

SETTING: *Nursery. Same as Scene 3.*
AT RISE: SARAH, *holding* BABY, *is pacing up and down.*

SARAH: Oh, where is the Hunter? The time is almost up. The little man will be here soon. Oh, dear. ... (HUNTER *enters.*)
HUNTER: Here I am, Your Majesty. (*Bows*)
SARAH: Did you find him?
HUNTER: I hunted the woods over. I hunted and searched and hunted and —
SARAH: Did you find him? Get on with it!
HUNTER: I came to a dark part of the forest where I had never been before, and there he was. I hid behind a tree and watched as he danced about and sang a little song. He said his name was ... ah ... Oh, dear. I forgot!
SARAH: Oh, no!
HUNTER (*To audience*): What was his name? (*Audience calls "Rumpelstiltskin."*) Yes, that's right. Rumpelstiltskin. Thank you ever so much.
SARAH: Rumpel— What did you say?
HUNTER: Rumpelstiltskin!
SARAH: Rumpelstiltskin! What an odd name. Thank you so much, Hunter.
HUNTER: You're welcome.
SARAH: Now you had better go. He will soon be here.
HUNTER: Yes, Your Majesty. Good day. (*He exits.*)
SARAH: Rumpelstiltskin — what a long, long name for such a little, little man! I will not forget this name. Never. (RUMPELSTILTSKIN *enters.*)

RUMPELSTILTSKIN: I've come for the child. Is she ready?

SARAH: I still have five minutes. I want my chance to guess your name.

RUMPELSTILTSKIN: You'll never guess. Give me the baby — quickly!

SARAH: No. I have five minutes. Is your name Oswald?

RUMPELSTILTSKIN: No! No! Give me the baby.

SARAH: Is it Thomas or Gerald or Geronimo?

RUMPELSTILTSKIN: No! No! Give me the baby, right away!

SARAH: Could it possibly be *Rumpelstiltskin?*

RUMPELSTILTSKIN: I want the — what? *What did you say?*

SARAH: I said, is your name Rumpelstiltskin?

RUMPELSTILTSKIN: How did you guess? Who told you? You found out! I'm so angry I could stamp my foot. (*Stamps foot*) I'm *so* angry! (*Stamps*) *So* angry! (*Stamps again*) *Angry!* (*Stamps so hard that he falls through floor and disappears, crying out*) Ah-h-h-h-h!

SARAH (*Crossing to where he disappeared*): My! He certainly did make a big hole in my new parquet floor. Poor little man. (KING *enters quickly.*)

KING: Sarah! Did I hear someone shouting? (*Sees hole*) And how did that hole get in the floor?

SARAH: I had a contest with a little man, and I'm afraid he lost.

KING: I guess he *is* lost.

SARAH: A little man tried to take our baby, and the earth just opened up and swallowed him.

KING: He must be clear to China by now. But our princess?

SARAH: She is just fine.

KING: But what was the man's name?

SARAH: Rumpelstiltskin.

KING (*Looking into hole*): Well, goodbye, Rumpelstiltskin. (*To audience*) And goodbye, everyone.

QUEEN (*To audience*): Goodbye! (*Bows, as curtains close*)

THE END

Production Notes

RUMPELSTILTSKIN

Number of Puppets: 7 puppets or marionettes.

Playing Time: 20 minutes.

Description of Puppets: Rumpelstiltskin is very short, with a beard, stocking cap and pointed elf's shoes. Hunter is dressed in green. King wears royal robes and crown. There should be two Sarah puppets, the first in a plain dress and apron, the second in royal robes, with a crown. Miller is dressed like a peasant.

Properties: Toy, basket of dark bread, toy rabbits and small rifle, toy spinning wheel, straw, golden cords.

Setting: For Scenes 1, 2, 3 and 5, the set should be a room in the palace with stone walls. Replace throne, used in Scene 1, with spinning wheel in Scene 2 and cradle in Scenes 3 and 5. Banners and tapestry may be changed also, if desired. Scene 4, the woods, may be played before curtain, or a painted backdrop of trees may be placed in front of palace set. In Scene 5, if puppets are used, Rumpelstiltskin falls behind stage at end. If using marionettes for this scene, build a raised section of the floor, through which he falls. In Scene 2, golden cord can be beneath stage and pulled up through a small hole in floor.

Lighting: No special effects.

JACK AND THE BEANSTALK

Characters

JACK
CHARLOTTE THE COW
BUTTERFLY
MOTHER
HAWKER
MRS. GIANT
MR. GIANT
MAGIC HEN
MAGIC HARP (PRINCESS MELODY)

Scene One

SETTING: *The garden of Jack's house.*

AT RISE: CHARLOTTE THE COW *is posing for* JACK, *who stands at his easel, drawing her.* BUTTERFLY *flies by.*

JACK (*Singing*):
>Old MacDonald had a farm,
>Eee-i, eee-i, oh,
>And on this farm he had a cow,
>Eee-i, eee-i, oh.
>With a—

Cow: Moo! Moo!

JACK (*Continuing song*):
>—here, and a—

Cow: Moo! Moo!

JACK (*Continuing song*):
>—there, here a—

MOTHER (*Calling from offstage*): Jack! What are you doing? Are you at your chores? Charlotte needs milking!

JACK: Charlotte is posing, Mother. (MOTHER *enters from house.*)

MOTHER: Posing? Are you drawing again? Put that silly easel away.

JACK: But, Mother, what makes the sky so blue? And why are butterflies' wings so colorful?

MOTHER: Jack, Jack, why do you always act like such a dumb-dumb when there's so much work to do? The landlord is coming to collect the rent tomorrow and here you are—playing with those useless crayons.

JACK: But, Mama, I like to draw.

MOTHER: Ever since your papa died we have grown poorer and poorer, and now we have no more money left at all. If we don't pay Mr. Bill Overdue, the landlord, we will be sent to the poorhouse! (*Sobs*)

JACK: Don't cry, Mama. Maybe I can sell my drawings.

MOTHER: Those useless things! (*She throws easel offstage.*) No! Take Charlotte to the county fair and sell her.

COW: *Mooooo!*

MOTHER: Yes, you, Charlotte!

JACK: Oh, no. Not Charlotte! Who will pose for me?

MOTHER: Never mind that. The cow must go. But come straight home. It is not safe to be out after dark. Just the other day the Princess was carried off, and goodness knows what has happened to her.

JACK: All right, Mother. Come along, Charlotte. (*He starts off, leading* Cow.)

COW (*Sadly*): Mooooo.

MOTHER: And get a good sum of money for her!

JACK: Goodbye, Mother.

MOTHER: Goodbye, Jack.

Cow (*Saying goodbye*): Moo-ooo! (*Jack leads* Cow *off and* Mother *exits. Curtain.*)

* * *

Scene Two

Setting: *At the fair. This scene is played before the curtain. Hawker's table is at center. There are three shells on it. There is a bag of beans on ground.*
At Rise: Hawker *stands behind table, calling.*

Hawker: Hurry! Hurry! See the shell game! (Jack *enters with* Cow *and they stand close to* Hawker.) Step aside, little man. (*Calling*) Try to guess which shell holds the magic beans. (*To* Jack) Go away, little boy. You bother me. (*Calls*) Hurry! Hurry! (Cow *eats bag of beans, making munching sounds. To* Jack) Your cow just ate my magic beans! She ate the whole bagful.
Jack: I'm sorry. But she was hungry!
Cow: Mooooo!
Hawker: Hungry, smungry. That's no excuse. I have only three magic beans left. You'll have to pay for the ones your cow ate.
Jack: But I have no money. All I have is this cow.
Hawker: Well, I'll tell you what I'm goin' to do. To show you my heart is in the right purse—er—place, I'm going to *give* you the last three magic beans, in exchange for your cow. (*Gives beans to* Jack)
Jack: Well—that seems fair. Mother will be pleased with these magic beans. They *are* magic, aren't they?
Hawker: Why, certainly. You don't think I'd cheat you, do you?

JACK: Oh, no. Well, I must go home now. Thank you, and goodbye. (HAWKER *begins to lead* Cow *off*.)

COW: Mooooo. . . .

JACK: Goodbye, Charlotte. (JACK *exits. Curtain.*)

*   *   *

Scene Three

SETTING: *The same as Scene 1.*

AT RISE: JACK *enters, carrying beans.*

JACK: Mother! I'm home.

MOTHER (*Entering*): Oh, there you are, Jack. Did you get a good price for the cow?

JACK: Yes. I met the strangest man at the fair. And in exchange for Charlotte he gave me these three magic beans. (*Gives her beans*) Aren't you proud of me?

MOTHER: Oh, Jack! How could you? What a dumb-dumb you are!

JACK: But these are magic beans.

MOTHER: Ridiculous! How can you be so gullible? (*Throws beans down*) *That* for your beans! Now go right to bed. There's nothing to eat for supper, anyway. (*Moans*) What shall we do? What shall we do? (MOTHER *and* JACK *exit. At rear, a huge beanstalk begins to grow up from below stage, slowly growing up past top of stage, out of sight. Lights dim to indicate passage of time. Sound of rooster crowing is heard from offstage.* JACK *enters, stretching.*)

JACK: Oh, what a good sleep I had. It's such a beautiful morning. Now I must find a way to earn some money. (*He sees beanstalk.*) What's this? I can't believe my eyes. The magic beans have grown up to the sky. They were magic beans, after all. (*He starts to climb beanstalk.* MOTHER *enters.*)

MOTHER: Jack! What are you doing up there? Where did that beanstalk come from? Come back!

JACK (*Still climbing*): I'll be back soon, Mother. Don't worry about me. The beans were magic, after all. (*Curtain.*)

* * *

Scene Four

SETTING: *At the door of the Giant's castle. Door is at center, before curtain. This scene is played in front of curtain.*

AT RISE: JACK *enters.*

JACK: I've been climbing for the longest time—right up into the clouds. And now I've come to a giant-sized castle. I'll just knock on the door and see who lives here. (*He knocks, waits.*) I'll knock harder. (*Knocks harder.*)

MRS. GIANT (*Opening door and looking out*): Mercy me! I thought I heard someone knocking but I don't see anyone here!

JACK (*Calling*): Here I am. Down here!

MRS. GIANT (*Not hearing him*): I guess I was imagining things. (*Slams door*)

JACK (*Knocking again*): Let me in!

MRS. GIANT (*Opening door*): I *did* hear a knocking. I'll bet it's that pesky raven knocking at my door.

JACK (*Shouting*): NO! IT'S ME! LOOK DOWN HERE!

MRS. GIANT: I don't—(*Sees him*) Oh! There is a little man on the doorstep. (*To* JACK) My, my. You are a little one.

You had better leave quickly or my husband, the Giant, will eat you for dinner.

JACK: Please let me in. I'm so hungry and tired from that long climb.

MRS. GIANT: Well! You do look undernourished. Come in and I'll give you some crumbs from the table.

JACK: Oh, thank you.

MRS. GIANT: But don't make any noise, for if the Giant finds you here it will be certain doom. You will be food for him. (JACK *enters, closing door behind him, and follows* MRS. GIANT *offstage, or through split in curtain.*)

*　　*　　*

Scene Five

SETTING: *The Giant's kitchen. An oversized table stands at center. Giant-sized stove is at rear, with dishes of food on it.*

AT RISE: MRS. GIANT *puts* JACK *on table.*

MRS. GIANT: Just sit here on the table. (*Pointing to tabletop*) Here are some crumbs.

JACK: Oh, thank you. You are so kind. (*Loud stamping noises are heard from offstage.*)

MRS. GIANT: I hear my husband, Mr. Giant, coming. Quickly! Hide! (JACK *hides under table.*)

MR. GIANT (*From offstage*): Fee, fi, fo, fum. I smell the blood of a little dumb-dumb. (GIANT *enters.*) I smell the presence of a stranger. Has anyone been here today?

MRS. GIANT: Don't be silly. You only smell the mutton stew in the oven.

213

GIANT: Well, it sure smells like a dumb-dumb to me. Give me my dinner, woman.

MRS. GIANT (*Going to stove for food*): Here you are—mutton (*Slams dish on table*), bread (*Places bread on table*), and cheese. (*Puts cheese on table.*)

GIANT: I sure am hungry. Now for the mutton. (*Eats*) Yum, yum! (JACK *stands, quickly takes bread, and hides under table again, unseen by* GIANT) That sure is good mutton! (*Looks for bread*) Where's that loaf of bread?

MRS. GIANT: Er . . . you ate it.

GIANT: I did? I don't remember. Hm-m-m. Guess I did. (*Eats more mutton*) Yum, yum! (JACK *takes cheese.*) Now for the cheese. (*Looks for cheese*) Why, it's gone! The cheese is gone!

MRS. GIANT: A mouse ate it!

GIANT: He did? Hm-m-m. Well, back to the mutton. Where's the pepper?

MRS. GIANT: Here! (*Hands him pepper shaker from stove.*)

GIANT: I like lots of pepper on my mutton. (*Shakes pepper generously.* JACK *sneezes.*) What was that?

MRS. GIANT: Just the cat sneezing. She has a cold.

GIANT: Oh. Now bring me my money. (MRS. GIANT *exits and re-enters with bag of gold coins.*)

MRS. GIANT: Here it is. (*She hands him bag and exits.*)

GIANT: Now to count my gold. (*Spills few coins out of bag onto table and starts to count them*) One, two, three, five —er—one, two, three—uh—six? That's not right. This is so hard! It makes me sleepy. I'll just take a little snooze. (GIANT *falls asleep and snores.*) Zzz-z-z-z-z-z.

JACK (*Coming out from under table*): Oh, look at all that money! (MRS. GIANT *enters.*) How pleased my mother would be if we had but a few gold coins to keep us from starving.

MRS. GIANT: Oh, you poor people! (*Hands bag of coins to* JACK) Here! Take the whole bag. My husband will never miss it. He has eleventy-seven more bags under his mattress.

JACK: Why, thank you! I'll never forget—

GIANT (*Waking up*): Ho-hum. (*Yawns*)

MRS. GIANT: Quick! Hide again! (JACK *hides under table.*)

GIANT: Wife, there's a thief in the house! My gold is missing.

MRS. GIANT: Don't be silly. I just put it back under your mattress so it would be safe.

GIANT: Well, I need more gold to fill that last bag, so bring me my Magic Hen that lays the golden eggs.

MRS. GIANT: Yes, dear. (*She exits and re-enters with* MAGIC HEN, *puts* HEN *on table and exits.*)

HEN: Cluck, cluck, cluck—

GIANT: Magic Hen, lay more golden eggs or I shall wring your neck.

HEN (*Loudly*): Cluck! Cluck! (*She lays golden egg.*)

GIANT: More! More golden eggs!

HEN: Cluck! Cluck! Cluck! (*Lays more eggs*)

GIANT: Good. That should be enough. I'm sleepy from all that hard work. (*He falls asleep again.*) Zzz-z-z-z. (JACK *comes out from under table again.*)

HEN: Cluck! Cluck! Jack! Please take me away with you. The Giant is so cruel to me. Cluck! Cluck! I'm sure he will kill me when I cannot lay enough eggs to satisfy his greed for gold. He grows more greedy every day. Oh, dear! Cluck-cluck-cluck!

JACK: I'll take you with me, Hen.

HEN: Oh, thank you, dear boy! Cluck! Cluck!

GIANT (*Waking up*): Ho-hum!

HEN: Let's hide. He's waking up. (*They hide under table.* MRS. GIANT *enters.*)

GIANT: What was that noise? I heard someone in here.

MRS. GIANT: Nonsense, dear. You were only having a bad dream.

GIANT: Well, I can't get back to sleep in this noisy castle. Bring me my Magic Harp. Maybe her soothing voice will make me sleep again.

MRS. GIANT: Yes, dear. (*Exits and re-enters at once with* MAGIC HARP, *which she puts down beside table.*) Here's your Magic Harp. Now, sleep tight.

GIANT: Play, Harp! Play! I command you! (*Harp music is heard from offstage.*)

HARP (*Chanting*):

> Although you have me in your spell,
> There must be someone I can tell.
> I'm really not a harp, you see,
> For I am Princess Melody.

GIANT (*Falling asleep*): Zzz-z-z-z-z-z-z.

JACK (*Coming out again*): Could it be true? Can this Harp really be the Princess Melody under an evil spell? (*To* HARP) How can I save you?

HARP (*Chanting*):

> You must escape the Giant's house,
> And be as quiet as a mouse.
> Take me with you when you flee,
> Or else there'll be no hope for me.

JACK: Of course, I'll take you with me. We'll go right away, before the Giant wakes. I'll just pick up the Hen (*Takes* HEN *from table*), and now you, Harp (*Takes* HARP), and now the bag of gold. . . . (*Drops bag. Coins spill with a clatter.* JACK *starts to exit, with* HEN *and* HARP, *abandoning gold coins.*)

GIANT (*Waking up*): What was that? (*Looks around*)

Someone has stolen my Magic Hen! (*Sees* JACK) There he goes with my Magic Hen and my Magic Harp! (*Chases* JACK *around and around stage*)

HEN (*Ad lib*): Hurry, Jack! Cluck, cluck! Hurry! Squawk! (*Etc.*)

HARP (*Chanting*):

> Now just see what you have done!
> You've spilled the gold coins, one by one.
> He's now awake and chasing us.
> I never have heard such a fuss.

MRS. GIANT: No, husband! Don't hurt him! He's so small. He will only give you indigestion! (JACK *exits with* HEN *and* HARP, *followed by* GIANT. *Curtain*)

* * *

Scene Six

SETTING: *Jack's garden, the same as Scene 1.*

AT RISE: JACK *is coming down the beanstalk with* HARP *and* HEN.

JACK (*Calling*): Mother!

MOTHER (*Entering*): What are you doing up there? Come down, Jack! You'll hurt yourself.

JACK: Quickly! Get an ax! (*Jumps off beanstalk, puts down* HEN *and* HARP)

MOTHER: This is no time to chop wood. Where have you been?

JACK: Mother, the Giant is coming!

MOTHER (*Terrified*): I'll do it! I'll get the ax! (*Exits and re-enters at once with ax*) I'll do it!

JACK: Please, Mother! I'd rather do it myself. (*He takes ax and chops at beanstalk.*)

GIANT (*From offstage*): Fee, fi, fo, fum! Wait till I catch that little dumb-dumb!

MOTHER: Hurry, Jack! Hurry! I can see his boots already!

JACK (*Still chopping*): I'm chopping as fast as I can. (*Chops again. Beanstalk falls to ground. GIANT shouts offstage, as if falling. There is a loud thud from offstage. MOTHER screams and hides her eyes.*) Mother, you can look now. It's all right—the Giant has fallen through the ground.

MOTHER: Oh, dear! He fell right through my cabbage patch. (*Sound of chord played on harp is heard from offstage. HARP is quickly removed and PRINCESS MELODY appears in its place.*)

JACK: Look what I've brought back, Mother. A Magic Hen, a Magic Harp (*Sees PRINCESS*)—er . . .

MOTHER: It's the Princess Melody!

JACK: Why, Princess. The spell is broken! You are no longer a harp.

PRINCESS: Thank you for rescuing me, Jack.

JACK (*Shyly*): It was nothing. Mother, I'm afraid I dropped the gold I was bringing back to you.

HEN: Never fear! Cluck, cluck. For if you will let me live here with you and your mother, I will gladly lay enough golden eggs to take care of all your needs.

MOTHER: You can move in right away.

PRINCESS: Now I must go home to my father, the King.

JACK: I will take you to your castle. Before we leave, I would like you to have this picture I drew of Charlotte. She was my friend. (*Hands her picture of COW from easel*)

PRINCESS (*Looking at picture*): Why, Jack. You are a fine artist. You must continue painting. I didn't know you loved horses.

MOTHER: But, Charlotte's not—

JACK (*Quickly*): We'd better leave before it gets dark.

MOTHER: Come right home, Jack. We're having beans for supper.

JACK: Magic beans? (*All laugh.*)

MOTHER: Goodbye, Princess Melody.

PRINCESS: Goodbye. (PRINCESS *and* JACK *exit.*)

MOTHER: Well—maybe my boy, Jack, isn't such a dumb-dumb after all! (*Curtain.*)

THE END

Production Notes

Jack and the Beanstalk

Number of Puppets: 10 hand puppets, rod puppets, or marionettes, or a combination. If desired, the Giants can be played by a boy and girl, instead of puppets. The actors stand in front of the puppet stage and use the stage apron for the kitchen table in Scene 5.

Playing Time: 15 minutes.

Description of Puppets: Jack and his mother wear shabby clothes with patches. Hawker is a sort of W. C. Fields character, with a top hat and tie. Mr. and Mrs. Giant are larger than other puppets or marionettes. Princess has a little crown, and flowing gown and robe. Harp is painted gold.

Properties: Beans, dish of mutton, cheese, bag containing gold coins, golden eggs, pepper shaker, harp, ax, and drawing of Cow.

Setting: Scenes 1, 3, and 6: The garden of Jack's house. There are flowers and one or two trees placed around stage. Jack's easel is downstage, with drawing on it. Jack's house is shown at rear, to one side. NOTE: Beanstalk can be made of paper or stiff cloth leaves sewn to a rope, which is pulled up on a heavy thread, through a screw eye or other holder above the stage. In Scene 6, release the thread quickly when Jack chops down the beanstalk. Scene 2: A fair. This scene is played before curtain. Hawker's table is center. Scene 4: At the door of Giant's castle. Door frame with working door is at center. Frame is made without a top, so that marionettes can walk through the frame when door is opened. The door can also be omitted, if necessary, and assumed to be offstage. Scene 5: Giant's kitchen, in the castle. An oversized table stands at center. Stove, also giant-sized, stands at rear. It holds dish of mutton, loaf of bread, cheese, and pepper shaker. Cloth covers table so Jack can hide beneath it. NOTE: If actors take parts of Giants, they stand in front of puppet stage and use the stage apron for the kitchen table. Food properties and bag of gold coins can then be easily handled by actors. If marionettes are used, put the hand properties on rods made of straightened coat hangers so that they can be manipulated from above.

Lighting: No special effects.

Sound: Harp music, as indicated in text. Music may also be played between scenes.

PINOCCHIO

Adapted from a story by Carlo Collodi

Characters

GEPPETTO, *an old wood carver*
PINOCCHIO, *the wooden puppet*
CREEKO THE CRICKET
BEGGAR WOMAN
BLUE FAIRY
BLACKBEARD, *a puppeteer*
PUNCHINELLO ⎫
HARLEQUIN ⎬ *his puppets*
FOX, *a crook*
CAT, *his accomplice*
FALCON
DOGFISH
PINOCCHIO, *the real boy*

Scene One

SETTING: *A sparsely furnished carpenter's shop. There is a window in the back, and a workbench with tools and an upright log on top of it. A couch is on one side.*
AT RISE: CREEKO THE CRICKET *comes in and addresses the audience.*

CREEKO: Once upon a time there was—a king, you exclaim? No, children, you are wrong. Once upon a time there was a piece of wood. It was not valuable. Just a plain stick of wood such as you have seen burned in a stove or fireplace. (GEPPETTO *enters.*) There was also a carpenter named Geppetto who owned this piece of wood. He lived in a little room with his carpentry tools and a few sticks of furniture, for he was very poor. (CREEKO *exits.*)

GEPPETTO: I suppose my friend Master Cherry thought I was crazy to want this wood to make a marionette, but I'm too poor to marry, and I've always wanted a boy of my own. So a puppet it shall be. (GEPPETTO *takes hammer and pounds away at log on table.* NOTE: *Log is really a hollow tube covering* PINOCCHIO. *As* GEPPETTO *hits the tube with his hammer, it slowly is lowered into table, gradually revealing* PINOCCHIO.) First the head. (*Head appears*) Wooden eyes—why do you stare at me? (*More hammering*) And now for the mouth. (*He hammers.* PINOCCHIO *laughs.*) What was that? (*He goes to window.*) Who's laughing at me? (PINOCCHIO *laughs again.* GEPPETTO *turns back to log.*) So it's you! Stop laughing, boy. Now to carve the arms and legs. (*Hammers some more*) Stop wiggling, you young rascal. You are not yet completed and already you are misbehaving. (*He reveals the rest of the puppet.*) And now the legs. . . . There! (PINOCCHIO *kicks him.*) Don't kick me, you bad boy. (PINOCCHIO *laughs.*) You should have a name. Hm-m-m. I'll call you Pinocchio. And now let's put you on the floor and see if you can walk. (*Puts* PINOCCHIO *on floor.*) One step at a time—left. . . . (PINOCCHIO *tries to walk.*) Right. . . . Fine! (PINOCCHIO *runs around room.*) Now you must learn to talk.

PINOCCHIO: Learn to talk? But I know how to talk already, Papa.

GEPPETTO: Amazing! But it will soon be dawn and you will have to go to school. I must buy you a spelling book. I'll be right back. (GEPPETTO *leaves.*)

PINOCCHIO: Ah! He's gone. Now I'll run away. I don't want to go to school.

CREEKO (*Entering*): Cree-cree-crik. . . .

PINOCCHIO: Who's calling me?

CREEKO: I am.

PINOCCHIO: Who are you?

CREEKO: I'm Creeko, the talking cricket. I am your conscience.

PINOCCHIO: Go away at once!

CREEKO: I will not go until I have told you a great truth.

PINOCCHIO: Tell it then, and be quick about it.

CREEKO: Woe to boys who rebel against their parents and run away from home. Sooner or later they will be sorry.

PINOCCHIO: Creeko Cricket, you keep still!

CREEKO: I will see you again, dear Pinocchio. (*He exits.*)

GEPPETTO (*Entering with a spelling book*): It's morning, Pinocchio, and time to go to school.

PINOCCHIO: I'm not dressed properly.

GEPPETTO: But you are clean! Remember that it is not fine clothes, but clean clothes that mark a gentleman.

PINOCCHIO: But to go to school I lack the most important thing.

GEPPETTO: What is that?

PINOCCHIO: A spelling book.

GEPPETTO: Ah, but I have one. I sold my coat to buy your spelling book. Now off to school, my boy. (*He gives book to* PINOCCHIO.)

PINOCCHIO: Goodbye, Papa.

GEPPETTO: Goodbye, Pinocchio. Come straight home for dinner. I'll be waiting for you. (*Curtain*)

* * *

Scene Two

SETTING: *A street. This scene may be played in front of the curtain.*

AT RISE: PINOCCHIO *skips onstage.*

PINOCCHIO (*Sing-song*): Off to school I go. Off to school I— (*He finds a penny on the street.*) I've found a penny! To-day is my lucky day. Today I will learn to read, tomorrow I will learn to write, and the next day to cipher. Then with all my education I shall earn a great deal of money, and I'll buy my papa a new coat of gold and silver with dia-mond buttons.

BEGGAR WOMAN (*Entering*): May I have a penny? I'm poor and very hungry.

PINOCCHIO: I need my penny to buy candy at school. Find your own penny. (BEGGAR WOMAN *turns into the* BLUE FAIRY. *See Production Notes.*) Where did the old beggar woman go? And who are you?

BLUE FAIRY: I am the Blue Fairy, your guardian. That old lady was hungry. You had breakfast this morning. You must learn not to be selfish, Pinocchio. When you are self-ish and greedy, you are many steps from becoming a real boy. For you to be a real boy would please your papa.

PINOCCHIO: And me, too. I want to be a real boy.

BLUE FAIRY: Then be good, and off to school with you.

PINOCCHIO: Goodbye, fair guardian. (*She exits.*) Off to school I go. (*Faint music is heard from offstage.*) Off to school. . . . (*Music gets louder.*) What can that music be? It's so pretty. (BLACKBEARD *enters, grinding a hand organ, which reads,* GREAT PUPPET THEATER.) Today I will listen to music. Tomorrow I will go to school. (*He goes up to* BLACKBEARD) What does that say on the side of your music box?

BLACKBEARD: It says, Great Puppet Theater!

PINOCCHIO: How much does it cost to get in? I have a penny.

BLACKBEARD: Two pence.

PINOCCHIO: Will you give me two pence for this new spelling book?

BLACKBEARD: I will buy the spelling book for two pence. (*They exchange book and coins.*)

PINOCCHIO: Hooray! I get to see the puppet show today. (*He exits with* BLACKBEARD.)

BLUE FAIRY (*From offstage*): Pinocchio—remember your papa's coat! (*Curtain.*)

* * *

Scene Three

SETTING: *Blackbeard's puppet theater. There is a miniature puppet stage at rear.*

AT RISE: HARLEQUIN *and* PUNCHINELLO, BLACKBEARD'S *puppets, are dancing on the miniature puppet stage in time to music.* PINOCCHIO *enters and watches them.*

HARLEQUIN (*Stopping his dance and pointing to* PINOCCHIO): Am I awake or dreaming? Surely that's Pinocchio!

PUNCHINELLO: It is indeed Pinocchio.

HARLEQUIN: It is! It is! It's our brother, Pinocchio!

PUNCHINELLO: Long live Pinocchio!

HARLEQUIN: Come up here and greet us, dear friend. (PINOCCHIO *runs up on the puppet stage and embraces them.*)

BLACKBEARD (*From offstage*): Go on with the play, puppets! (BLACKBEARD *comes onstage*. *To* PINOCCHIO) Why have you come to raise a disturbance in my theater? Come with me. (*He picks up* PINOCCHIO.)

PUNCHINELLO: Oh, poor Pinocchio.

HARLEQUIN: It's our fault.

BLACKBEARD: There is not enough wood for roasting my sheep tonight. Pinocchio is made of very dry wood and will make a beautiful blaze for my roast.

PINOCCHIO: Papa! Papa! Save me! I don't want to die! I don't want to die! (*All three puppets cry.*)

BLACKBEARD (*Sneezing*): Ah-h-h-h-choo! Ah-h-h-choo!

HARLEQUIN (*To* PUNCHINELLO): Good news. Blackbeard sneezed. That is a sign that he pities Pinocchio and will spare him.

BLACKBEARD: Ah-h-h-h-choo!

PINOCCHIO (*To* BLACKBEARD): Bless you!

BLACKBEARD: Thank you. Your papa and mama—are they still alive?

PINOCCHIO: Papa, yes. My mama I have never known.

BLACKBEARD: What a sorrow it would have been for the poor man if I had thrown you on the burning coals. Instead, I will burn a puppet belonging to my company. Ah! Which one? I know! (*He grabs* HARLEQUIN.)

HARLEQUIN: No! No! Not me!

PINOCCHIO (*On his knees*): Have pity! Sir Blackbeard!

BLACKBEARD: What do you want of me?

PINOCCHIO: I beg of you to pardon poor Harlequin.

BLACKBEARD: Impossible. I have spared you, so he must be put on the fire—for I am determined to have my mutton well roasted.

PINOCCHIO: Then in that case I know my duty. Throw me

into the flames. It is not just that my true friend Harlequin should die for me. (*All puppets cry.*)

BLACKBEARD: Ah-h-h-choo! Ah-h-h-choo! You are a good brave boy, Pinocchio.

HARLEQUIN: Then I'm free?

BLACKBEARD: You are free. Tonight I will resign myself to eating my mutton half-raw.

PINOCCHIO, HARLEQUIN *and* PUNCHINELLO: Hooray!

BLACKBEARD: What is your Papa's name, Pinocchio?

PINOCCHIO: Geppetto.

BLACKBEARD: Is he poor?

PINOCCHIO: Very poor.

BLACKBEARD: Poor fellow. I'm sorry for him. Here! Take these five gold pieces and give them to him with my compliments. (BLACKBEARD *gives* PINOCCHIO *a bag of gold.*)

PINOCCHIO: I thank you a thousand times. Now I must go home. Goodbye, my friends.

ALL: Goodbye, Pinocchio. (PINOCCHIO *exits. Curtain.*)

*　　*　　*

Scene Four

SETTING: *A street, played before the curtain as in Scene 2.*
AT RISE: PINOCCHIO *enters.*

PINOCCHIO: Home I go, to see my papa again! (Fox *and* CAT *enter.* Fox *has a crutch under his arm, and* CAT *wears dark glasses.*)

FOX: Good evening, Pinocchio.

PINOCCHIO: How do you know my name?

Fox: I know your father well. I saw him a while ago, shivering in the doorway of his house, looking for you.

Pinocchio: Poor Papa. But in the future he will not need to shiver.

Cat: Not shiver? Why, Pinocchio?

Pinocchio: Because I have become a gentleman.

Fox *and* Cat (*Laughing*): You?

Pinocchio: There is nothing to laugh at. If you know money when you see it, you will know that these are five gold pieces. (*He shows them the bag of gold. Fox lifts his crutch and the Cat raises his dark glasses.*)

Fox: Hm-m-m-m. And what are you going to do with all that money?

Pinocchio: I shall buy my papa a new coat, and a spelling book for myself—for I wish to go to school to study.

Fox: Look at me. Through my foolish desire to study I became lame.

Cat: And look at me. Because I was so fond of study I lost the sight of both my eyes.

Pinocchio (*Gullibly*): Really?

Fox: Would you like to double your money? Would you like to turn your five miserable gold pieces into a hundred . . . a thousand . . . two thousand?

Pinocchio: Yes, of course, but how?

Fox: Easy enough. Instead of going home, you must go with us to the field of miracles.

Pinocchio: The field of miracles?

Cat: The field of miracles!

Fox: Come. We will show you the way.

Pinocchio: When I'm rich I'll give each of you 500 gold coins to show my appreciation.

Fox: To us? We do not work for profit. We work only to help others.

CAT: Yes. . . . to help others. (*They all exit together.*)

BLUE FAIRY (*Entering*): Pinocchio! Come back! Your papa is looking for you. (*Curtain.*)

* * *

Scene Five

SETTING: *The field of miracles. There are a tree and two pails onstage.*

AT RISE: PINOCCHIO *enters with* FOX *and* CAT.

FOX: Ah—here we are, at last.

PINOCCHIO: That was a long walk and I'm tired.

CAT: But it will be worth it to you.

FOX: We will leave you now. Plant your coins right here, under this tree. Pour two buckets of water on them and one pinch of salt. Then leave them for a short while.

CAT: When you return you will have your fortune growing on a tree.

FOX: Goodbye. And remember—plant them *right here!*

PINOCCHIO: Thank you ever so much, friends. (*They exit, leaving* PINOCCHIO.) Now—I'll just drop my five gold coins into this hole, and . . .

CREEKO (*Entering*): Beware, Pinocchio!

PINOCCHIO: Who is it?

CREEKO: It's Creeko, the Cricket, again.

PINOCCHIO: What do you want this time?

CREEKO: Turn back and take the five gold pieces to your poor papa, who is crying because you have not returned to him.

PINOCCHIO: Tomorrow my papa will be a gentleman. By then these five coins will have become five thousand.

CREEKO: Don't trust those who promise to make you rich in a day. Go back.

PINOCCHIO: I don't need your advice. Good night, Creeko Cricket.

CREEKO: Good night, Pinocchio. Heaven keep you from robbers. (CREEKO *exits.*)

PINOCCHIO: And good riddance. And now to plant my gold. (*He drops the bag of gold into a hole under the tree.*) There! And now the two pails of water. (*Pretends to pour water from pails*) And now a pinch of salt. (*Pretends to sprinkle salt*) There! Now I'll walk around this field of miracles and wait for my gold tree to grow. By the time I come back this way it should be fully grown and I'll just pull the gold right off. Papa and I are going to be rich! (PINOCCHIO *exits.* CAT *and* FOX *re-enter and take the bag of gold.*)

FOX: The stupid, wooden-headed fool! (FOX *and* CAT *exit.*)

PINOCCHIO (*Entering*): My tree should be grown by now. I . . . (*Looks for the gold tree*) Perhaps I'm too early . . . or maybe I didn't plant them right. I'll try a different spot. (*He looks for the bag of gold.*) Oh, no! The gold isn't here. What happened?

BLUE FAIRY (*Entering*): What's wrong, Pinocchio? Where is the gold for your papa?

PINOCCHIO: I gave my gold to the poor. (*His nose grows longer.*)

BLUE FAIRY: Now, Pinocchio, look at your nose. You aren't telling me the truth.

PINOCCHIO: Well—I lost the money in the river. (*His nose grows still longer.*)

BLUE FAIRY: Look again. Your nose grows even more.

PINOCCHIO: Oh! I swallowed the gold coins. . . . (*Nose grows even longer*)

BLUE FAIRY: You see—the more you tell lies, the longer your nose grows.

PINOCCHIO: Oh, my beautiful Blue Fairy, the Fox and Cat told me to bury the gold to make more money, and now they are gone—Fox, Cat, and the money.

BLUE FAIRY: You are a very stupid puppet. At this rate you will never be a real boy. But now you must hurry to save your papa. He has gone to sea looking for you and he is in great danger. (*She claps and her* FALCON *enters.*) Get on my falcon's back and fly out to sea to save your father.

PINOCCHIO: Yes, Blue Fairy! Yes! I must save him. Goodbye. (PINOCCHIO *gets on* FALCON'*s back and they fly about.*)

BLUE FAIRY: Goodbye, Pinocchio. (*They exit. Curtain.*)

* * *

Scene Six

SETTING: *At sea.*

AT RISE: FALCON, *with* PINOCCHIO *on his back, flies in.*

PINOCCHIO: Where is my papa? (*Calls*) Papa! Papa!

FALCON: Caw! Caw! Out to sea. Caw!

PINOCCHIO: Take me to him. (*Calling*) Papa! Papa! (*They fly about.*) Where's my papa?

FALCON: The gulls say his boat sank and the dogfish swallowed him.

PINOCCHIO: I must help him! (PINOCCHIO *jumps from* FALCON'*s back into ocean.* FALCON *flies offstage.*) Papa! Papa! (PINOCCHIO *swims about.* DOGFISH *enters and swallows* PINOCCHIO. *Curtain.*)

* * *

Scene Seven

SETTING: *Inside Dogfish's stomach.*

AT RISE: GEPPETTO *is on one side of the stage.* PINOCCHIO *enters.*

PINOCCHIO: It's so dark in here. I must be in the dogfish's stomach. But, wait—who is that? There is someone else in here with me.

GEPPETTO: It is only Geppetto, once a poor wood carver, but now food for the dogfish.

PINOCCHIO: Papa! My dear papa! I have found you at last. I will never, never leave you again. (*Crosses to* GEPPETTO)

GEPPETTO: Can I believe my eyes? Are you really my boy, Pinocchio?

PINOCCHIO: Yes! Yes! I am really your wooden puppet. Have you forgiven me?

GEPPETTO: Oh, my dear boy! (*They embrace.*)

PINOCCHIO: I've had such a time and have such a tale to tell. But we must escape through the mouth of the dogfish and swim away.

GEPPETTO: But I cannot swim.

PINOCCHIO: I will carry you on my shoulders. I am made of wood and can float. Now, come. The dogfish is asleep with his mouth open. (*They exit through teeth at front. Curtain.*)

*   *   *

Scene Eight

SETTING: *Geppetto's workshop, as in Scene 1.*
AT RISE: GEPPETTO, *sick, is lying on couch.* PINOCCHIO *stands by him.*

PINOCCHIO: Poor Papa. Please get well. I've worked every day since we returned from the sea. I've gone to school, too, and now you must get well. Here are some copper farthings I've earned drawing water for the farmers next door. Get well, Papa.

BLUE FAIRY (*Entering*): Pinocchio!

PINOCCHIO: My Blue Fairy has returned.

BLUE FAIRY: I see that you are a good puppet now. And you have been taking care of your papa. Would you like to be a real boy now?

PINOCCHIO: I would rather see my papa well, Blue Fairy.

GEPPETTO (*Weakly*): Pinocchio. . . .

PINOCCHIO: Yes, Papa?

GEPPETTO: Would you get me a glass of cool water?

PINOCCHIO: Yes, Papa. (PINOCCHIO *exits.*)

BLUE FAIRY: And now it is time for the real boy. Sit up, old Geppetto. (*He sits.*)

GEPPETTO: Suddenly I feel so much better!

BLUE FAIRY: Now, greet your boy, Papa Geppetto.

GEPPETTO: What? Who's there? (PINOCCHIO, *the boy, enters.*)

PINOCCHIO: It's me, Papa! Look at me!

GEPPETTO: My *son!* You're a real boy!

BLUE FAIRY: Well done, Pinocchio. To reward you for your kind heart I will forgive you for all that is past. Try to be good in the future and you will be happy. Goodbye, Pinocchio.

PINOCCHIO: Goodbye, my dear Blue Fairy. And thank you! (*She exits.* PINOCCHIO *and* GEPPETTO *exit in the opposite direction.* CREEKO THE CRICKET *enters.*)

CREEKO (*Calling*): Pinocchio! Pinocchio! Ah . . . I guess he doesn't need a conscience any more. Well. . . . Perhaps there's someone out there who needs me more! (*Peers out into audience, as curtains close.*)

THE END

Production Notes

PINOCCHIO

Number of Puppets: 13 puppets or marionettes. The Beggar
Woman may be quickly exchanged for Blue Fairy, or else
a turn-around puppet may be made, with Beggar Woman
on one side and Blue Fairy on the other.

Playing Time: 15 minutes.

Description of Puppets: Pinocchio is a small puppet, and
wears a bright jacket and short pants. Pinocchio's nose
should be made so that it pulls out of his head, or else
longer noses can be added. Creeko wears a jacket and top
hat. Harlequin and Punchinello are small puppets, and they
wear white costumes. Harlequin's has diamond-shaped
patches. Blackbeard has a long black beard and is very tall.
Fox carries a crutch and Cat wears dark glasses. Falcon is
a white bird. If a marionette is used, it can be made to fly
easily, otherwise a puppet on a long stick can be worked
from below. The boy Pinocchio is dressed like the puppet,
but is taller.

Properties: Hammer; miniature hand organ, reading GREAT
PUPPET THEATER; penny; bag of gold pieces; two pails.

Setting: Scene 1: Geppetto's workshop, with a carpenter's
bench, tools and an upright, hollow tube, painted to resem-
ble a log, which conceals Pinocchio. Tube is gradually low-
ered through hole in carpenter's bench to reveal Pinocchio.
There are a window and a couch at rear. Scene 2: A street.
This scene may be played before the curtain. Scene 3: The
Great Puppet Theater. A miniature puppet stage is at rear.
Scene 4: A street. Scene may be played before the curtain.
Scene 5: The field of miracles. A tree is at one side, and

two pails stand nearby. Scene 6: At sea. A backdrop of the sea, with waves, etc., is used. Scene 7: Inside the Dogfish's stomach. Two rows of jagged teeth are at top and bottom of stage. Red paper may be used as backdrop, lighted from behind. Scene 8: Geppetto's workshop, the same as Scene 1.

Lighting: Special effects in Scene 7, as indicated above.

THE TALE OF PETER RABBIT

Adapted from the story by Beatrix Potter

Characters

NARRATOR
PETER RABBIT
FLOPSY
MOPSY
COTTONTAIL
MRS. RABBIT
MR. McGREGOR
THREE SPARROWS
OLD MOUSE
WHITE CAT

SCENE 1

BEFORE RISE: NARRATOR *enters and speaks to audience.*

NARRATOR: Once upon a time, there were four little rabbits, and their names were Flopsy (FLOPSY *enters in front of curtain*), Mopsy (*Enters*), Cottontail (*Enters*) and Peter (*Enters*). They lived with their mother in a sand bank underneath the root of a very big fir tree. (*Curtain opens. Rabbits remain onstage.*)

*　　*　　*

SETTING: *Interior of Mrs. Rabbit's home.*

AT RISE: MRS. RABBIT *enters and speaks to others.*

MRS. RABBIT: Now, my dears, this morning you may go into the fields or down the lane, but don't go into Mr. McGregor's garden. Your father had an accident there. He was put in a pie by Mrs. McGregor.

FLOPSY: We are good little bunnies...

MOPSY: We are going down the lane...

COTTONTAIL: To gather blackberries.

MRS. RABBIT: Run along, now, and don't get into mischief. I am going out.

FLOPSY (*Handing her hat*): Here is your bonnet.

MOPSY (*Handing her basket*): And here is your basket...

COTTONTAIL (*Handing her umbrella*): And your umbrella.

MRS. RABBIT: I am off to the baker's. I'm going to buy a loaf of brown bread and five currant buns. Goodbye, children. Behave yourself, Peter.

ALL: Goodbye, Mama. (MRS. RABBIT *exits*.)

FLOPSY: Let's go to pick berries, Peter.

PETER: No! I'm going to Mr. McGregor's garden.

FLOPSY: Mama will be angry.

MOPSY: Shame on you.

COTTONTAIL: You'll be sorry. (PETER *runs off.*)

ALL: You'll be sorry, Peter! (*Curtain*)

*   *   *   *   *

SCENE 2

SETTING: *Mr. McGregor's garden. Some netting is at one side.*

AT RISE: PETER *enters and starts to nibble vegetables as* NARRATOR *speaks.*

NARRATOR: Peter, who *was* very naughty, ran straight away to Mr. McGregor's garden and squeezed under the gate.

PETER: Oh, boy. Do these vegetables look good! First I'll eat some lettuce. (*Nibbles*) Mm-m-m, good. And some French beans. (*Nibbles*) Yum, yum. And then I'll eat some radishes. (*Nibbles*) Oh-h-h, my tummy! I feel a little sick. I should be able to find some parsley to make me feel better. (*Exits.* MR. MCGREGOR *enters on opposite side.*)

MR. MCGREGOR: Another work day in my garden. I must pick some beans and radishes for Mrs. McGregor. I sure have a nice garden when those pesky rabbits aren't stealing from me. (*He looks over garden.*) What's this? My garden has been picked over. There has been a pesky rabbit here and just recently, too. I'll find him. (*Exits*)

PETER (*Entering and looking around*): Ah...now that I've had some parsley, my tummy feels much better. (PETER *starts to nibble, and backs across stage.* MR. MCGREGOR *enters, walking backwards as if searching for* PETER. *They back into each other and turn.*)

MR. MCGREGOR: What's this? Stop, thief! (MR. MCGREGOR *chases* PETER *about stage and off, then onstage again for a chase back and forth.*) Stop, you pesky rabbit! Stop, thief! (*They exit.*)

NARRATOR: Peter was most dreadfully frightened. He rushed all over the garden, for he had forgotten the way back to the gate. He lost one of his shoes among the cabbages and the other shoe among the potatoes. (PETER *and* MR. MCGREGOR *rush in, then out again.*) After losing his shoes, he ran on four legs, and went so fast that I think he might have gotten away altogether if he had not unfortunately run into a gooseberry net and gotten caught by the large buttons on his jacket. (PETER *runs in alone and runs into netting*) It was a blue jacket with brass buttons — quite new.

PETER: Oh, dear, I'm caught in this net. I'm lost for sure. (THREE SPARROWS *fly in.*)

SPARROWS: Poor Peter . . . we implore you . . . exert yourself. Pull, pull. Oh-oh, here comes Mr. McGregor. (*They fly away.*)

MR. McGREGOR (*Entering*): Ah, there you are! Now I have you. (*He starts for* PETER, *and holds him by coat, but* PETER *pulls out of his coat and runs offstage.*) Come back, come back. Oh, well. I'll just use this little blue jacket and those little shoes for a scarecrow to frighten the blackbirds away. (PETER *runs across stage again and off.*) There's that rabbit again. He went into the tool shed. Now I have him! (*Exits. Curtain*)

*   *   *   *   *

SCENE 3

SETTING: *The tool shed. Large watering can and three potted geraniums are onstage.*

AT RISE: PETER *enters.*

PETER: Where can I hide? Ah! The watering can! (*He jumps inside watering can. With hollow voice*) Brrr! This would have been a beautiful place to hide if there weren't so much water in it.

MR. McGREGOR (*Entering*): I'm quite sure he is somewhere in this tool shed. Perhaps he is hidden underneath a flower pot. (*Picks up each pot*) Not this one. Not under this. Not here either. Where can he be?

PETER (*Sneezing*): Kerchoo!

MR. McGREGOR: Aha! He's in the watering can. (PETER *jumps out.*) Come back here! (PETER *knocks down geranium pots and runs offstage*). Now look what he's

241

done. He's broken my potted geraniums. Oh, I'm tired of running after him. I think he's good and scared anyway. I'd better get back to work. (*He exits. Curtain.*)

*   *   *   *   *

SCENE 4

SETTING: *The same as Scene 2.*
AT RISE: PETER *runs in and sits down.*

NARRATOR: Peter sat down to rest. He was out of breath and trembling with fright, and he had not the least idea which way to go. Also, he was very damp from sitting in that watering can. (OLD MOUSE *enters with a pea in her mouth.*)
PETER: Dear little Mrs. Mouse, can you tell me the way to the gate?
NARRATOR: Unfortunately, Mrs. Mouse had in her mouth such a large pea she was taking to her family, that she couldn't answer.
MOUSE: Mmm-m-m. Mmmm.
PETER: You can't talk with your mouth full. Won't you please tell me the way?
MOUSE: Hm-m-m. M-m-m. (*Runs off*)
PETER (*Crying*): Now I'll never get out of the garden. (WHITE CAT *enters and sits at center.*)
CAT: Meow-w-w.
PETER: Maybe I can ask that pretty white cat the way out.
CAT: Meow-w-w. (*Swishes tail*)
PETER: No — it's best I don't speak to her. My cousin, Benjamin Bunny, told me all about cats.
CAT: Meow-w-w. (*Swishes tail again and exits*)

242

PETER (*Looking around*): Oh, there's the gate at last! (*Scratching noise is heard, and* MR. MCGREGOR *backs in, hoeing.*) How can I get past Mr. McGregor to the gate? Oh, dear, I'll have to run for it. (PETER *runs by* MR. MCGREGOR *and off.*)

MR. MCGREGOR: Come back, you bad little rabbit! Come back here! (*Starts after him.*) Oh, he got under the gate. (*Rushes out. Curtain*)

NARRATOR: Peter never stopped running nor did he look behind him until he got home to the big fir tree.

*   *   *   *   *

SCENE 5

SETTING: *The same as Scene 1.*

AT RISE: MRS. RABBIT *is cooking at stove.* PETER *enters, panting.*

MRS. RABBIT: Peter, where have you been? What happened to your clothes? This is the second little jacket and pair of shoes you have lost in a fortnight.

PETER (*Weakly*): Mama, I don't feel very well. (*Moans*) Oh-h-h!

MRS. RABBIT: Well, you had better go right to bed. (PETER *lies down, and* MRS. RABBIT *covers him with coverlet.*) Now, lie there and be still. (*She gets out tea kettle and cup*) And here is some chamomile tea to make you feel better. "One tablespoonful to be taken at bedtime!" (FLOPSY, MOPSY *and* COTTONTAIL *run in.*)

ALL: We are home, Mama!

MRS. RABBIT: Get ready for supper. (*To* PETER) Flopsy, Mopsy and Cottontail are having bread, milk and blackberries for supper, but you shall have none at all. Now will you learn to be a good little rabbit, Peter?

243

PETER (*Groaning*): Yes, Mama. (*Others gather around* MRS. RABBIT *as curtains close slowly*)

NARRATOR: We *hope* that Peter learned his lesson — what do you think?

THE END

Production Notes

The Tale of Peter Rabbit

Number of Puppets: 11 hand or rod puppets or marionettes.

Characters: 1 male or female for Narrator. If desired, Mr.
McGregor could be an actor, with the rest of the cast
puppets.

Playing Time: 15 minutes.

Description of Puppets: The Beatrix Potter illustrations
will give you ideas for the puppets. Peter should have a
blue jacket with big brass buttons. You may wish to
redesign the show altogether, so use your imagination.

Properties: Bonnet, basket and umbrella, crepe paper
lettuce and other vegetables, coverlet, tea kettle and cup,
hoe.

Setting: Scenes 1 and 5: Interior of Mrs. Rabbit's home.
Scenes 2 and 4: Mr. McGregor's garden. Lettuce,
radishes, other vegetables may be growing in rows. Some
netting is at one side — the gooseberry net. Scene 3: The
tool shed. A large watering can, and three potted
geraniums are onstage. Illustrations in the Beatrix Potter
book will give you ideas for the setting.

Lighting: No special effects.

Sound: Simple piano music, perhaps "In a Country
Garden," might be used.

THREE BILLY GOATS GRUFF

Characters

GRANNIE OLSEŃ
BILLY
GRETA
LITTLE GOAT
MIDDLE GOAT
BIG GOAT
TROLL

SCENE 1

SETTING: *Grannie Olsen's little house, in Norway.*
AT RISE: GRANNIE *is rocking in her rocking chair, knitting.* BILLY *and* GRETA *are building a bridge from wooden blocks.* GRETA *has a toy goat.*

BILLY (*Grabbing the goat*): Give me that goat. It's mine. I want to make him walk across the bridge. Greta, let go!
GRETA (*Pulling goat back*): But I only want to... (BILLY *pulls goat*)
BILLY: I don't care. It's mine, and I can do what I want with it.
GRETA: Then you can't play with my blocks.
BILLY: Here.... Take your old blocks. (*Knocks over bridge*)
GRETA: All right for you, Billy.
GRANNIE: Now, children, don't be so greedy. It's not nice. Come, sit here next to Grannie Olsen, and I'll tell you a story about sharing and being kind to each other.

GRETA: Oh, goody. I love stories.

BILLY: Well, O.K. Just so it isn't mushy.

GRANNIE: Oh, it's exciting. You see, it's about goats and bridges and...a troll!

GRETA *and* BILLY: Oh-h-h! Tell us, please.

BILLY: Trolls are ugly and fierce and mean.

GRANNIE: This troll was all of those things, but the Three Billy Goats Gruff taught him a lesson. Now, sit here by my side and I'll begin my story, and when I'm through, it's off to bed for both of you. Once upon a time... (*Curtain*)

* * * * *

SCENE 2

BEFORE RISE: GRANNIE *speaks offstage, or in front of curtain, while stage is being set up.*

GRANNIE: Once upon a time, there lived a family of three goats on the side of a peaceful hill. Every day when the sun became too hot they would move across a little bridge to another hill where it was cooler and shadier. But one day...(*Curtains open*)

* * *

SETTING: *Two hills connected by a bridge at center. A shady tree is on one side. The other side is sunny.*

AT RISE: LITTLE GOAT *is grazing on the sunny side.*

LITTLE GOAT (*Singing to tune of "Over the River"*):
Over the river, across the bridge,
To the shady side I go.
I know the way,

'Cause that's where I play
When the sun's too hot, you know.
Over the river, across the bridge,
That's where I'll play all day.
My brothers will come
And join in the fun
Till the sunshine goes away.

Oh, my. The sun is very hot today. I can't wait to get to my favorite shady spot on the other side of the bridge. (*Walks across bridge. Sounds of clip, clop, clip, clop are heard.* TROLL *appears under bridge as* LITTLE GOAT *gets halfway across.*)

TROLL: Hey — who's that on my roof?

LITTLE GOAT (*Stopping*): I beg your pardon?

TROLL: Can't you see where you're going? You're on my roof!

LITTLE GOAT: What do you mean, your roof?

TROLL: Goof? Who's a goof? I ought to eat you up for that.

LITTLE GOAT: For your information, this is a bridge.

TROLL: A what?

LITTLE GOAT (*Loudly*): A bridge!

TROLL: It is, is it? Well, whatever it is, it's my home now, and if you want to cross, you'll have to pay!

LITTLE GOAT: But, but...this is a free bridge — for everyone.

TROLL: Not anymore. Now it's a...*troll* bridge. (*Laughs*) Ha, ha, ha!

LITTLE GOAT: Oh, dear. I haven't any money with me.

TROLL: Honey? I don't want honey. I want gold. Or I'll eat you up.

LITTLE GOAT: Oh, please don't do that, Mr. Troll. My brother is coming soon, and he may have some gold to pay you.

TROLL: Oh, goody.

LITTLE GOAT: Besides, he's bigger and fatter than I am.

TROLL: You are awfully scrawny. Where is he, did you say?

LITTLE GOAT: He's up there on the sunny hill, near the big bush.

TROLL (*Looking*): What bush?

LITTLE GOAT: The one next to the big rock. (LITTLE GOAT *edges across bridge as* TROLL *looks.*)

TROLL: What rock?

LITTLE GOAT: Hmm.... I know he's up there.

TROLL: Oh, very well. I'll wait for him to go across. Hurry before I change my mind about you.

LITTLE GOAT: Oh, thank you, Mr. Troll. I'll hurry! (*Runs across bridge and off*)

TROLL: Worry? You don't have to worry. It's your brother who has to worry. (*Laughs and goes back under bridge.* MIDDLE GOAT *appears.*)

MIDDLE GOAT (*Singing or speaking*):
>Some like the heat, but I'm no fool.
>I like to go where it is cool.
>I like to rest beneath a tree,
>All alone or with company.
>Clippety-clop, clippety-clop, clippety-clop....

Ah, that nice shady spot on the other side of the bridge looks so cool and refreshing. It will be a good spot for a nap this afternoon. (*Starts to cross bridge. Clip, clop, clip, clop sound is heard.*)

TROLL (*Appearing under bridge*): Hey! Stop! (MIDDLE GOAT *stops in middle of bridge*) Can't you see you're on private property?

MIDDLE GOAT: I am? Funny, I never noticed before. I thought it was free.

TROLL: Tea? Tea? Sorry, we don't serve refreshments, and you have to pay to cross, or else I get to eat you up.

MIDDLE GOAT: Some choice! But I'll tell you what I'm going to do, Mr. Troll.

TROLL: Yes?

MIDDLE GOAT: I'll pick a number from one to ten. If you can guess it, you get my money, and you can eat me up, too. If you don't guess it, I can cross the bridge for nothing.

TROLL: Oh, boy. I love games — but I get three guesses.

MIDDLE GOAT: Well...all right.

TROLL: Is it six?

MIDDLE GOAT: Nope.

TROLL: Three?

MIDDLE GOAT: Sorry.

TROLL: Ah-ha! It must be eight.

MIDDLE GOAT: Wrong again. But you were very close.

TROLL: Five?

MIDDLE GOAT: Well, don't feel too bad. (*Starts across bridge again*) My big brother will be coming by soon. He always crosses this bridge about this time each day. You'll like him. He's *really* big and fat.

TROLL: Oh, neato! How will I recognize him?

MIDDLE GOAT: By his big horns.

TROLL: Oh, how nice. I love tubas and trombones. They send me!

MIDDLE GOAT: These will send you, all right.

TROLL: I'll bet you didn't think I looked like the musical type.

MIDDLE GOAT: Oh, but you do. You really do.

TROLL: Aww.... Well, hurry across. I'll wait for your brother.

MIDDLE GOAT (*Crossing*): So long, and have a nice trip. (*Exits*)

TROLL: Now where did he get the idea I was going on a trip? Must be hard of hearing. Well, I'll just wait for that nice fat goat with his musical instruments. Nothing nicer than having music with your meals. (*Singing to tune of "Little Brown Jug"*)

Oh, I like music when I dine,
And tuba tunes are just divine.
It makes my meals digest just fine.
Oh, I like music when I dine.

(*Disappears under bridge.* BIG GOAT, *who has great curling horns on his head, enters.*)

BIG GOAT: Ho-hum. Now for a nice, cool nap on the other hill. (*Singing to the tune of "Pepsi-Cola Hits the Spot"*)
Ho-ho-hum, my work is done,
Time to leave the noonday sun,
And find a shady place to rest
Across the bridge, that's where it's best.

(*Starts across bridge.* TROLL *leaps up from under bridge and holds onto* BIG GOAT)

TROLL: Ah-ha! Gotcha! (*Suddenly noticing* GOAT's *size and horns*) Er...I mean, excuse me!

BIG GOAT (*Fiercely*): You got me what?

TROLL: Er — a free pass. That's it, a free pass over the bridge. You're the third goat to cross this bridge today, and you get a free pass.

BIG GOAT (*Butting* TROLL *with horns*): You had better get out of my way, or you'll be getting a free pass — with my horns.

TROLL: Yes, yes. By all means. Good day. (*Disappears*)

BIG GOAT (*Crossing bridge*): The things that litter the roads these days. Ho-hum. (*Exits*)

TROLL (*Reappearing*): Has he gone? Good. This certainly hasn't been my day. The moon must be in the wrong cycle. First I misplace my ear trumpet, then my glasses disappear, and now I have to go without lunch. What a price to pay, just for having a troll bridge.

LITTLE GOAT *and* MIDDLE GOAT (*Entering*): Yoo-hoo, Mr. Troll.

LITTLE GOAT: Did you lose this ear trumpet? (*Hands* TROLL *large ear trumpet*)

TROLL: Why, yes I did.

MIDDLE GOAT: And are these your spectacles? (*Hands glasses to him*) We found them over there by the well.

TROLL: My goodness, yes. Goodie. Now I can see again and hear again. And now, for lunch, I'm going to —

LITTLE GOAT (*Quickly*): Here, we picked some dandelion greens and some apples for your lunch.

TROLL: For me? Aww....

MIDDLE GOAT: And here are some wild strawberries for dessert.

TROLL: Oh, my. How kind. I promise never to charge anyone a toll to cross my bridge.

BIG GOAT (*Entering*): And you won't eat the pedestrians?

TROLL: No — never again. Unless maybe they jaywalk.

LITTLE GOAT:

> It's nice to be good neighbors,
> And cheer up someone sad.
> It's nice to help each other.
> It sure beats being bad.

MIDDLE GOAT:

> 'Cause when you help each other
> It brightens up the day.
> It cheers up those who need it
> And chases blues away.

BIG GOAT:

> So if you meet a person
> Who's sad or acting rough,
> Be kind, and try to help him —
> Don't be a goat that's gruff!

GOATS: This is the end, and no butts about it! (*Curtain*)

THE END

Production Notes

THREE BILLY GOATS GRUFF

Number of Puppets: 7 hand or rod puppets or marionettes.

Playing Time: 15 minutes.

Description of Puppets: Fairytale or costume books will give you ideas for Norwegian costumes for Grannie and children. Troll might also be dressed this way — but he is not too neat and is quite ugly and funny looking. The three goats are small, medium and large sized.

Properties: Knitting, small toy bridge (should only look as if it were made of blocks; it is really one piece), toy goat, ear trumpet, eyeglasses, dandelion greens, apples, strawberries.

Setting: Scene 1: Grannie Olsen's little house in Norway. There is a rocking chair. Scene 2: Two hills, connected by bridge at center. For a hand or rod puppet show, this can be a cut-out attached to front of stage. One hill has a tree and is shady, the other is sunny.

Lighting: No special effects.

Sound: "Morning" and "In the Hall of the Mountain King" from Grieg's *Peer Gynt Suite* might be used.

THE PIED PIPER OF HAMELIN

From the poem by Robert Browning

Characters

MICHAEL RAT
UNCLE THEODORE RAT
FRITZ, *boy*
GERTY, *girl*
FRAU UBERNASE
DOCTOR SCHNITZEL
MAYOR GROSSMAN
PIED PIPER
HERMAN, *crippled boy*
RATS
CHILDREN

SCENE 1

BEFORE RISE: MICHAEL RAT *enters with a sack over his shoulder.*

MICHAEL (*Calling*): Uncle Theodore! (UNCLE THEODORE *enters. He carries old-fashioned ear trumpet.*)

UNCLE THEODORE: Yes, Michael? Are you ready to see the world?

MICHAEL: All ready. My sack is packed.

THEODORE: What? (*Holds up ear trumpet*)

MICHAEL (*Loudly*): I'm all ready to go.

THEODORE: Oh, yes. Well, you're old enough to sow your oats, young rat. Where are you going?

MICHAEL: I thought I'd go to Paris —

THEODORE (*Interrupting*): What?

MICHAEL (*Loudly*): I thought *Paris* — then London, to visit the King. But on my way, I'll stop in Hamelin Town.

THEODORE: What did you say? Oh, Paris — fine. London, O.K. But, by no means stop in Hamelin.

MICHAEL: Why not? Aren't you from Hamelin, Uncle?

THEODORE: Yes, but you must never go there. I lost my family in that place, and I would be dead, too, if I weren't hard of hearing.

MICHAEL: What happened?

THEODORE: Come, I'll tell you. (*They start to walk off.*) You see, long ago there was a plague of rats in Hamelin ... (*They exit.*)

*　　*　　*

TIME: *Long ago.*

SETTING: *Interior of Town Hall in Hamelin.*

AT RISE: RATS *are scampering all about. They hide as* FRITZ *enters.*

FRITZ: I'm going to hide and surprise Gerty. But where can I hide? (*Looks about, points to left corner.*) Over here will do. (*He runs to left corner and hides.*)

GERTY (*Entering, carrying a doll*): Where are you, Fritz? I know he's here somewhere. (*She looks around.*) Is he hiding in the corner? (*Looks into right corner*) No. Maybe over here. (*Runs center*)

FRITZ (*Jumping out*): Boo! (GERTY *jumps in fright.* FRITZ *laughs.*)

GERTY: Oh, I knew where you were all the time.

FRITZ: What will we play now?

GERTY: Let's count the panes in the Town Hall windows.

FRITZ: No. I can't count very high yet.

GERTY: We could play with my dolly. (*She holds up doll.*)

FRITZ: No, that's no fun. Let's look for more rats. There are rats here in the Town Hall, too. Aren't they funny? I think I'll catch one.

GERTY: Oh, ugh! Leave them alone. Mama says they are dirty things, hiding everywhere — even in our kitchen.

FRITZ: Oh, well, never mind. Let's find Herman and play outside. We're not supposed to be in the Town Hall, anyway.

GERTY: But there are more rats outside! (*Reluctantly*) Oh, all right. (*They exit. In a moment,* DOCTOR SCHNITZEL *and* FRAU UBERNASE *enter.*)

FRAU UBERNASE: Where is the Mayor? This rat situation is growing worse all the time. He simply must do something about it.

DOCTOR SCHNITZEL: Yes. There are rats in my desk, and my medicine cabinet, and everywhere! (MAYOR GROSS-MAN *enters.*)

MAYOR GROSSMAN: Good afternoon, Frau Ubernase, Doctor Schnitzel.

FRAU: Good afternoon, indeed! You promised to rid us of the horrible rats in this town.

DOCTOR: Yes. You are the Mayor. You promised!

MAYOR: I've had traps set, and poison put out ...

FRAU: Yes — and the rats spring the traps without getting caught, and grow fat on the poisoned barley.

DOCTOR: They are running away with our town. We are being eaten out of house and home!

MAYOR: What can we do? What can I do? (PIED PIPER *enters, carrying flute.*)

PIED PIPER: Good day, Herr Mayor.

MAYOR: Who are you, and what do you want here?

PIPER: I am the Pied Piper.

FRAU: With all our troubles, the last thing we need is music.

DOCTOR: Off with you. We have enough pests as it is.

PIPER: Perhaps I can help you. I see you have rat problems.

MAYOR: Too many rat problems.

PIPER: Perhaps I can solve your dilemma.

MAYOR, FRAU *and* DOCTOR (*Ad lib; excitedly*): How? What do you mean? Tell us! (*Etc.*)

PIPER: Pay me one thousand guilders and I'll rid Hamelin Town of all its rats.

MAYOR: We'll pay you five thousand guilders if you can do that.

DOCTOR: Oh, yes. Anything!

FRAU: Please help!

PIED PIPER: One thousand guilders will be fine. Tomorrow all the rats will be gone. So, until tomorrow — goodbye. (*He quickly exits.*)

FRAU: Our hero. (*She exits.*)

DOCTOR SCHNITZEL: What a genius. (*He exits.*)

MAYOR: Hmm. Let's wait and see. (*Follows them off. Curtain.*)

*   *   *   *   *

SCENE 2

TIME: *Next day.*

SETTING: *Street in Hamelin. Backdrop shows Bavarian-style buildings.*

AT RISE: RATS *are scampering about, as* FRITZ *and* GERTY *enter.*

FRITZ: What shall we play? Pin the tail on the rat?

GERTY: That's not funny. Oh, Fritz, let's go home. There are just too many rats out here. (*She runs off.*)

FRITZ (*Calling after her*): Don't let them bother you. (HER-

257

MAN, *the crippled boy, limps onstage with his crutch under one arm*) Hi, Herman. Want to play ball?

HERMAN: I can't catch with this crutch. Come over to my house, and we'll have something to eat, instead.

FRITZ: Good idea. I'm sorry you have to use that crutch, Herman. (*They exit, arm in arm.* FRAU *and* DOCTOR *enter.*)

FRAU: He should start soon. The Piper promised he would get rid of the rats by noon.

DOCTOR (*Pointing offstage*): Here comes the Mayor.

MAYOR (*Entering*): Good morning, everybody.

DOCTOR: Where is he? Where is the Piper?

MAYOR: He's on his way. Let's go to the edge of the river and watch the rats disappear. (*All exit.* PIPER *enters, with flute.*)

PIPER: Now's the time. Here's my pipe to play.... (*Plays pipe and dances about. Flute music is heard from off-stage.* RATS *start to enter.* PIPER *dances in a circle, with* RATS *following, then exits.* RATS *follow him off, and other* RATS *enter and cross the stage, following* PIPER *off.*)

MAYOR (*From offstage*): Look! Here they come!

DOCTOR (*From offstage*): Stand aside, everyone.

FRAU (*From offstage*): Look! They are entering the water by the dozens. (*More* RATS *cross stage.*)

MAYOR, FRAU *and* DOCTOR (*From offstage, cheering*): Hooray! (*Last* RATS *cross stage and exit. Music stops.* MAYOR, FRAU *and* DOCTOR *enter.* MAYOR *is carrying small bag.*)

MAYOR: Three cheers for the Pied Piper! (PIPER *enters.*)

DOCTOR, MAYOR *and* FRAU: Hooray! Hooray! Hooray!

PIPER: Thanks for your bravos, but I must be on my way. Just give me my one thousand guilders and I'll be gone.

MAYOR: Pay that sum to a wandering gypsy? Never. Our business together is done, Piper.

DOCTOR: We're not ones to shirk from duty, but one thousand guilders ...

FRAU: Our losses have made us thrifty.

MAYOR (*Handing* PIPER *bag*): Here — take fifty guilders.

PIPER: Folks who cheat me may find me piping to another tune.

MAYOR (*Getting angry*): That's all you'll get!

FRAU: Take that or nothing at all.

PIPER: One thousand — a bargain is a bargain. . . .

DOCTOR: Off with you, and never return.

MAYOR: Or we will chase you away. You — threaten us? Do your worst! Blow your pipe, there, till you burst! Now, get out of here. (*They exit, leaving* PIPER *alone.*)

PIPER (*Calling after them*): Don't say I didn't warn you! (*He plays flute. Music is heard from offstage.* FRITZ *and* GERTY *enter.*)

GERTY: Listen to that beautiful music. It seems to be calling me.

FRITZ: Look at that funny-looking piper. Let's follow him. (*Calls offstage*) Come on, everybody. Come follow the Pied Piper and let's see where he will go. (CHILDREN *enter.* GERTY *and* FRITZ *follow* PIPER *offstage, and* CHILDREN *follow them off. Finally* HERMAN *enters, leaning on his crutch.*)

HERMAN: Wait for me! (*Crosses slowly and exits. Curtain.*)

*   *   *   *   *

SCENE 3

SETTING: *In front of Koppelberg Hill. This scene is played before curtain.*

AT RISE: PIPER, *still playing, leads* FRITZ, GERTY *and* CHILDREN *in from one side of stage and exits with them through curtain, into Koppelberg Hill.* MICHAEL *and* THEODORE *enter.*

259

THEODORE: And so, the Piper led all the children of Hamelin into the base of Koppelberg Hill with the magic of his piping. It was as if they were under a spell. (HERMAN *enters slowly, on his crutch.*)

MICHAEL: Here comes Herman, the crippled boy. Does he go into the mountain, too?

HERMAN (*Calling*): Wait for me! (*Offstage music stops.*) Where am I? Why am I here — in front of Koppelberg Hill? Where are my friends? I must have been in a trance. I'd better go home now. (*Turns and slowly exits.*)

MICHAEL: What happened to the children?

THEODORE: They were never seen again.

MICHAEL: How do you know all this, Uncle Theodore?

THEODORE: I was there. You see, I was hard of hearing then, also, and could not hear the music of the Pied Piper. Now, off you go. Have a good time, Michael.

MICHAEL: Goodbye, Uncle. (*Starts off, waving*) Goodbye! (*Exits*)

THEODORE (*Waving*): Goodbye! (*Exits in opposite direction.*)

THE END

Production Notes

THE PIED PIPER OF HAMELIN

Number of Puppets: 9 hand or rod puppets, and cut-outs of
  Rats and Children on rods.
Playing Time: 10 minutes.
Description of Puppets: Frau, Doctor, Mayor, Fritz and
  Gerty are dressed in old German costumes. A rod puppet
  would be especially good for the Pied Piper, who should be
  tall and skinny. He wears long coat, half yellow and half
  red, has blue eyes and a merry smile. His hands should be
  attached to the flute with a string that pulls the flute up to
  his mouth when he plays. Michael and Uncle Theodore
  should look like mice, with old German hats and jackets
  (optional). Herman has a crutch attached under his arm.
Properties: Small bag, doll, old-fashioned ear trumpet.
Setting: Scene 1, Interior of Town Hall in Hamelin, painted
  on backdrop. Scene 2, Street, with Bavarian buildings
  painted on backdrop. Scene 3, Koppelberg Hill, painted
  on the front curtain, divided in the middle to let Piper and
  Children enter.
Lighting: No special effects.
Sound: Offstage flute or recorder music, as indicated in text.

RAPUNZEL'S TOWER

Characters

NARRATOR
NAOMI WOODCUTTER
ROGER WOODCUTTER
BABY RAPUNZEL, *their child*
WITCH
LUCIFER, *the dog*
RAPUNZEL, *at 21*
PRINCE

SCENE 1

SETTING: *In front of the Woodcutters' house.*
AT RISE: ROGER *is chopping wood.*

NARRATOR: There once was a poor woodcutter who lived happily with his wife and baby in a little cottage at the edge of the forest. (NAOMI *and* BABY RAPUNZEL *enter and sit in front of house.*) One day....

ROGER (*Chopping wood*): Good morning, Naomi. How's our little baby, Rapunzel, today?

NAOMI: She's just as cute as ever. And she's beginning to crawl. I just caught her crawling out of our garden into the one next door.

ROGER: You had better be careful! That's where the old witch lives.

NAOMI: I know. I'm taking Rapunzel indoors now. Breakfast is ready. Come in soon.

ROGER: I will, just as soon as I finish this pile of wood. (*Chops.* NAOMI *and* BABY *enter house.*) Such a good wife, and we are so happy to have such a sweet little child. No problem at all ... well, not yet. (LUCIFER *romps in and barks.*)

LUCIFER: Arf! Arf! (*Pants.* NAOMI *re-enters with* BABY.)

NAOMI: Look, Roger. What a sweet little dog.

ROGER: Come here, boy.

LUCIFER (*Panting*): Arf! Arf!

NAOMI: He's such a nice dog, and he'd be fine company for Rapunzel. And a good watchdog for us, too!

ROGER: Now, Naomi, remember that he probably belongs to somebody. Don't get too attached to him. (BABY *crawls up to* LUCIFER, *hugs him, pulls his ears, giggles and coos.*)

NAOMI: Look, Roger. How nicely they play together. We simply must keep him. I insist.

ROGER: Well, it goes against my better judgment, but if it will make you happy, my love ...

NAOMI: Oh, thank you, Roger.

ROGER: Come inside, pooch. We'll give you some breakfast.

LUCIFER: Arf! Arf! (*Jumps up and kisses* ROGER) Smack!

ROGER (*Laughing*): Get down! (*All laugh and exit into house. Curtain*)

* * * * *

SCENE 2

SETTING: *Witch's garden.*

AT RISE: WITCH *is in garden, with hoe, working on radish patch.*

NARRATOR: And so the little dog stayed with Roger and Naomi and Baby Rapunzel and became a loving member of the family. A few weeks passed, and then, one dark and gloomy afternoon . . .

WITCH: Oh, my, the garden is doing so nicely. (*Laughs gaily*) Look how big the cabbages are getting. The rhubarb is shooting up so high! And the radishes . . . ! Wait until Mama sees them! (*Laughs gleefully*) I hope no one comes into my garden and digs them up. The Woodcutter family next door lives awfully close, and with that baby, they probably eat a lot. Hm-m-m. Just so they keep out of my garden. (*Exits.* BABY RAPUNZEL *enters crawling. Giggling and cooing, she starts to pull up radishes. See Production Notes. She eats them with smacking sounds and an occasional burp. She also pulls up lettuce and scatters it about.*)

LUCIFER (*Running in*): Arf! Arf! (*He tries to pull* BABY *back, but she hits him with radish and continues pulling up vegetables.* LUCIFER *gives up and exits.*)

WITCH (*Entering*): Oh, no! Look what that child has done to my garden. Come with me, you naughty girl. (WITCH *picks up* BABY *and exits with* BABY *crying. Curtain*)

*　　*　　*　　*　　*

SCENE 3

SETTING: *The same as Scene 1.*
AT RISE: NAOMI *enters, then* WITCH *appears with* BABY.

WITCH: Yoo-hoo! Anybody home? Oh, there you are.
NAOMI: Yes? May I be of any help?
WITCH (*Sweetly*): Indeed you may, my dear. You can answer a small question I have, if you don't mind.

NAOMI: Well, if I can . . .

WITCH: Tell me, dearie (*Angrily*), does this belong to you? (*Holds up* BABY)

NAOMI: Oh! It's my baby. Where did you find her? She was here playing with the dog a minute ago.

WITCH: She was in my radish patch, that's where! (BABY *burps*) And she ate up twenty-one of my biggest, reddest radishes. I was saving them for a big radish pie for Mama's birthday. She will be three hundred next week. (*She cries*) Boo-hoo!

NAOMI: Don't cry. I'll be glad to pay for the radishes . . . but I'm afraid we don't have any money now. Perhaps in a few months.

WITCH: Months? *Months?* I want my radishes now. (*Cries again.*)

LUCIFER (*Appearing*): Arf! Arf!

NAOMI: Oh, here's our dog now. Bad dog! Why didn't you keep better watch over Rapunzel?

WITCH: *Your* dog? Why, that's *my* dog! First your daughter steals my radishes, and now I find it's you who have taken my dog!

NAOMI: But we didn't take him . . .

WITCH: Enough! Enough! Don't say another word, or I'll cast an evil spell on you. And I don't want to do that. I promised Mother I'd stop doing evil things.

NAOMI: Oh, dear!

WITCH: Come, Lucifer.

LUCIFER (*Growling*): Grrrr!

WITCH: Now see what you've done. You've turned my own dog against me. He doesn't want to come with me.

NAOMI: No. He wants to be with Rapunzel. He loves her. (BABY *pulls on* LUCIFER'S *ears.*)

WITCH: Wants to be with Rapunzel, does he? Ah-ha! That's it. And fair payment, too. Since you took my dog, and then your daughter took my twenty-one radishes, I shall now take my dog, *and* your daughter ... and keep her for twenty-one years. One year for every radish!

NAOMI: Oh, you wouldn't do that!

ROGER (*Entering*): I overheard everything. You wouldn't do such a thing, would you?

WITCH: I'm within my rights.

NAOMI: You mean ...?

ROGER: Yes, dear. What's right is right! Rapunzel must stay with the witch for twenty-one years. One year for every radish.

WITCH: Ha! A very sensible decision. I'm glad there are still some honest people left in the world.

NAOMI: But will we be able to visit Rapunzel?

WITCH: No! Not a chance. And don't try to sneak a visit when I'm not home, because I plan to hide her where I will be the only person she sees for twenty-one years. (*Laughs evilly*) Heh, heh, heh!

NAOMI: Oh, dear!

WITCH: So, until then ... bye-bye! Come, Rapunzel. Come, Lucifer. (*They exit.*)

NAOMI: What shall we do now? Oh, dear! Oh, dear!

ROGER: Now, now, Naomi. Everything will be all right. Besides, there's no way we can talk a witch out of doing what she pleases. At least we won't have to worry about the company Rapunzel keeps — she won't be having any for twenty-one years. (*They exit. Curtain*)

*   *   *   *   *

SCENE 4

SETTING: *The tower.*

AT RISE: RAPUNZEL, *now 21, is looking out tower window with her back to audience.* LUCIFER *is next to her.*

NARRATOR: Years passed, and Baby Rapunzel grew up into a lovely young lady. The witch kept her locked up inside the top of a tower somewhere deep in the forest. Rapunzel's only companion in all those twenty-one years was her faithful dog Lucifer . . .

RAPUNZEL (*Singing to the tune of "I'm Only a Bird in a Gilded Cage"*):

        I'm only a girl in a golden tower
        Alone, and so lonely, too.
        Won't someone please come, and take me away,
        Or I'll end up feeling so blue.
        (*She and* LUCIFER *face audience.*)
        Yes, I'm only a girl in a golden tower
        And I don't know what to do.
        I can't escape and no one knows
        Just where I am, do you?

(*Speaks*) Oh, Lucifer, I don't know what I'd do without you. (*She hugs dog and cries.*) Boo-hoo!

LUCIFER: Woof! Woof!

WITCH (*Offstage*): Rapunzel, Rapunzel, let down your golden hair.

RAPUNZEL: Oh, dear. It's the witch. And I haven't finished mending her broomstick. (*She drops her braids down outside window.*) Here you are, Witch. Ouch! Go gently! Owwww!

WITCH (*Appearing at window*): Well, dearie. Is my broomstick done? I'm tired of climbing your hair every day to get into this tower.

RAPUNZEL: No . . . er — I have a few more straws to fasten.

WITCH: Well, be quick. I must get to the market. They're having a sale on pumpkins.

RAPUNZEL (*Working on broom*): There! Finished! Here. (*Hands broom to* WITCH)

WITCH (*Inspecting broom*): Hm-m-m. They don't make them like they used to — cheap straw, poor quality wood. Oh, well, I must be off!

RAPUNZEL: Yes. You certainly are.

WITCH: What? What did you say?

RAPUNZEL: I said — er — oh, look at that star! (*Pointing out window*)

WITCH: Stars — already? I am late. I have an appointment at the beauty parlor at midnight. Bye-bye! (*She flies out window on broomstick.*)

RAPUNZEL: Alone again. (*Sighs*) At least she is company for me. Someone to talk to. (*Sings to tune of "Twinkle, Twinkle, Little Star"*)

> Little stars, my only friends
> Tell me where this huge world ends.
> From my tower way up high
> All I see is endless sky. (*She and* LUCIFER *look out window. Curtain*)

* * * * *

SCENE 5

SETTING: *The forest.*

AT RISE: PRINCE, *in his hunting garb, enters.*

PRINCE (*Singing to tune of "Twinkle, Twinkle, Little Star"*):

> Hunting, fishing, always play,
> Isn't there a place to stay?
> Where a maiden, young, can help
> Guide this lost and forlorn whelp.
> Forest show me where to find
> A wife that's just and good and kind.

Is there none that will appear
That I can call sweetie, dear?
(*He laughs*) Enough of this silly singing. I had better get back to my hunting. Look! There's a rabbit. Maybe I can catch him and keep him for a pet. (LUCIFER *runs in. He barks and pants.*) Why, it's a doggie, right here in the woods. Are you a pet of someone nearby?

LUCIFER (*Barking and nodding*): Woof! Woof!

PRINCE: Where does that someone live? (LUCIFER *barks again and points offstage.*)

WITCH (*Offstage*): Rapunzel! Rapunzel! Let down your golden hair.

PRINCE: Listen! Someone is calling. Oh, I see! An old lady is at the bottom of that golden tower. And she's climbing up on two beautiful golden braids. Let's see what that's all about. (PRINCE *and* LUCIFER *exit. Curtain*)

*　　*　　*　　*　　*

SCENE 6

SETTING: *The tower.*

AT RISE: RAPUNZEL *is at window, singing.*

RAPUNZEL (*Singing to tune of "Twinkle, Twinkle, Little Star"*):
>From my tower, way up high
>All I see is endless sky.

PRINCE (*Offstage*): Rapunzel! Rapunzel! Let down your golden hair.

RAPUNZEL: What's this? The witch returning so soon? She must have forgotten something, or maybe her broomstick conked out. Here, Witch! (*She puts her braids out the window and* PRINCE *climbs them and appears at window.*) Oh! Who are you? *What* are you?

269

PRINCE: I am a prince, fair lady. I was riding through the forest when suddenly I saw an old lady shouting to Rapunzel. Two beautiful golden braids appeared from the tower window. After she climbed up them, I heard your beautiful voice, and I knew I had to see you.

RAPUNZEL: Oh, I am so happy you did. It is so lonely here with no one to talk with all day — every day.

PRINCE: Then why don't you leave?

RAPUNZEL: I can't. There are no stairs to or from the tower, and I can't climb down my own hair. And besides, I belong to the old witch until twenty-one years have passed.

PRINCE: Could I come to visit you every day? We could talk and I could tell you all about the outside world.

RAPUNZEL: Oh, would you? That would be wonderful. Only don't let the witch catch you. She is very protective and jealous.

PRINCE: Until tomorrow then. Farewell! (*He starts to climb out the window.*)

RAPUNZEL: Don't you think you'd better wait until I dangle my hair out the window?

PRINCE (*Looking below*): Oh, yes. I forgot.

RAPUNZEL (*Dropping hair out window*): There!

PRINCE (*Climbing down*): Farewell, again. (*He exits.*)

RAPUNZEL: Auf Wiedersehen! (*She exits.*)

NARRATOR: And so the Prince faithfully visited Rapunzel every day for many months and then one day . . .

WITCH (*Offstage*): Rapunzel! Rapunzel! Let down your golden hair.

RAPUNZEL (*Entering and going to window*): Right away, my prince. (*Lets her hair down*) What news have you brought me today?

WITCH (*Appearing*): News? Prince? So, you have been having visitors behind my back.

RAPUNZEL: Oh, dear, it's you. Where's your broom?

WITCH: It conked out. It was an old model anyhow. But don't change the subject. Who is this prince?

RAPUNZEL: He just happened by one day. Now he visits me daily, and I'm afraid I've fallen in love with him.

WITCH: Love! In love with a prince? Hmmmph! Such luck. The only person who ever visited me was a bill collector. Well ... it must stop! We simply can't have it! You belong to me!

RAPUNZEL: If you're going to be like that, I suppose I'll have to tell you.

WITCH: Tell me what?

RAPUNZEL: My twenty-one years were up three months ago. I no longer belong to you.

WITCH: They are? You don't? Why didn't you say something three months ago?

RAPUNZEL: I have become very fond of you and I would miss your company.

WITCH: You have? You would?

RAPUNZEL: Yes, because I ... love you.

WITCH: Awwwww!

RAPUNZEL: But I love the Prince also. And I wish to marry him.

WITCH: If it will make you happy. And besides, Mama has been feeling poorly lately. I should go stay with her.

PRINCE (*Offstage*): Rapunzel! Rapunzel! Let down your golden hair!

WITCH: Oh, oh! There's your boyfriend now.

RAPUNZEL: Here! (*Throws down her braids*) Climb up quickly!

PRINCE (*Appearing*): Rapunzel — who's this?

WITCH: Never mind. I was just leaving. And for a wedding present I'd like to leave you kids with this tower. Good apartments are hard to find nowadays. Bye-bye! (*She *picks up her broom. To audience*) And you thought I was going to be nasty, didn't you? (*She laughs and flies off*)

PRINCE: Wedding? Did she say wedding?

RAPUNZEL: Yes, my prince.

PRINCE: Then, will you? I mean, are we going to ...?

RAPUNZEL: Yes, my prince.

PRINCE: Wow!

RAPUNZEL: Oh, dear!

PRINCE: What is it?

RAPUNZEL: If we live here in this tower, how will we get in and out?

PRINCE: Well, I've noticed that men are wearing their hair longer these days. If I let mine grow as long as yours, we can take turns going out.

RAPUNZEL: But we won't be able to go out together. And I'd like to introduce you to my parents, at least.

PRINCE: Maybe your parents would like to come and live with us.

RAPUNZEL: What a wonderful idea! I'm sure that Mother and Father would both enjoy letting their hair down, too. (*They laugh, then dance about.* LUCIFER *comes in and jumps about, barking.*)

NARRATOR: And so Rapunzel and the Prince were married, and they lived happily ever after in the tower with Rapunzel's long-lost mother and father. And everyone agreed to grow long hair and let it all hang out. (*Curtain*)

THE END

Production Notes

Rapunzel's Tower

Number of Puppets: 7 hand or rod puppets or marionettes.
Characters: 1 male or female for Narrator.
Playing Time: 15 minutes.
Description of Puppets: Roger and Naomi wear peasant costumes, as does the Witch, but she should wear dark colors and a tall hat with wide brim. Witch should not be too ugly or mean looking but funny. She might wear glasses. Lucifer is soft and cuddly and also funny looking. Baby wears a long white gown, and the grown-up Rapunzel is dressed in a plain, pretty gown. She has long blonde braids with bows at the ends. Prince wears hunting clothes.
Properties: Ax, bits of green paper for lettuce, hoe, broom.
Setting: Scenes 1 and 3: In front of Woodcutters' house. There is a pile of wood. Scene 2: The Witch's garden. There might be trees in the background and a suggestion of her house. There is a row of vegetables — cabbage, rhubarb, lettuce and radishes painted on a long flat. Scenes 4 and 6: The tower. There is a small window at back. There should be a hidden door at the base if you are using hand or rod puppets. Window should be open to the top if you are using marionettes. A small bed and chair might complete furnishings. Scene 5: The forest.
Lighting: No special effects.
Special Effects: When Baby pulls up radishes, one radish is sewn to her hand, so that it looks as if she's pulling up many.

THE TABLE, THE DONKEY AND THE STICK

Adapted from the German folk tale by the Brothers Grimm

Characters

FATHER, *a poor tailor*
JOHANN, *his older son*
KARL, *his younger son*
ANNA, *his daughter*
CARPENTER
INNKEEPER
WEAVER
DONKEY
NARRATOR

SCENE 1

SETTING: *The tailor's cottage, a room crowded with furniture.*

NARRATOR: There once was a poor tailor who had two sons and one daughter. They lived happily together in their little cottage, until one day the father spoke to his son, Johann.

FATHER: Johann, my son, we cannot go on much longer unless I find more work. The people in this village are poor and there is little for us to do here. I'm afraid I will have to sell our cottage unless one of us goes to the big city to earn some money.

JOHANN: I will go, Father. I will try to find work as a carpenter, for I am very good with tools.

FATHER: I was hoping you would say that, son, for I am too old to find another job.

JOHANN: Do not worry, Father. I will leave at once. I have nothing to pack. Say goodbye to Karl and Anna for me. I hate tearful farewells, and you know that Anna always weeps when she is sad. Goodbye, Father.

FATHER: Farewell, son. Come back home as soon as possible. (JOHANN *exits and* FATHER *follows him offstage.*)

NARRATOR: One year passed. (*Part of the furniture is removed.* FATHER *re-enters with* KARL *and* ANNA.)

FATHER: Ah, children. A whole year has passed since Johann left to seek his fortune, and still not a word from him. I am afraid your brother has failed and is too ashamed to return home.

ANNA: Do not fear, Father. Surely we will hear from Johann soon.

FATHER: Perhaps, Anna, but alas—business has not improved, and I can no longer afford to buy food for all of us.

KARL: Never fear, Father. I have decided that it is my turn to go to seek my fortune. I will try to get a job grooming horses on the King's estate. I hear they are looking for a new stable boy.

FATHER: Yes, Karl. That sounds like an excellent idea. Perhaps you will succeed where your poor brother has failed.

ANNA: Do not say that, Father. Johann will return. You'll see. And Karl will help us.

KARL: Yes. I'd better leave now, before someone else gets the stable boy's job.

FATHER: Goodbye, son, and good luck.

ANNA: Goodbye, Karl. (*She weeps.* KARL *exits.* FATHER *and* ANNA *follow him offstage.*)

NARRATOR: Another year passes. (*Most of the remaining furniture is removed.* FATHER *and* ANNA *re-enter.*)

FATHER: Oh, Anna, my daughter, what are we going to do? We have not heard a word from either of your brothers. We have sold most of the furniture and all of your late mother's beautiful dishes. And still I have barely enough money to buy food.

ANNA: Never mind, Father. I have made up my mind to go to the city and try my luck as a weaver in the tapestry factory.

FATHER: But, Anna, you are too young to go by yourself to the city.

ANNA: I am twenty-three, Father, and old enough to be able to take care of myself.

FATHER: Very well. Go, if you must, Anna. But write to me—and come to see me often.

ANNA: I will, Father. Don't worry. You must take care of yourself while I am gone. Goodbye.

FATHER: Goodbye, sweet Anna. Don't be like your brothers. (*She exits. Curtain.*)

*　　*　　*

SCENE 2

SETTING: *Carpenter's shop, with workbench onstage, holding wood and tools. Scene may be played in front of curtain.*

AT RISE: CARPENTER *and* JOHANN *are onstage.*

CARPENTER: You have worked for me as a carpenter's apprentice for two years, Johann. You have learned your trade very well.

JOHANN: Thank you, sir. I have tried to do my best.

CARPENTER: I have nothing else to teach you. It is time for you to go out on your own and open your own shop.

JOHANN: It makes me happy to hear that, sir. I am anxious to return home to my family.

CARPENTER: Before you leave, Johann, I would like to give you a token of my appreciation for your hard work. (*Gets table*)

JOHANN (*In surprise*): A table? (*Without enthusiasm*) Thank you, sir. That is kind of you.

CARPENTER: Do not look so disappointed. This is no ordinary, common table, I assure you.

JOHANN: What do you mean?

CARPENTER: This is a magic table. Watch. (*Recites*) "Table, be covered." (*The table is filled with food.*)

JOHANN (*Amazed*): Why, it is magic! The table was bare at first, but now it is covered with a tablecloth, and holds dishes of fine roast meat, and drink. It is truly amazing!

CARPENTER: This table will satisfy your needs for the rest of your life, Johann. Whenever you are hungry, all you have to say is, "Table, be covered," and you will have all the food you want.

JOHANN (*Excited*): Thank you. Thank you! Father will be pleased. He needed a way to find food for our family.

CARPENTER: Good. Now, be off with you. And good luck.

JOHANN: Goodbye, sir. And thank you. Thank you! (JOHANN *exits, with table. Curtain.*)

* * *

SCENE 3

SETTING: *In front of an inn.*

AT RISE: JOHANN *enters, carrying table.*

JOHANN: I think I will stop and rest at this inn before I go home to Father. This table is heavy. (INNKEEPER *comes out of the inn.*)

INNKEEPER: Good day, my friend. Can I offer you something to drink? You look tired and thirsty.

JOHANN: No—but I can offer you something. (*Recites*) "Table, be covered." (*Food appears on table.*)

INNKEEPER: Heavens! How did you do that?

JOHANN: It's a magic table. It will give me food whenever I command.

INNKEEPER: My! What a lucky fellow you are.

JOHANN: Yes. I'm taking the table home to my poor father. But I still have a long way to go, and I am tired.

INNKEEPER: Don't worry. I will let you stay here at my inn tonight free. Having such an important person here will be good for business.

JOHANN: Why, how kind of you.

INNKEEPER: It's nothing. Just follow me. I will give you my best room. (*Exits with* JOHANN, *then re-enters*) Ha! Good. He sleeps. Now I will take that magic table and put another in its place. Such a table will make my inn prosper. (*He switches tables, then exits. Lights dim, or curtains close briefly, to indicate passage of time. Sound of birds singing is heard.*)

JOHANN (*Entering with* INNKEEPER): Your room was comfortable, and the service excellent. How can I ever repay you?

INNKEEPER: Oh, you have, my young friend! You have. Just by staying here.

JOHANN: You're very kind. Well, I must be going now. I'll take my table, here, and be off. (*He lifts table.*) That's strange. It seems to be much lighter today.

INNKEEPER: That's because you had a good night's sleep and are not so tired.

JOHANN: Yes, perhaps you are right. Well, goodbye.
INNKEEPER: Farewell. (JOHANN *exits. Curtain.*)

* * *

SCENE 4

TIME: *The next day.*
SETTING: *The same as Scene 1. All the furniture is gone.*
AT RISE: JOHANN *enters, with table.*

JOHANN: Father! I'm home. It's Johann.
FATHER (*Entering*): Johann, my son! How good it is to see you! I had almost given you up for lost. Where have you been?
JOHANN: It's a long story, Father. But, look, look, what I have brought you!
FATHER: A table? How nice. This will be useful. I don't have any table or chairs now. I had to sell all the furniture.
JOHANN: This is not just an ordinary table, Father. It's a magic table.
FATHER: Magic? I don't believe it!
JOHANN: No? Well, watch. (*Recites*) "Table, be covered." (*Nothing happens.*)
FATHER: Well? Is something supposed to happen?
JOHANN: Wait. Maybe I didn't say it right. (*Shouts*) "Table, be covered."
FATHER: I'm waiting.
JOHANN (*Disappointed*): Oh, no! The magic must have worn off. (*Sadly*) I knew it was too good to be true.
FATHER: Don't look so sad, son. At least I have a table to eat on now, and best of all, I have you with me again.

279

JOHANN: I'm happy to be home, Father. (*They embrace. Curtain.*)

*   *   *

<h2 style="text-align:center">SCENE 5</h2>

SETTING: *Same as Scene 3.*
AT RISE: KARL *enters with* DONKEY.

KARL: I cannot believe my good luck. I have been away from home for only one year, and already I am the richest person in the kingdom . . . thanks to my magic donkey, here.

INNKEEPER (*Entering*): Welcome to my inn, young man. Did I hear you say that you had a magic donkey?

KARL: Yes, I did say that, Innkeeper. I have been working at the King's stables for one year and he liked my work so well that he gave me this magic donkey.

INNKEEPER (*Sneakily*): Ho! In what way is he magic?

KARL: I'll show you. Watch! All you have to do is pull his ear and say, "Brickelbrit," and gold pours from his mouth.

INNKEEPER (*Greedily*): What are you waiting for? Do it! Do it!

KARL: Very well. (*He pulls* DONKEY's *ear.*) "Brickelbrit."

DONKEY: Hee-haw. (DONKEY's *mouth opens, and gold pieces pour out.*)

INNKEEPER: My, that is an easy way to get money! A donkey like that is a rare and wonderful gift.

KARL: Yes! I am taking it home to my poor father, so that he will never have to work again.

INNKEEPER: What a thoughtful son you are. But you look

tired. With all that money of yours, you should stay here for the night and rest. You can get off to a fresh start in the morning.

KARL: That's a fine idea. I'll take the best room in the inn. Here are some gold coins for you—please see that my donkey is fed and well cared for.

INNKEEPER: Oh, I'll take care of him, all right. Come, I'll show you to your room. (*They exit, leaving* DONKEY *on-stage.*)

DONKEY: Hee-haw.

INNKEEPER (*Re-entering*): Good! He's asleep. The fool! How could he be so trusting? I'll take his donkey and replace it with the one in my stable. He won't even know the difference. (*He leads* DONKEY *off, then enters leading another* DONKEY.) There! Now I will have all the gold I need. Ho, ho, ho! (*He exits. Lights dim to indicate passage of time. Sound of birds singing is heard.* KARL *and* INNKEEPER *enter.*)

KARL: What a good sleep I had! You have a fine inn here, and I would like to show my appreciation by giving you some more gold.

INNKEEPER: Oh, that won't be necessary. You have already given me enough, and besides, it is an honor to have such a rich gentleman staying at my inn.

KARL: How honest you are! Thank you. I must be on my way home now. (*Goes to* DONKEY)

INNKEEPER: Have a safe journey. (KARL *and* DONKEY *exit. Curtain.*)

*   *   *

SCENE 6

TIME: *The next day.*
SETTING: *The bare cottage, as in Scene 4.*
AT RISE: KARL *enters.*

KARL: Father! I've returned!

FATHER (*Entering*): Karl, my son! You're home at last! You look well and happy.

JOHANN (*Entering*): Brother! Welcome home.

FATHER: Have you brought anything home from your travels?

KARL (*Nonchalantly*): Nothing but a donkey.

FATHER (*Disappointed*): A donkey? A goat would have been more useful.

KARL: You won't think that when you see *this* donkey. He's magic.

FATHER: Oh, no! More magic again.

JOHANN: I hope your magic will last longer than mine did.

FATHER: What does the donkey do—give you food, too, I suppose?

KARL: Better than that, Father. Whenever I pull the donkey's ear and say, "Brickelbrit," gold coins pour from his mouth.

JOHANN (*In disbelief*): I don't believe it! Bring your donkey in!

KARL: Very well. (*Brings in* DONKEY) Now, watch. (*Pulls* DONKEY's *ear*) "Brickelbrit."

DONKEY: Hee-haw. (*Nothing happens.*)

FATHER: Where is the gold, Karl?

KARL: I don't know. Something must have gone wrong.

JOHANN: Your magic disappeared just as quickly as mine did!

FATHER: Don't worry. I am happy to have my two sons home. Now, if only your sister were here, too! But she has been gone for months now, seeking her fortune.

KARL: Yes, I hope that Anna is well. But I'm worried about her because she is frail and helpless.

JOHANN: Don't worry. Anna will be fine. She can take care of herself. (*Curtain*)

*   *   *

SCENE 7

SETTING: *The tapestry factory, with loom. Scene may be played in front of curtain.*

AT RISE: WEAVER *and* ANNA *are onstage, talking together.*

WEAVER: You have done a fine job here, Anna. You are the best weaver we have had for many years. I am sorry to see you leave.

ANNA: I am sorry to leave, too, but now that I have saved money, I must go home to my father.

WEAVER: It is dangerous to travel alone through these parts, Anna. Please take this to protect yourself. (*Hands* ANNA *a stick*) It is a token of my appreciation and affection for you.

ANNA: Thank you. (*Without enthusiasm*) That will be a great help.

WEAVER: This is not an ordinary stick, Anna, but a magic stick which will protect you against any danger.

ANNA (*Surprised*): A magic stick! How does it work?

WEAVER: If ever you are in danger, just say, "Stick, protect me," and the stick will begin to strike your attackers. It will not stop until you say, "Stick—stop."

ANNA (*Excited*): My, what a wonderful stick! How can I ever thank you? Now I shall be safe on my journey home. Goodbye—and thank you again.

WEAVER: Goodbye, Anna. Have a safe journey. (*Curtain*)

*   *   *

SCENE 8

TIME: *That evening.*

SETTING: *Same as Scene 3.*

AT RISE: ANNA *enters, holding her magic stick.* INNKEEPER *appears from the inn.*

ANNA: I have been walking for many hours. I must sit down for a while to rest.

INNKEEPER: Good evening, young lady. Why is a young girl like you traveling alone? Don't you know it isn't safe?

ANNA: Don't worry about me! I can take care of myself.

INNKEEPER: Yes, if you say so. But why don't you stay here and work at my inn?

ANNA: Thank you, sir, but I'm on my way home.

INNKEEPER: You'll change your mind when you hear how clever I am. Listen. Just this week I tricked two foolish lads who came by here on the way to their father's cottage in Sneiderdorf.

ANNA (*Aside*): Sneiderdorf! That's where I live.

INNKEEPER: One of them had a magic table, and the other, a magic donkey. I stole them and gave the two men a false table and donkey instead.

ANNA (*Aside*): They must have been my brothers.

INNKEEPER: So, you see, I am clever, and rich, too. Why not work here for a time?

284

ANNA: I'll have to think about it. Where are the magic table and donkey?

INNKEEPER: I am hiding them in my barn. I don't want anyone to know about them.

ANNA (*Coyly*): My! How clever of you!

INNKEEPER: Now, come inside, and I will give you something to eat.

ANNA: I really must be on my way, sir.

INNKEEPER (*Insisting*): Yes, yes, come in.

ANNA: No, I can't. I must go.

INNKEEPER (*Pulling* ANNA's *arm*): Just come in for one minute.

ANNA: Stop! Let me go! (*Calls*) "Stick, protect me." (*Stick hits* INNKEEPER *over and over.*)

INNKEEPER: Ouch, ooh, make it stop! Get it off me! Ow! Ooh! Stop! Stop!

ANNA: First you must promise me that you'll let me have the table and donkey. They belong to my brothers.

INNKEEPER (*Still being hit by stick*): I promise! I promise! Just make this stick stop!

ANNA: Then you must promise me that you'll never trick or cheat any other customers.

INNKEEPER: I promise! Only make the stick stop!

ANNA: Very well. "Stick—stop." (*Stick stops.*)

INNKEEPER (*In pain*): Oh, my poor head.

ANNA: That should teach you never to be dishonest again. Now come and help me put the table on the donkey's back. I must return home.

INNKEEPER: Yes, I'm coming. But please don't set that stick on me again. (*They exit. Curtain.*)

*   *   *

SCENE 9

TIME: *The next day.*
SETTING: *The bare cottage again, as in Scene 4.*
AT RISE: ANNA *enters.*

ANNA: Father! Father! It's Anna! I've come back!

FATHER (*Entering*): My child! How good to see you!

KARL (*Entering*): Anna, dear sister, you're home! I have been worried about you.

JOHANN (*Entering*): See, Karl! I was right. I told you we didn't have to worry about her.

ANNA: It's wonderful to see you all again—and from now on, we will have no more worries. (*Brings on table and donkey*) Karl and Johann, I have returned with the real magic table and donkey. The thieving innkeeper stole these from you, and gave you false ones in their place.

JOHANN: So the Innkeeper is to blame!

KARL: He tricked us both. I can't believe it!

FATHER: The table and donkey are magic, after all. Karl and Johann, I should never have doubted you.

ANNA: Father, many of our friends and neighbors have been kind and helpful to you while we were gone. Call them together and we shall eat and drink to our heart's content. I shall fill all their pockets with gold, too.

FATHER: What a splendid idea! It's so good to have my wonderful family with me again. (*Curtain*)

THE END

The Table, the Donkey and the Stick

PRODUCTION NOTES

Number of puppets: 8 hand or rod puppets or marionettes (the same Donkey can be used for each role).

Playing Time: 25 minutes.

Costumes: Typical German country dress, such as dirndls and *lederhosen*.

Properties: Cottage furniture, built in three separate units so that each can be removed as a section, as directed in Scene 1; carpenter's bench, with wood and tools on it; magic table, which has a second top hinged to the back edge, so that it can be flipped quickly to reveal "food" glued to this hidden top (use the same table for the second table); gold coins threaded together (placed inside head of Donkey and pulled out of Donkey's mouth as indicated); magic stick, which should be large and on a heavy, strong wire for good control.

Setting: Simplify all the scenery because of the nine scene changes. The cottage interior is the main back set. The inn can be a painted drop in front of the curtain. The carpenter's shop and the tapestry factory scenes can be done in front of the curtain. For the carpentry shop, use a workbench to suggest the set, and for the tapestry shop, a loom.

Lighting: Lower the lights and bring them up again, to indicate the passage of time, in the scenes at the inn.

Sound: No special effects. German folk dances may be played as background music, if desired.

ALICE'S ADVENTURES IN WONDERLAND

Adapted from the book by Lewis Carroll

Characters

NARRATOR
ALICE
ALICE'S SISTER
WHITE RABBIT
FISH FOOTMAN
FROG FOOTMAN
DUCHESS
COOK
BABY
CHESHIRE CAT
MARCH HARE
MAD HATTER
DORMOUSE
QUEEN OF HEARTS
KING OF HEARTS
CARDS

Scene One

SETTING: *A riverbank.*
AT RISE: ALICE'S SISTER *is sitting down, reading from a book to* ALICE, *who sits nearby.*

ALICE'S SISTER:
>A boat, beneath a sunny sky,
>Lingering onward dreamily,

In an evening of July—
Children three that nestle near,
Eager eye and willing ear,
Pleased a simple tale to hear—

ALICE: Dear sister, I don't really know why you read that
book. What use is a book without pictures or conversation?
(*To herself*) Oh, dear. This hot day is making me very
sleepy. (*She lies down.* ALICE's SISTER *exits.* WHITE RAB-
BIT *runs in, looking at his watch.*)

WHITE RABBIT: Oh, dear! Oh, dear! I shall be late! (*He
exits.*)

ALICE: Late? I wonder what for? A rabbit with a waistcoat
and watch! Most peculiar. (*She gets up and peers offstage
after* WHITE RABBIT.) He's gone down that rabbit hole.
I'll just see where he goes. (*She exits. From offstage*)
Oh-h-h! I'm falling! (*Curtain*)

*　　*　　*

Scene Two

SETTING: *In the rabbit hole.*

AT RISE: ALICE *is floating in mid-air. Bookcases and shelves
pass by her as she falls.*

ALICE: I seem to be falling down a very deep well. Or else
I'm falling very slowly. It's too dark to see where I'm going. All the cupboards and bookshelves are filled. (*Turns*)
Let's see—here is some orange marmalade. After such a
fall as this I shall think nothing of tumbling down stairs!
I wonder how many miles I've fallen by this time? I must
be getting somewhere near the center of the earth. I hope
they remember to feed Dinah her saucer of milk at tea

time. There are no mice in the air, I'm afraid, but you might catch a bat, Dinah. And that's very like a mouse, you know. But do cats eat bats, I wonder? (*She yawns.*) Do cats eat bats? Do cats eat bats? Do bats eat cats? (ALICE *lands on the ground.*) Oh! (*She gets up.*) I don't seem to be a bit hurt from that fall. (*Looks offstage*) Why, there goes the White Rabbit! I'll follow him. (*She runs off, as curtains close.*)

*   *   *

Scene Three

SETTING: *In front of the Duchess's house. There is a door-way, with a sign over it reading,* THE DUCHESS. *This scene may be played before the curtain.*
AT RISE: WHITE RABBIT *runs in.*

RABBIT: Oh, my ears and whiskers, how late it's getting! I'll be late for the Queen's game. She will be furious. (*He exits.* ALICE *runs in.*)

ALICE (*Calling to* RABBIT): Wait! Wait for me! Oh, dear. He's gone again. (*Looks around*) Here's a little house. Perhaps they can help me. (*She watches as* FISH FOOTMAN *enters, carrying large envelope, crosses to door, and knocks.* FROG FOOTMAN *enters, goes to door and opens it.*)

FISH FOOTMAN (*Presenting envelope to* FROG FOOTMAN): For the Duchess. An invitation from the Queen to play croquet. (*They bow and knock heads together. Both fall over backward, then get up.*)

FROG FOOTMAN: For the Duchess. An invitation from the Queen to play croquet. (*They bow again, knock heads, fall over, then get up.* FISH FOOTMAN *exits, as* ALICE laughs. *She crosses to door. From offstage, sounds of howling, sneezing and crashing are heard.* ALICE *knocks on door.*) There's no sort of use in knocking. And that for two reasons. First, because I'm on the same side of the door as you are. Secondly, because they're making such a noise inside, no one could possibly hear you. (*Offstage noises grow louder.*)

ALICE: Please, then. How am I to get in?

FROG FOOTMAN: There might be some sense in your knocking if we had the door between us. For instance, if you were inside, you might knock and I could let you out, you know. (FROG FOOTMAN *sits on stoop of door.*)

ALICE (*More firmly*): How am I to get in?

FROG FOOTMAN: I shall sit here till tomorrow. . . .

ALICE: It's really dreadful the way all the creatures here argue. It's enough to drive one crazy. Oh, there's no use talking to him. (ALICE *enters the door. Curtain.*)

*   *   *

Scene Four

SETTING: *The Duchess's kitchen.*

AT RISE: COOK *is stirring a pot on the stove and sprinkling pepper in it with her other hand.* DUCHESS *is sitting on a stool holding* BABY, *who howls.* CHESHIRE CAT *is sitting on stove.* ALICE *enters and looks around.*

ALICE (*Sneezing*): There's certainly too much pepper in that soup! (*Sneezes again. To* DUCHESS) Please, would you tell me why your cat grins like that?

DUCHESS (*Bouncing* BABY): It's a Cheshire Cat. That's why. (*To* BABY) Pig! (BABY *continues to howl.*)

ALICE: I didn't know that Cheshire Cats always grinned. In fact, I didn't know that cats could grin.

DUCHESS: They all can and most of 'em do.

ALICE: I don't know of any that do.

DUCHESS: You don't know much, and that's a fact. (COOK *suddenly begins to throw pots and pans at* DUCHESS *and* BABY. DUCHESS *ignores them.* BABY *continues to howl.*)

ALICE: Oh, Cook! Please mind what you're doing. There goes the baby's precious nose.

DUCHESS: If everybody minded their own business the world would go 'round a great deal faster than it does.

ALICE (*Brightly*): Which would not be an advantage. Just think what work it would make with the day and night. You see, the Earth takes twenty-four hours to turn round on its axis—

DUCHESS: Talking of axes—chop off her head!

ALICE: Twenty-four hours, I think; or is it twelve?

DUCHESS: Oh, don't bother me. I never could abide figures. (*She sings to the tune of "Pop Goes the Weasel."*)

> Speak roughly to your little boy,
> And beat him when he sneezes.
> He only does it to annoy
> Because he knows it teases.

(*Speaks*) Chorus.

DUCHESS *and* COOK: Wow! Wow! Wow! (DUCHESS *tosses* BABY *in the air.*)

DUCHESS (*Singing again*):

> I speak severely to my boy,
> I beat him when he sneezes,
> For he can thoroughly enjoy
> The pepper when he pleases.

(*Speaks*) Chorus.

DUCHESS *and* COOK: Wow! Wow! Wow!

DUCHESS: Here! (*She hands* BABY *to* ALICE.) You may hold it a bit, if you like! I must go get ready to play croquet with the Queen. (ALICE *takes* BABY *and exits.* DUCHESS *exits the other way as* COOK *throws another pot at her. Curtain.*)

*   *   *

Scene Five

SETTING: *In the woods.*

AT RISE: CHESHIRE CAT *is sitting in branches of tree at one side of stage.* ALICE *enters, carrying* BABY, *which snorts.*

ALICE: The poor little thing is snorting away like a steam engine! I can hardly hold it. But if I don't take this child away with me, they're sure to kill it in a day or two. (BABY *grunts like a pig.*) Don't grunt! That's not at all a proper way of expressing yourself. (*Looks closely at* BABY) It has a turned-up nose, much more like a snout than a real nose. Also its eyes are very small for a baby's.

BABY (*Snorting*): Oink! Oink!

ALICE: If you are going to turn into a pig, my dear, I'll have nothing more to do with you. Mind now! (BABY *turns into a pig and runs away. See Production Notes.*)

BABY (*Grunting as it exits*): Oink! Oink!

ALICE: If it had grown up, it would have made a dreadfully ugly child; but it makes a rather handsome pig, I think. I've known other children who might do very well as pigs, if one only knew the right way to change them. (ALICE *sees* CHESHIRE CAT *in the tree and walks over to it.*) Cheshire-Puss. Would you tell me, please, which way I ought to go from here?

CHESHIRE CAT: In one direction lives a Hatter. And in the other direction lives a March Hare. Visit either you like: they're both mad.

ALICE: But I don't want to go among mad people.

CHESHIRE CAT: Oh, you can't help that. We're all mad here. Do you play croquet with the Queen today?

ALICE: I should like that very much, but I haven't been invited yet.

CHESHIRE CAT: You'll see me there. By the bye, what became of the baby? I'd nearly forgotten to ask.

ALICE: It turned into a pig.

CHESHIRE CAT: I thought it would. (CAT *disappears*.)

ALICE: I've seen hatters before. The March Hare will be much the most interesting, and perhaps, as this is May, it won't be raving—at least not so much as it was in March.

CHESHIRE CAT (*Reappearing*): Did you say pig or fig?

ALICE: I said *pig!* And I wish you wouldn't keep appearing and vanishing so suddenly. You make me quite giddy.

CHESHIRE CAT: All right! (*He disappears slowly, leaving only his grin. See Production Notes.*)

ALICE: Well! I've often seen a cat without a grin, but a grin without a cat! It's the most curious thing I ever saw in all my life. (ALICE *exits. Curtain.*)

*   *   *

Scene Six

SETTING: *The March Hare's tea party. The March Hare's house is in the background. It has a pair of long ears on its roof. There is a long table at center, with teacups and saucers on it, and a large teapot with its lid off.*

AT RISE: MARCH HARE *and* MAD HATTER *sit at table, arguing and leaning on* DORMOUSE, *who sits between them, sleeping.* ALICE *enters.*

ALICE: Oh, there they are. That must be the March Hare and the Mad Hatter. And look . . . they are resting their elbows on a dormouse. I suppose it doesn't mind.

HATTER *and* MARCH HARE (*Shouting at* ALICE): No room! No room!

ALICE: There's plenty of room.

HATTER: What day of the month is it? (*Holds up his watch*)

ALICE: The fourth.

HATTER: Two days wrong. I told you butter wouldn't suit the works, March Hare.

MARCH HARE: It's the best butter.

HATTER: Yes, but some crumbs must have got in as well. You shouldn't have put it in with the bread knife. (ALICE *looks at watch.*)

ALICE: What a funny watch! It tells the day of the month and doesn't tell what o'clock it is.

HATTER: Why should it? Does your watch tell you what year it is?

ALICE: Of course not. But that's because it stays the same year for such a long time.

HATTER: Which is just the case with mine. We quarreled about it last March, just before *he* went mad, you know. It was at the great concert given by the Queen of Hearts and I had to sing. (HATTER *stands on table and sings, to tune of "Twinkle, Twinkle, Little Star"*)

　　　　Twinkle, twinkle, little bat.

　　　　How I wonder what you're at.

(*To* ALICE, *speaking*) You've heard the song?

ALICE: Something like it.

HATTER (*Continuing to sing*):

> Up above the world you fly,
> Like a tea-tray in the sky,
> Twinkle, twinkle—

DORMOUSE (*Waking up and singing*): Twinkle, twinkle. . . .

HATTER (*Getting down off table*): Well, I hardly finished the first verse when the Queen bawled out, "He's murdering the time. Off with his head!"

ALICE: How dreadfully savage!

HATTER: And ever since that, he won't do a thing I ask. It's always six o'clock now.

ALICE: Is that the reason so many tea things are put out here?

MARCH HARE: Yes—that's it. It's always tea time and we've no time to wash the cups in between.

ALICE: Then you keep moving 'round, I suppose?

HATTER: Exactly so. As the things get used up. I want a clean cup. Let's all move one place on. (HATTER *and* MARCH HARE *get up and move, carrying* DORMOUSE *with them, and knocking over dishes.*)

ALICE: Ugh! You've spilled the milk jug!

MARCH HARE: Into the teapot with 'im! (MARCH HARE *and* HATTER *lift* DORMOUSE *and try to stuff it into teapot.*)

ALICE: Well, really, now! It's the stupidest tea party I ever was at in all my life! (*She walks away.*) Everything's curious today. I think I may as well go on to the croquet game. (*Exits. Curtain.*)

* * *

Scene Seven

SETTING: *Queen of Hearts's flower gardens.*

AT RISE: CARDS *march onstage and line up against back-ground.* ALICE *enters and looks about.* WHITE RABBIT *enters.*

RABBIT (*Announcing*): Their Royal Majesties, the King and Queen of Hearts! (KING *and* QUEEN OF HEARTS *enter.*)

QUEEN: Off with their heads! Off with their heads! (*Pointing to* ALICE) Who is that girl?

RABBIT: I don't know, Your Majesty.

QUEEN: Idiot! (*To* ALICE) What is your name, child?

ALICE: My name is Alice, so please Your Majesty. (*To herself*) Why, they are only a pack of cards. I needn't be afraid of them.

QUEEN: And why do the rose bushes have white roses? They should be red. Where are the gardeners? Off with their heads!

KING: Their heads are gone, dear.

QUEEN: That's right. (*To* ALICE) Can you play croquet?

ALICE: Yes.

QUEEN: Come then. (*She walks away.*)

ALICE: (*To* WHITE RABBIT): Where's the Duchess?

RABBIT: Sh-h-h! She's under sentence of execution.

ALICE: For what?

RABBIT: She boxed the Queen's ears. (ALICE *laughs softly.*) Hush! The Queen will hear you.

QUEEN: Get to your places! (CARDS *begin to dash about.* QUEEN *continues to bellow.*) Off with their heads! Off with their heads! (*Sounds of* CARDS *muttering are heard.*)

ALICE (*To* RABBIT): They are dreadfully fond of beheading people here.

CHESHIRE CAT (*Appearing*): How do you like the Queen?

ALICE: Not at all. She's so extremely—oh, the Queen is listening—ah . . . likely to win at this game that it's hardly worthwhile playing. (CARDS *continue to scamper about. Muttering sounds increase.*)

QUEEN: Has the Duchess had her head removed?

KING: Let the jury consider their verdict first.

QUEEN: No! No! Sentence first—verdict afterward.

ALICE (*Shouting*): Stuff and nonsense! The idea of having the sentence first!

QUEEN: Hold your tongue!

ALICE: I won't!

QUEEN (*Shouting*): Off with her head!

ALICE: Who cares for you? You're nothing but a pack of cards! (CARDS, KING *and* QUEEN *fly at* ALICE. *She tries to beat them off.* CHESHIRE CAT *disappears and* WHITE RABBIT *exits.* ALICE *falls onto the ground and lies as she did in Scene 1. Curtain.*)

*   *   *

Scene Eight

SETTING: *The same as Scene 1.*

AT RISE: ALICE *lies sleeping, in same position as in previous scene.* ALICE's SISTER *stands nearby, calling to her.*

SISTER: Wake up, Alice dear. Why, what a long sleep you've had.

ALICE (*Waking up and yawning*): Oh! I've had such a curious dream. I must tell you about my strange adventures. There was a rabbit in a waistcoat, and . . .

SISTER: I'm sure it was a curious dream, but now run in to
your tea; it's getting late.

ALICE: All right, sister dear. (ALICE *exits*. SISTER *continues
to sit*.)

NARRATOR: And so Alice went to tea and her sister sat a long
time in the cool grass watching the sun go down. There
was a distant rabbit running in the fields—a frightened
mouse splashed his way nearby—and she heard the rattle
of teacups, half believing she was in Wonderland too.
Open her eyes and she would be back to the confused
clamor of the busy countryside. But she knew that her
little sister, Alice, would always keep the simple and loving
heart of childhood and would gather children around her
to tell them the strange tale of her dream of Wonderland,
remembering her own childhood and the happy summer
days. (*Curtain*.)

THE END

Production Notes

ALICE'S ADVENTURES IN WONDERLAND

Number of Puppets: 13 hand puppets, rod puppets, or marionettes, and 4 or more stick puppets for Cards.

Playing Time: 20 minutes.

Description of Puppets: Model the puppets for this show after the original Tenniel illustrations for *Alice's Adventures in Wonderland,* if you like, or design your own puppets and costumes. Use cut-out figures mounted on rods or heavy wire for the Cards. The Dormouse should be a stuffed toy. The baby is a trick puppet with a baby's head on one end of its body, and a pig's head on the other. A dress covers the pig's head, and dress is flipped over to cover baby's head when baby turns into pig. The Cheshire Cat is a cut-out cardboard figure used on the stove in Scene 4. For Scenes 5 and 7, attach the cut-out to the backdrop, behind a sliding panel.

Properties: Book, pots and pans for the Cook (mounted on wires so that you can control them when the Cook "throws" them), pepper shaker and spoon sewn to Cook's hands, and watch, sewn to White Rabbit's hands.

Setting: Use simple sets, with cut-outs on plain black or blue background. Scene 1, A riverbank—a willow tree on a green, grassy knoll. Scene 2, Down by the rabbit hole— a treadmill band of scenery, showing shelves and bookcases. Roll this behind Alice until she falls to the ground. Scene 3, In front of the Duchess's house—a door frame with a working door, and a sign over it reading THE DUCHESS. This scene may be played before the curtain, without scenery, if desired. Scene 4, The Duchess's kitchen

300

—cut-out of a big, black stove with Cheshire Cat on it. There is a stool center for Duchess. Scene 5, In the woods —a cut-out of a large tree, with a sliding panel in the branches which can be operated from backstage. Behind the panel is the cut-out Cheshire Cat, and on the panel is a drawing of the Cat's "smile"—two rows of teeth arranged in a grin. By sliding the panel you hide the cat and show only the grin. Scene 6, The March Hare's tea party. There is a table center, with six or more chairs arranged behind it. Toy teacups, saucers, and teapot are glued to table. A cut-out of the March Hare's House, with chimneys shaped like long ears, is on the backdrop (this may be omitted). Scene 7, Queen of Hearts's flower garden—background has cut-out rose bushes on it with white roses. Cheshire Cat is on sliding panel in background. Scene 8, Riverbank, as in Scene 1.

Lighting: No special effects.

Sound: Crowd noises, in Scene 7, as indicated in text (use recordings if desired).

HOW TO PRODUCE A PUPPET SHOW

HOW TO PRODUCE A PUPPET SHOW

The following pages are meant to help you produce the twelve plays in this book. Although there have been many "how-to" books on puppet construction and the production of a puppet show, the following is meant to show you the easy way for beginners and the young.

Most of the plays can be done as hand puppet, rod puppet, or marionette shows. Produce the play as you see fit, and would enjoy doing it. A lot depends on the time you have to produce the show—hand puppets take less time than marionettes, for example. Some stories lend themselves better to one kind of puppet than another, also.

Puppet plays are lots of fun to do and see, and you can learn much about theater and how to get along with each other through this wonderful world of puppets.

Designs for Simple Puppets

Here are some ideas for easy puppets that would be fun to make. They can be made in a short time from household utensils, wooden spoons, handkerchiefs, fly swatters, flip-top cigarette boxes, milk cartons, cracker or cereal boxes, paper bags, paper cups, gloves, crepe paper, cardboard, old toys,

Designs for simple puppets: A. Fly swatter puppet; B. Milk carton puppet with handkerchief blanket; C. Paper bag puppet; D. Cereal box puppet with cloth tube neck; E. Paper doll puppet backed with cardboard and with paper fasteners at leg and arm joints, mounted on a rod or string; F. Flip-top cigarette box puppet with rubber band at jaw, and mounted on stick; G. Paper sculpture puppet on a stick; H. Glove puppet with furry ball and eyes; I. Finger puppet; J. Wooden spoon puppet with cloth skirt.

vegetables, and similar materials. See if you can find some interesting objects around the house and make puppets out of them.

Making Papier-Mâché Puppet Heads

Paper-covered puppet heads are inexpensive and easy to make. There are three types of bases on which you can build your *papier-mâché* puppet heads: a styrofoam ball; a crumpled newspaper ball; an inflated balloon. Before applying paste and paper to the styrofoam or newspaper balls, put a cardboard tube (from wax paper, paper towels, etc.) into the center for a neck. (Put the tube into the balloon head after *papier-mâché* is dry and break the balloon.) Be sure your index finger fits the tube. Tear newspaper into small pieces, apply flour-and-water paste or school paste to each piece and apply them to the puppet head until the head is covered with three or four layers of the torn paper. Be sure to bring the paper strips down onto the tube for strength. Next add the nose, ears, brows, eyes, and chin with more paper.

Papier-mâché puppet heads.

There is a commercial pulp *papier-mâché* called "Papier-Mâché Clay" that you can buy in most craft, art or hobby shops. You add only water because the adhesive is already in it. Apply this directly to a styrofoam ball, but for newspaper balls or balloons, apply a layer of torn paper strips and paste before applying the Clay. It is very good for facial features, because it molds easily, like putty or modeling clay. Be careful to apply a *thin* coat of Papier-Mâché Clay so that it dries quickly and doesn't crack. Use poster paints or acrylics to paint the head.

If you are making a marionette head, put heavy wire loops on each side of the head for strings. Also, glue a short dowel into the neck tube and put a screw eye in the exposed end of the dowel so that the body can be attached to the head.

Yarn, cord, or unraveled rope makes good hair. You can also use construction paper cut into fringe, felt, or a steelwool pad for a wig. Save corks, buttons and beads to use for eyes and noses.

Simple Hand Puppets

There are two kinds of simple hand puppet body patterns you can try. Use soft fabrics such as muslin or cotton so that the puppet moves easily. It would be wise to make a simple sketch of the costume first.

The shaped hand puppet body: Cut two pieces of fabric in the shape shown in the drawing. Note that the front piece is narrower than the back. The front piece is approximately 4″ across at the waist. The back is approximately 5″ across at the waist. Sew these two pieces together, leaving the neck and the bottom open. Then glue the neck tube of the puppet head into the neck opening of the puppet body. Cut felt hands and fit them over the ends of the arms on the puppet body.

The shaped hand puppet body.

The flat hand puppet body, with head.

If you wish, you can make the puppet body out of muslin, attach the hands and head to this, and then dress the hand puppet over the muslin. You can add capes, aprons, collars, belts, ribbons, buttons, or any other trim to complete the costume.

The flat hand puppet body, with head: Cut two pieces of a heavy fabric, such as felt, in the shape shown in the drawing. Note that the head is part of the body pattern and that the two pieces are the same size. Sew the two pieces together, leaving the bottom open. Stuff the head with cotton batting, then decorate the puppet with felt trim, buttons, costume jewelry, etc. This simple puppet pattern is excellent for making animals like cats, owls, dogs, mice, etc. People puppets may also be constructed in this fashion.

Fundamentals of Hand Puppet Manipulation

There are two ways to place your hand inside a hand puppet, both illustrated here:

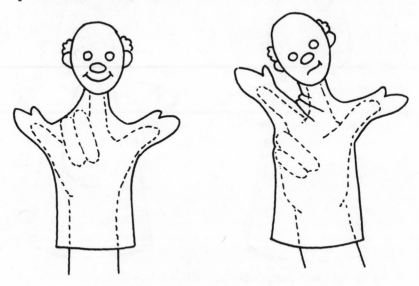

In the first, which is our choice, place your index (pointing) finger in the puppet's head, and your thumb and little finger in the hands of the puppet. This way the figure stands straight and does not look out of shape, nor does it lean. It is more comfortable, and the second and third fingers fill out the chest, so the puppet seems more erect.

The second method is the old European hand puppet position. Perhaps this method is best for you if your little finger is small and you do not have good control of it. Put your index finger in the puppet's head, and your thumb and second finger in his hands. Comfort is the most important consideration in deciding which method to use.

Basic movements

Standing: Hold the puppet erect with your thumb and little finger crooked. Try to hold the puppet's hands out in front of it, but with the hands facing forward.

Bowing: Bend from your wrist, which is your puppet's waist. *Never* bend the whole puppet forward from your elbow—it will look as if it is falling forward with its legs straight. Remember this when the puppet picks up a prop.

Nodding: Bend the first two joints of your index finger.

Turning head from side to side: Either turn the entire body to the side, or else place the upstage puppet hand against the cheek and turn the head with your finger. You can also make the head tube wide enough for two fingers, and the tube long enough inside the costume for the second finger to twist.

Clapping: Close your thumb and little finger together, and return to the spread hand position. *Never* crumple your fingers together to "crush in" the puppet's body. Always think "full chest."

Walking: Use a soft up-and-down motion as you move the

puppet along to convey walking. There are many other rhythms and motions you can try, too, depending upon the age, mood and kind of character your puppet is portraying.

Running: Lean your puppet forward a bit as you quickly move it up and down and forward. This motion, like walking, varies with the kind of puppet it is.

In general, remember that your hand is the whole body of the puppet and not just an extension of your own body movements. Try to show crying, laughing, being angry, and all the other emotions and body movements you can think of. In a rehearsal, think through the action required, and block the broad movements for a scene first. Then smooth out the little movements and reactions to what is being said. Keep the action going. And, above all, practice—practice—*practice!*

The Sock Puppet

The sock puppet is a favorite with children because its mouth moves. You can buy new socks to make it, but well-worn soft socks do just as well. Make a cut in the toe of the sock about 3″ deep, as shown, and turn the sock inside out. Cut out a felt mouthpiece in the shape of a large oval, sew a tongue to this if desired (see drawing), and pin the felt oval into the opening in the cut sock. Sew in place by hand or machine, stitching felt teeth into place at the same time if desired, then turn the sock right side out. Now sew eyes, brows, ears, scales, etc., onto the sock. Felt or any other heavy material may be used for this. Shiny buttons or fake jewels may be used for eyes.

Instead of a sock, you can also use a tube of fake fur, wool felt, or jersey, following the method described above. Experiment to make wonderful, imaginative animals or monsters.

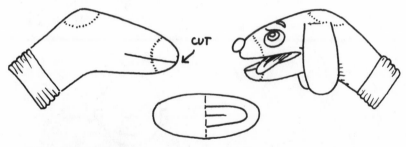

The sock puppet.

When the puppet is finished, put your hand in it and try talking at the same time as you move its mouth. Can you lip sync—that is, move the puppet's mouth to fit your words? Work at it. You'll be surprised how much fun it can be.

The Rag Doll Marionette

If you like to sew, you may enjoy making a rag doll marionette for your performance. Follow the simple design on page 180. The body, legs, and feet are cut in one piece, and the arms and head are separate. Either make a *papier-mâché* head as previously described, or make a stuffed rag doll head, following the drawing.

Sew the back and front pieces of the body section together, turn right side out, and fill the feet with sand. Make two rows of stitches across the ankles, then stuff with cotton to the knees. Make another double row of stitches, stuff to the hips, and make two more rows of stitching. Stuff the body and sew the shoulders closed by hand. Sew and reverse the arm and hand pieces. Stuff the hands with sand and make a double row of stitches at the wrists. Stuff to the elbows with cotton, and stitch twice. Stuff just a bit to fill out the upper arm and attach it to the shoulder of the body section. If you

313

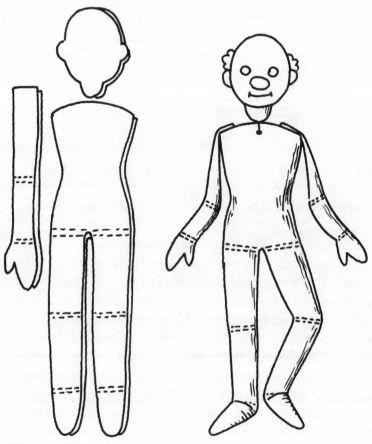

The rag doll marionette.

are using a stuffed head, sew, reverse, and stuff, then attach to the center of the shoulder area.

Paint the face and hands. Then attach the wig and dress your marionette. To complete the feet, sew them at right angles to the ankles, and either paint shoes on them, or cover with felt.

The Marionette Control and How to Use It

When your marionette is completed, the next step is to make a marionette control and string the marionette. The marionette control consists of three wooden sticks. Molding strips ½″ × ¾″ are ideal, though you can use laths as well. The main bar with which you hold the control is 9″ long. The shortest bar is 5″ long and is for the head strings. Nail this to the main bar about three inches from the front (see drawing on page 182). The third bar is 7″ long. It is for the leg strings, and must be detachable in order to "walk" the marionette. Drill a hole in the middle of the bar, and put a nail or peg in the front of the main bar to hold the third bar when it is not in use.

Attach black, dark blue, or gray carpet thread to the marionette on each side of its head, on each shoulder, on each knee, on each wrist, and on the back. If you use a *papier-mâché* puppet head, you will probably need to insert a loop of heavy wire on each side of the head above the ears. For cloth heads, sew strings directly on each side above the ears. The strings should be at least 2′ long, or longer, if your backdrops are high. Attach the strings to the control with staples, or else tie the strings to the control bars and glue in place. Always start with the head strings and hang the marionette during the rest of the stringing.

Try working your marionette. Hold it standing erect with its feet just touching the floor. Bend the control forward for

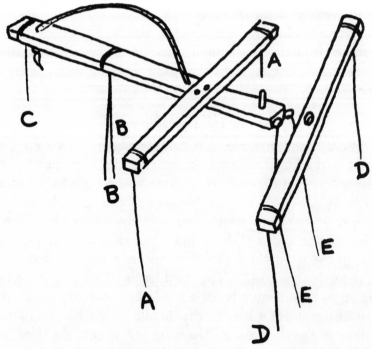

The marionette control, showing strings: A—the head strings; B—the shoulder strings; C—the back string; D—the knee strings; E—the hand strings.

bowing. Try sitting the marionette down on a low box, or on your foot. Keep its knees up. Try working its hands. Now use your other hand to take the leg bar off its peg and try walking the marionette. It's tricky, but with practice, you'll succeed. Bob the marionette up and down ever so slightly as you tilt its leg bar from side to side while moving the whole control forward. Turn the marionette's head from side to side by bending it forward, taking the weight off the head strings, and then turning the main bar from side to side.

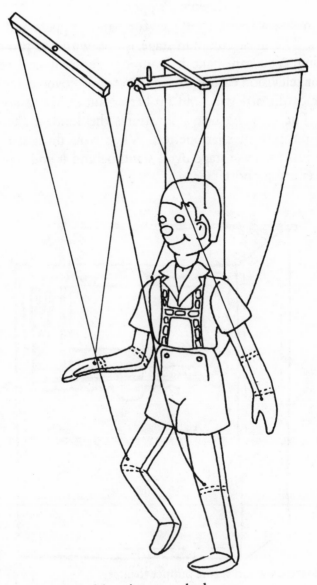

The marionette with strings attached.

Simple Puppet Stages

Here are a few easy stages for hand puppets and marionettes. The most common stage is one with the proscenium opening. You can make it from a large cardboard refrigerator or television carton. A wooden frame covered with muslin or cardboard will hold up better under heavy use, however. The drawing below illustrates this kind of theater for hand puppets or marionettes. When you do a marionette show just turn the stage over, stand behind it and work over the scenery support.

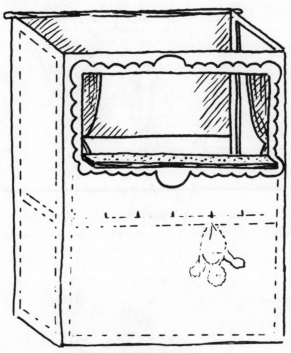

Cardboard or wood frame puppet theater.

To construct the theater, make three rectangles of wood strips as in the drawing, glue muslin or cardboard to each wooden frame, and paint. Cut out the proscenium opening, and hang a curtain rod and curtains to cover the opening, if you wish. Also hang a light background curtain at back.

Another important feature of this stage is the "playboard" or apron. This is a board about 4" wide across the bottom of the proscenium on which props and puppet furniture can be placed. The playboard is not necessary for marionette shows, when the stage is turned upside down.

Another type of puppet theater is the "open proscenium" hand puppet stage (below) that is excellent for plays requir-

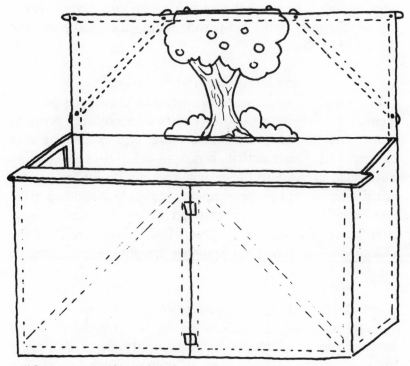

"Open proscenium" hand or rod puppet stage.

ing a large number of puppeteers. With this type of stage, there is an unlimited view of the action (the closed proscenium theater does have limited sight lines). Set pieces and scenery are hung from the back support and placed on the playboard. The bottom section is in four pieces, built like the stage above, and it should be hinged so that it can be folded when not in use. This stage front should be high enough to hide the tallest puppeteer and low enough to enable the littlest puppeteer to hold his puppet in view.

To make a quick puppet stage: Fasten a blanket or sheet to a stick, and have two children hold the ends of the stick up; put a tension curtain rod in a doorway and hang a curtain from it—use the open area above it for your proscenium opening; get a large cardboard box or packing crate, cut the top off it, and have the puppeteers stand inside and play over the top of the box.

Props for the Puppet Stage

Props and scenery can be as much fun to make as puppets themselves. Save boxes of many sizes to make such props as chairs, couches, thrones, chests, tables and cabinets. Easter baskets, Halloween noisemakers, and other toys make good small hand props. Shrubbery and trees can be cut from cardboard, painted and propped up on a stand. You can also make interesting greenery from crushed newspaper, and flowers from tissue or construction paper. Old sponges are good for making bushes, too. Real branches are always intriguing to the eye.

Scenery

You can paint backdrops on brown wrapping paper, butcher paper, or muslin, but to simplify the stage design, use a set piece—a single piece of scenery, such as a tree or house front cut out of cardboard, which leaves the rest of the stage free for easy action. For example, a throne room would have just one large impressive throne—and a banner or two to add color. A whole forest can be suggested with one large tree and a dark background or green cloth. Change the background to a light color, and you have a garden. Even a fence with flowers on it tells the audience it is a friendly outdoor place. Perhaps your play may call for no scenery at all if it is short and the puppets are delightful to look at.

Materials and Supplies and Where to Get Them

Felt is good for making puppet heads, hands and other parts of the puppet body. You can also use it for hats, vests, shoes, and just about any part of the costumes or trim. Use the half-wool, half-synthetic blend of felt. It's cheaper and easier to work with. Felt usually comes 72" wide in a very large range of colors, including four or five flesh tones from light pink or champagne to beige or tan. Small felt squares are also excellent when you need only a small quantity of one color. Felt is available at department stores, variety shops, craft and art supply stores and dime stores.

Yarn, embroidery floss, raffia and burlap all make good puppet hair. Cotton rug yarn is cheap and goes a long way. Other wool yarns are good, too, but more expensive. Stores mentioned above usually carry these products too.

Wood can be used for many things in puppetry. A soft, good grade of pine is best for almost everything you might want to build or carve. Local lumber yards carry it in just the width and thickness you need. Plywood is excellent for thin, strong joints. Never use balsa wood, however—it is seldom strong enough.

Styrofoam is good for many things. It comes in ¼" to 2" thicknesses, and in various ball and egg shapes. Although it may be a bit expensive, it is very light, easy to handle, and cuts down your work. You can buy it at craft or hobby stores, flower supply houses, decorator and display houses, and the dime stores.

Paint is an important material in puppetry. Buy a good grade of latex white house paint. Mix cheap liquid or powder temperas (poster paints) into small amounts of the latex white paint for puppet heads, scenery, props, costumes and just about everything. It can be scrubbed when dirty and dries fast; it is opaque and doesn't crack if it is not put on too thickly. All paint stores carry the latex household paints.

Costume fabrics should be light-weight for easy movement of the puppet. The best fabrics are jerseys, cottons, light velvets, silks, satins and soft, rough-textured materials. If necessary, wash the fabric before cutting it to make the material softer. Keep your patterns small and in scale to the puppet. Yard goods shops, department stores, and dime stores carry many of the fabrics you can use.

Scenery fabric can be inexpensive unbleached muslin, which comes in various widths and paints well. Use this for backdrops, covering frames, and making scenery and props.

Charcoal pencils are excellent for sketching in your scenery before painting. They are easier to see than ordinary pencil and not so messy as chalk. You can buy them at your local art or craft supplies dealer. School supply houses may carry them, too.

Black light and black-light paints are luminous products which are fun to use for special effects when you want things to glow in the dark. If you have a costume supply house in your town, it will probably carry these products, or write Shannon Luminous Materials Co., 7356 Santa Monica Blvd., Los Angeles, Calif. 90046.

Papier-mâché clay is a paper pulp with glue already in it.

It comes in a powdery form, and all you add is water to get a putty-like working material. It's great for forming features on puppet heads, hands or feet, hats, and many other puppet items. The thinner it is, the faster it dries. If it is used thick, it is probably best to dry it in a warm oven to take out the moisture. There are a number of brands of varying qualities, but the best is "Celluclay" because of its smooth texture. Most art and craft or hobby shops carry this product.

"*Sculpey*" is a modeling plastic that stays soft indefinitely or bakes hard in fifteen minutes in your oven. Polyform Products (9420 Bryon St., Schiller Park, Ill. 60176) is the firm that makes it, but it may be found in art, hobby or craft shops. This material is also good for molding features on puppet heads.

How to Get the Most Out of Your Rehearsals

You can't just make a set of puppets, wiggle them in front of an audience, and expect your play to be a success. A good production is like a chain—each link is important to make a good show. Let's assume you have the following: (1) a good puppet script or storyline; (2) puppets that look good from a distance and work easily and well; (3) scenery or set pieces that look good from a distance and carry out the mood of your show; (4) lights that give your show good visibility and create the proper mood; (5) sufficient practice in working a puppet. Now you're ready to start your rehearsals. Here are a few simple rules to follow to get the most out of them:

I. The director should (a) listen to the recorded tape of the show or know the script well if the dialogue is to be live; (b) plot the action so he knows who is going where and when; (c) understand about the particular movements of the characters—i.e., an old man moves slowly, a child skips along, etc.; (d) figure out any dances the puppets might have to do; and (e) think about the action of the curtains, lights and scenery.

II. With the puppeteers (a) sit down and listen to the recorded tape with the scripts. If the show is to be live, the puppeteers should memorize their lines and be able to speak their parts without the scripts; (b) decide which puppeteers should do what parts. Also include all curtain pulling and scenery changing as part of the action of the puppeteers. Sometimes non-puppeteers can be assigned to do these specific jobs; (c) have the puppeteers try the puppets or marionettes they are to use, and check the following—(1) are the marionettes' strings long enough when they lie down? (2) do the puppeteers understand the marionette controls? (3) are the hand puppets large enough and do the hand puppets' hands fit the fingers of the operator for easy hand movement?

III. Have the puppeteers "walk through" the show with the puppets to get a general idea of pace (how fast the show moves). First, try it without the recorded tape of speeches, then with it. Next, for each scene, carefully figure out the action and blocking, that is, the arranging of characters on stage for importance of character and good spacing and grouping. Be sure to *use the whole stage.* Use the back area as well as the front of your stage. If there are to be any dances, set them aside until the whole action of the play has been thought out, and then go back and rehearse them.

IV. Assemble the show. Put all the separate parts of rehearsals together, and rehearse, rehearse, and *rehearse again!* Remember, the movement of the scenery and curtains is an essential part of the show, too. Don't have dead spaces of time when nothing is happening onstage. Keep the time between scenes very short. Your scene changes should not take more than thirty seconds. You can also change scenery in front of the audience—this gives them something to look at and can on occasion provide more action than the puppets themselves in the course of the play. If necessary, rehearse with the few puppeteers that need more practice, or with those that are doing the longer parts. Those not rehearsing can be working on scenery or props.

V. The dress rehearsal is really like a first performance. All the puppets, scenery, props and lights should be assembled and tested to see if they are all in good working order. Then go straight through the show without stopping. Perhaps you can have some friends in the audience to tell you what seems wrong or doesn't look right to them. Take their criticisms seriously. You can't think of everything! Remember, they are there to enjoy the show and to help you.

Always cooperate with each other backstage. Puppeteers are usually anxious to please, and have come to enjoy themselves. Try not to lose your temper. Usually you will know who is the best puppeteer for the most important part. Where possible, share equally all the good roles, and remember that *the show is the thing*. As the director, listen to what others have to say, and then use your own good judgment. You have the final say! Stress that the puppeteers must keep cool. If you or anyone else makes a mistake during a performance, *do not panic!* Try to keep from breaking the train of thought. The show must continue, no matter what, and especially if the dialogue and narration are on tape.

It is sometimes difficult to remain calm, but real professionalism emerges when something accidental happens— a puppet's head or leg falling off, strings getting tangled, or the myriad other catastrophes that can occur. Remember, keep cool, and go on with the show!

Music in Puppetry

Music is an important part of your puppet production. Whether you use live or recorded music, you should plan carefully to use some kind of musical accompaniment with your show. It creates the right atmosphere and bridges the gap between the scenes. It can be used to change the mood during acts, as background for action, and as rhythm for dances or pantomimes.

The musical interludes should never be so long as to slow down the action of your play. They should serve as background and never become overpowering or get in the way of the words or action.

Usually you should use music that fits the size of the puppet stage—small musical groups or single instruments like piano, guitar, or recorder. Music boxes or recordings of them are ideal. Sometimes orchestra suites or music from ballets are especially suitable. It depends on the mood or effect you want for your production. To summarize, remember that music should be used in your productions for the following reasons:

(1) Mood—to help bring out the emotional feeling or atmosphere of your play. Ask yourself, is it a happy play, a sad story, a fast-moving story, a silly play, or a serious one? Will the music help or detract from the play? How much music should be used?

(2) Bridges—the music you play while changing scenery. You mustn't let your audience grow restless while you change the scenery or when the action lags.

(3) Songs or dances—try to find just the right dance or song accompaniment for the style of your show. Perhaps children's songs, new or old, might be just right for your

story, even though you might have to change the lyrics to fit the action.

(4) Background—sometimes added music will enhance the action, as when the story is spooky or sad.

(5) Opening music—to get your show off to a good start.

Below are some suggestions for recordings or musical ideas you might wish to try for the plays in this book. Most of them are popular enough to be found in your local record stores. The record dealer may also be able to give you some suggestions, if you tell him the type of mood you are trying to achieve in the play.

Pinocchio—Neapolitan Mandolins, RCA Victor FSP-115

The Frog Prince—Bird Fancier's Delight, VOX PL 12-750

Jack and the Beanstalk—Modern Times (movie sound track) UAL 4049

Snow White and the Seven Dwarfs—Wood Dove & Golden Spinning Wheel, Artia, ALP 200

Alice's Adventures in Wonderland—All in a Garden Green, Counterpoint/Esoteric M-2658-616

The Wizard of Oz—La Boutique Fantasque, Rossini/Respighi (several recordings)

The Reluctant Dragon—Symphonies and Fanfares for the King's Supper, Nonesuch H-71009

You may use live music, if there is someone in your group who plays the piano, guitar, or recorder (or even simple instruments such as the mouth organ, or paper-over-comb). You may wish to add other instruments such as tambourines, rhythm sticks, bells or drums. Be original and create your own moods with sound!